THE ASHES
A CENTENARY

THE ASHES

A CENTENARY

Ray Illingworth
and
Kenneth Gregory

COLLINS
London and Sydney
1982

William Collins Sons and Co Ltd
London · Glasgow · Sydney · Auckland
Toronto · Johannesburg

Illingworth, Ray
   The Ashes: a centenary
   1. Cricket – England – History
   2. Cricket – Australia – History
   I. Title II. Gregory, Kenneth
   796.35'865   GV923
   ISBN 0 00 216542 2

First published 1982
© Ray Illingworth and Kenneth Gregory 1982

Photoset in Ehrhardt

Made and Printed in Great Britain by
William Collins Sons and Co Ltd Glasgow

TO
THE CRICKETERS OF
ENGLAND AND AUSTRALIA

ACKNOWLEDGEMENTS

We are greatly indebted to the Earl of Darnley for permission to reproduce his grandfather's autograph, the pictures of his grandparents and of his grandfather's 1882–3 team in Australia;

to Lord Clifton for the cartoon 'To be or not to be';

to Mrs Beryl Llewellyn for permission to reproduce the caricatures of Armstrong and Macartney by her father, Arthur Mailey;

to Mr D. B. H. Wells for all the other autographs of winning captains at the front of the book;

to Mr Leslie Ames, CBE and Mr Jim Laker for their help over certain points;

and to the curator of the MCC, Mr Stephen Green and his secretary, Mrs Fay Ashmore.

We also acknowledge gratefully permission granted by the Home Office to reproduce the England badge and by the Australian Cricket Board that of Australia.

CONTENTS

ILLUSTRATIONS

THE ASHES WINNING CAPTAINS
AUSTRALIA

Will L. Murdoch, 1882

John McCarthy Blackham, 1891–92

Harry Trott, 1897–98

Joe Darling, 1899, 1901–02, 1902

Hugh Trumble, 1901–02

M. A. Noble, 1907–08, 1909

W. W. Armstrong, 1920–21, 1921

H. L. Collins, 1924–25

W. M. Woodfull, 1930, 1934

Don Bradman, 1936–37, 1946–47, 1948

A. L. Hassett, 1950–51

R. Benaud, 1958–59, 1961

Bob Simpson, 1964

Ian Chappell, 1974–75, 1975

THE ASHES WINNING CAPTAINS

ENGLAND

Ivo Bligh, 1882–83

Lord Harris, 1884

Arthur Shrewsbury, 1884–85, 1886–87

Allan G. Steel, 1886

W. G. Grace, 1888, 1890, 1893, 1896

A. E. Stoddart, 1894–5

P. F. Warner, 1903–04

F. Stanley Jackson, 1905

John W. H. Douglas, 1911–12

Charles B. Fry, 1912

A. P. F. Chapman, 1926, 1928–29

D. R. Jardine, 1932–33

Len Hutton, 1953, 1954–55

P. B. H. May, 1956

Ray Illingworth, 1970–71

Mike Brierley, 1977, 1978–79, 1981

During MCC's tour of Australia in 1958–9
the United States met Australia in the Challenge Round
of the Davis Cup at Brisbane.
The Americans were successful.
Australians therefore spoke of other matters,
in particular the fight for the Ashes,
where they were doing very well.
The non-playing captain of the US Davis Cup team
listened intently, then asked:
    'What, precisely, is an Ash?'

CHAPTER ONE

The Beginning

Dr W. G. Grace was bloody.

He must have been bloody because he was a conscientious general practitioner, and in the circumstances which prevailed at Kennington Oval just before 3.30 on the afternoon of Tuesday, 29 August 1882, any conscientious GP would have been bloody. Once we have grasped this fact, and noted its repercussions, the history of the Ashes will fall into perspective. Dr Grace – by temperament and skill England's opening bat – was called out on a case when he should have been padding up; this not only caused a hitherto unexplained delay of 10 minutes, it also demoralized one great England batsman and rendered him incapable of carrying the fight to Australia. For having examined his patient, Dr Grace gave certain instructions which proved fatal to England's cause. A few days later the *Sporting Times* printed an obituary notice:

In Affectionate Remembrance
of
ENGLISH CRICKET
which died at The Oval
on
29th August 1882.
Deeply lamented by a large circle of
Sorrowing Friends and Acquaintances
RIP

NB – The body will be cremated and
the Ashes taken to Australia.

The talking point at the Oval in late August 1882 was *not* cricket. Far away in Egypt a British army was about to engage the enemy, at home the newspapers devoted pages to the heroic spirit of sixteen thousand men under the command of General Sir Garnet Wolseley. Sir Garnet's frequent telegrams to the War Office were copied in the press and made splendid reading; at the Oval in late August spectators waited for play to begin by immersing themselves in the thoughts of a great soldier – 'Delay due to guns in the wrong place' and 'Very hot. Sixteen men 4th Dragoon Guards disabled by sunstroke.' Before long more mysterious telegrams appeared: 'Locomotives arrived safely. Now waiting for camels' and 'I am just off to the front. Will telegraph again when I get there.' If we wonder why the newspapers of 1882 did not devote more space to a cricket match – and explain some of the points which baffle us – the answer is they had more important things to dwell upon.

Our knowledge of the 1882 match is derived mainly from two classic reconstructions: by H. S. Altham in his, and E. W. Swanton's, *A History of Cricket*, and by Neville Cardus in his essay *The Greatest Test Match*. But neither mentions nor explains the 10 minutes when there was no play (Altham, by implication, denies there was any such hiatus), neither touches upon an odd discrepancy in the Australian bowling analysis; both take it for granted there was nothing unusual in one of England's finest batsmen, C. T. Studd, 'walking round the pavilion with a blanket round him'. Another source assures us that the No. 11, Peate, could totter to the crease only after being dosed with champagne. Peate was a Yorkshireman; Yorkshire captains do not dose any of their men with champagne but tell them to 'B— well get out there and bat!'

One very obvious reason for England's demoralization at the Oval was an Australian. George Giffen related how, in the preceding April, passengers on board the P & O *Assam* had attended a fancy dress ball and blenched at the sight of an undeniably authentic Mephistopheles – six foot two inches tall, sinewy, with eyes that burned. Twelve Australian cricketers were momentarily aghast until they recognized Frederick Robert Spofforth. Yet the gaze of this Devil in red was benign (or so Giffen insisted) compared to that of the Demon in white who bowled against England at the Oval. But acknowledging Spofforth's skills and aspect, there was on 29 August 1882 a malignant spirit abroad which undermined England.

Her selectors had chosen both well and diplomatically; to defend an unbeaten home record against Australia (it consisted of one game won by five wickets), they had named six amateurs and five professionals, six from the North of England and Nottinghamshire and five from the South. If two Etonians, Lyttelton and Studd, suggested bias, the captain was a Harrovian; Marlborough in the person of Steel and Uppingham in Lucas added weight. So did Dame Trotman's Dame School which had taught W. G. Grace to read and write. The teams were:

ENGLAND		AUSTRALIA	
A. N. Hornby (captain)	*Lancashire*	W. L. Murdoch (captain)	*NSW*
R. G. Barlow	*Lancashire*	A. C. Bannerman	*NSW*
W. Barnes	*Nottinghamshire*	J. M. Blackham	*Victoria*
Dr W. G. Grace	*Gloucestershire*	G. J. Bonnor	*Victoria*
A. P. Lucas	*Surrey*	H. F. Boyle	*Victoria*
Hon A. Lyttelton	*Middlesex*	T. W. Garrett	*NSW*
E. Peate	*Yorkshire*	G. Giffen	*S. Australia*
J. M. Read	*Surrey*	T. Horan	*Victoria*
A. G. Steel	*Lancashire*	S. P. Jones	*NSW*
C. T. Studd	*Middlesex*	H. H. Massie	*NSW*
G. Ulyett	*Yorkshire*	F. R. Spofforth	*NSW*

The player to have most influence, if not on the game of cricket, then on cricket literature, was Horan, who later wrote for the *Australasian* under the name of 'Felix'. At the Oval he fielded at short-leg to Spofforth and also managed to keep an eye on twenty thousand spectators. His recollections of the game are still accepted today. As we shall see, Horan was a graphic writer but not entirely accurate.

At 11.45 on the morning of Monday, 28 August 1882, a bell was rung. Let the ground be cleared! Play would commence at ten minutes past midday. Thousands approved the news. Why play should start at ten minutes past the hour rather than on the hour or half-, even quarter-hour, nobody knew. It was common knowledge the Australians had insisted on shortened hours of play for their tour but this ten minutes past the hour baffled. Murdoch was glad to have won the toss, for with rain about the pitch could only worsen. Hornby led England out; the dominant figure W. G. looked cheerful, and the two finest brains on the England side, Steel and Lyttelton (both future QCs), chatted together. A cheer welcomed the Australian openers, Alec Bannerman and Hugh Massie, the former to receive first ball from . . . of course! Ted Peate, the great Yorkshire slow left-arm bowler. Peate from the gasometer end. Hornby waved his forces here and there – Read right back at long-off, just in case. A lady emerged briefly from her furs to ask why all the Englishmen were on one side of the field.

'My dear, I thought I'd told you at breakfast. Peate bowls the off-theory.'

The lady regained the comfort of her furs; perhaps the weather would improve by mid-afternoon. It did, the temperature rising to 58°F.

The summer of 1882 had been depressingly wet until a week or two before the Oval match when a spell of dry, cool weather caused the pitch to harden but insufficiently to make batting an enviable pastime. Peate dropped the ball where he chose, so did another left-hander, Barlow. Both turned it appreciably. The sunshine of Melbourne and Sydney seemed far distant. At lunch, taken after 100 minutes, Australia had poked, groped and pushed their way to 41 for 6. To the combined skills of Yorkshire and Lancashire there was no answer. The head thus severed, the tail did not wag: Australia out for 63 off 80 four-ball overs. Peate and Barlow triumphant, the off-theory had been vindicated.

PEATE'S FIELD

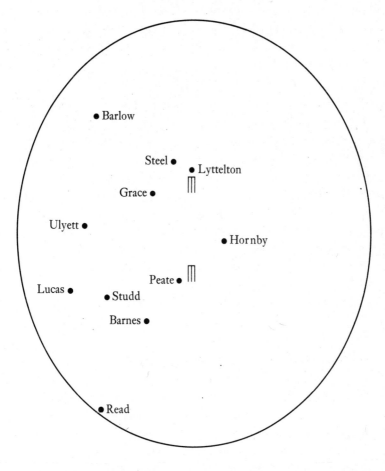

Note: The only essential difference between this field and that shown in
P. F. Warner's *Book of Cricket* (1934) for Rhodes, Blythe, Parker
and Verity, is that 'Barlow' moves to second slip when the ball is
turning, otherwise to forward short-leg – 'Hornby' dropping
deeper.

Eleven unhappy visitors admitted they had hoped to do much better whatever the conditions. Should England make 150 or more, Australia faced an innings defeat. Why, just to think of the England batting made the crowd feel warmer: ten men able to score hundreds, Hornby's only problem was to decide his order. In the event Hornby's problem was solved for him by Spofforth. Yorking W. G. leg stump after the Champion had made only 4, Spofforth carried all before him and bowled unchanged.

Here we must glance over the shoulder of the Australian scorer. Today, when elementary methods are still employed in club cricket, the balls of an over are recorded in this order: $\begin{smallmatrix}1&4\\2&5\\3&6\end{smallmatrix}$. But in the first decade of the present century scorers preferred: $\begin{smallmatrix}1&2\\3&4\\5&6\end{smallmatrix}$. In 1882 the four-ball over was still in use, a maiden naturally being recorded as . . . . and an over from which four boundaries were taken as 4 4 4 4. This will strike the reader as being insultingly simple. Not so if he wishes to know from which ball in the over the 4 was made. Take an over set down as . 1 . . and translate into modern terms; the single was taken not from the second ball but the *fourth*. Similarly . . 1 . meant a single from the over's *first* ball. Why the scorer in 1882 should have chosen to record an over's balls in the order 3 4 1 2 doubtless had a ready explanation but one not apparent to the authors of this book. Conclusive proof that W . 1 W meant an over's first ball had yielded a single, the second and third balls wickets, and the fourth had not been scored off will be presented later. Readers wishing to investigate the mystery are advised to consult the 1883 *Wisden*, having first armed themselves with a pint of strong black coffee. The *Wisden* in question had availed itself of sundry details taken from the Australian scorebook, so prompting the question, 'Then what was the state of the England scorebook?'

Now we must draw attention to the first apparently strange discrepancy in the Australian scorebook. Garrett 16 and Boyle 19 between them sent down 35 overs. When Spofforth ended the England innings he was halfway through his 37th over.

At five minutes to six o'clock, England were all out for 101.

The Australians returned to the Tavistock Hotel. Only a few hundred yards away at the Savoy Theatre the first run of *Patience* was drawing the town. The tourists ignored temptation and, in the manner of Australians, had an early night.

Next morning, soon after breakfast, Mrs Eliza Spendlove, of 191 Brook Road, Kennington, handed some sandwiches to her husband George. He bade his wife goodbye, collected a friend Edwin John Dyne from 24 Pollock Road, and set out for the Oval. Rain had fallen during the night; before long a downpour threatened to stop cricket for the day. Shortly before eleven o'clock it eased, leaving the field a treadable bog. Something in the sky suggested sun; this token effort noted, the sun disappeared for the day. A slight breeze sprang up. Spendlove and Dyne chatted, the groundsman and his staff removed mud from the creases and filled the holes with sawdust. Conditions were impossible, but as another twenty thousand spectators had gathered, a prompt start was made at 12.10.

This time the bowling was opened by Barlow and Ulyett at medium pace, Peate's ability to spin a piece of soap being called in question. At once the Australians showed their hand. While Bannerman scarcely lifted his bat, Massie sprang to attack almost every ball. He was lucky – or so men said, and they may have said it half an hour later. In Ulyett's second over Massie drove hard to the off. Read chased and collected the ball, then threw – or did he? – to the wrong end. Let us say that Massie *might* have been out. He now proclaimed himself. A cut off Barlow, a sweep, and then a pull: three precious boundary hits. Twenty runs came in a quarter of an hour. A double change of bowling, Peate and Studd being introduced. Massie on-drove Studd for 4 . . . the way that ball jumped! . . . then clove Peate savagely past mid-off. Another on-drive – the arrears of 38 had been wiped off in half an hour. When the bowlers confronted Bannerman they impelled a fine batsman to fight for survival; against Massie they were helpless. Barnes took over and induced Massie to drive too soon. The ball soared high to long-on where Lucas positioned himself perfectly – then dropped the catch. Cold, hard soap! Lucas heard the crowd's wrath and hung his head in shame. Still Massie attacked: 50 for none in 40 minutes. A majestic on-drive to the boundary off Peate saw the field adjusted; Massie thrashed the next ball through the now vacant space. Hornby called up Steel who could break the ball both ways. Massie swung him for yet another 4. Steel changed his grip. For no good reason at all, Massie was bowled. 66–1–55. A great innings: nine 4s, two 3s, three 2s, and seven singles.

With Australia 28 ahead, Billy Murdoch hastened in. When he left the pavilion, one Australian was smiling satanically and snapping his fingers. If Murdoch batted superbly, eight other Australians hardly batted at all, contributing 19 between them. A shower saw the players take an early lunch, after which Garrett called his captain for an impossible run. Hornby's return made the appeal a formality. So at 3.25 in the afternoon Australia were out for 122, setting England 85 for victory. Sensing his finest hour, Hornby said he would go in first with W. G.

It was now that George Eber Spendlove made his bid for immortality. Telling Edwin Dyne he did not feel well, he rose to his feet. No sooner had he done that than he fell to the ground, blood pouring from his mouth. Mr Dyne at once yelled 'Doctor!' a cry taken up by others in the vicinity. Above the throng a black beard and MCC cap hove into sight. Seconds before their owner had been walking from the field preparatory to donning pads and gloves. One glance at the stricken Spendlove was enough.

'Carry him to the room above the pavilion.'

Within minutes Dr Grace had lost a patient. As he was a conscientious GP, and as investigation of a haemorrhage is a messy business, there can be little doubt that on his return to the England dressing room W. G. was bloody. Doubtless he asked for soap and a bucket of water.*

---

* The writer's maternal grandmother, when a child, was taken ill. The family physician, Dr Henry Grace, being on holiday, his locum called. A beard and a beam filled the sick room. 'Little girl in bed? Measles. Have an acid drop.' His patient's family still regard Dr W. G. Grace as the greatest of diagnosticians, the little girl living to be a hundred. – K.G.

DR WILLIAM GILBERT GRACE, 1880–99
The Champion

'Perhaps some old cricketer who remembers Spofforth will
let us know how this great bowler placed his field: did he
bowl from round the wicket to a semi-circle of fieldsmen
close to the batsmen's leg-side?'

Neville Cardus, *The Summer Game,* 1929

The Hon Ivo Bligh described the Spofforth of 1882: 'long lean
arms whirling through the air from a commanding height, and a
long stride coming down with great force and damaging effect *on
a very awkward spot for a breaking-back ball bowled at the other
end*' (our italics). Which would seem to prove beyond doubt that
Spofforth bowled round the wicket. His pace in 1882 was well
above medium, though occasionally he would send down a
genuinely slow delivery or a very fast yorker on the leg stump –
all with an identical action. His stock ball (if it can be so termed)
came back from the off anything from a couple of inches to two
feet. Inevitably the most skilled batsman did not know whether
to play for a small or greater degree of turn; if the latter, and the
ball deviated little, the result was an outside edge. But at the Oval
– and certainly in England's second innings – Spofforth was
bowling balls that sometimes shot or, just as often, lifted head-
high (A. G. Steel's testimony). Field placements were therefore
simple: two slips, two silly points, very short square-leg and silly
mid-on. The prince of wicketkeepers, Blackham, generally stood
up, his 1882 tour-de-force being stumpings from fast yorkers
that missed the leg stump.

Dr Grace dried his hands, then reached for his pads. Word had
been passed to the Australian dressing room – 'W. G.
professionally engaged. Won't be long.' It was natural for H. S.
Altham to write of 'the breathless 10 minutes that divided the
innings' because he had been reading Horan's reminiscences of
the occasion committed to paper years later. Horan concentrated
the excitement towards the close of England's second innings
when 'the strain, even for spectators, was so severe, that one
onlooker dropped down dead . . .' Contemporary press reports
agree that Australia's second innings ended at 3.25 and that

FREDERICK ROBERT SPOFFORTH, 1876–87
The Demon Mk. I

England went in at 3.45. The accounts of Mr Spendlove's inquest explain why the interval was 20 and not 10 minutes. It was for 20 minutes that Spofforth inspired the other Australians by intoning, 'This thing can be done.'

We do not know how much Mr Spendlove's misfortune shook the England side. But it is unlikely that the sight of men bearing a near corpse, and accompanied by Dr Grace, would have passed without comment. All we have been told, by C. I. Thornton, is that before long Studd was pacing the dressing room with a blanket thrown round him – this same Studd whose cricket career was brief and who became a missionary in China. Certainly his two 1882 hundreds against the Australians suggested he was a fine batsman. It was surely Hornby's duty to send him in early before nerves were transformed into complete disintegration. Hornby failed as a leader. With the advantage afforded by posterity, we see that the England selectors had also failed; a badly damaged wicket, the bowlers pitching in one another's footmarks, and Arthur Shrewsbury – the first great master of pad play – not in the team. Granted that in 1882 Shrewsbury had not yet perfected pad play, but he knew what his legs were for.

At 3.45 Spofforth bowled the first over of England's second innings from the gasometer end. W. G. played out a maiden. Garrett attacked with the pavilion behind him. A single to Hornby, a single to Grace. Only 83 to win: the crowd felt much better. (Spofforth would bowl 28 overs in this innings; opposite him Garrett 7 and Boyle 20 totalled 27. The last wicket fell to the final ball of Boyle's 20th over. How, then, did Spofforth's overs exceed those bowled at the other end? If he kept on throughout at the gasometer end, the tally should have been the same for both Spofforth and Garrett-Boyle. But if Spofforth changed ends, and the last over was bowled by Boyle, then Spofforth's overs should have totalled one *fewer* than those of Garrett-Boyle.)

England were 14 without loss after 8 overs. 71 to win. The first ball of Spofforth's 5th over W. G. pushed for a single, the next knocked Hornby's off stump out of the ground.

15–1–9.

In the previous over from Spofforth Hornby had on-driven a splendid boundary; clearly his intention had been to score runs. But now he sent in Barlow, the Lancashire stonewaller. This was surely a time for a stroke-maker like Studd. It still was – for Barlow was out first ball.

15–2–0.

As George Ulyett walked in, the crowd relaxed. Yorkshire for a crisis. The crowd shuddered: Ulyett played and missed, the ball grazing the stumps. In the Australian scorebook the over was inscribed W . 1 W, proof of the methods employed in 1882.

At the non-striker's end the Champion stood self-confident. He recalled pitches far worse than this in the orchard at Downend. Mama was less dangerous than Spoff? Not indoors she wasn't!

'Run up!'

Grace on-drove Spofforth for 4. While the ball was being retrieved, Horan stared at the vast crowd. Nearly twenty thousand paid for admission on the first day. How would he feel were he one of them? Horan's memory was beginning to stock up. Grace next on-drove Spofforth for 3. Murdoch had a word with the Demon who nodded. Garrett's 7th over yielded two singles, Spofforth's 8th was a maiden to Ulyett. At its conclusion he walked down the pitch, measured out his run at the pavilion end – and bowled his 9th over.

'Can't have it! Shan't have it! Won't have it!'

This was not the occasion when Dr Grace spoke the most awful words ever heard on a cricket field. In 1882 Law VIII stated, among other things, that 'No bowler shall bowl more than two overs in succession.' (The Law was amended in 1889 so as to prohibit a bowler from bowling two overs in succession *in the same innings*. In the Old Trafford Test of 1921 Warwick Armstrong bowled two overs in succession when, as it were, the umpires had been baffled and bewildered by Warwick Armstrong.)

Boyle took over from Spofforth at the gasometer end. Both '

SPOFFORTH'S FIELD

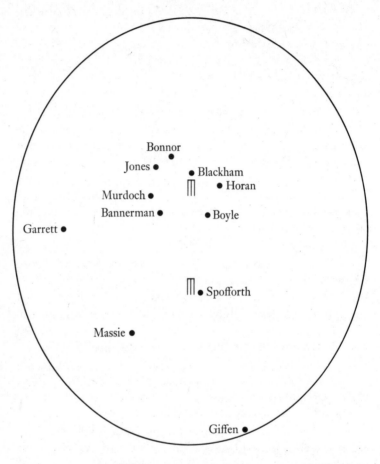

Note: (i) In the 1930s W. J. O'Reilly bowled with W. A. Brown and J. H. Fingleton in something like the Horan-Boyle positions.

(ii) Spofforth employed a long-on just as Larwood often did when bowling to Woolley.

batsmen played their strokes. George Giffen later declared this innings of W. G.'s a masterpiece. A tremendous cheer greeted the half-century. Colonial cheek to think they could take on England! Only 35 to win. Then, at 51, Spofforth bowled a very fast ball to Ulyett who played inside it. Blackham's appeal suggested conviction and relief. A very fine stand, England were almost home and dry. 'Dry' perhaps not the word in these conditions. The crowd prepared to welcome Studd. Lucas came in. Either Hornby was mad or Studd had put his head in a bucket.

51–3–11.

The runs had come in even time off 88 balls. The question was asked: Could seven men defend their stumps while the great Doctor carried England to victory? A 2 off Boyle: to the next ball Grace pushed his left leg forward and drove. Not to the pitch! Caught by Bannerman at mid-off. Men will not agree that W. G. made an error of judgement. It was Boyle pitching in Spofforth's follow-through. All right, Garrett's – the same thing. Unfair!

53–4–32.

The Hon Alfred Lyttelton stalked to the wicket. Clearly Studd refused to leave the comfort afforded by his blanket.

In the 26th over Lucas hit a single; his second scoring stroke was delayed for 25 overs. Lyttelton snicked Boyle for 2, then swung Spofforth for 4.

Twelve maiden overs followed. England's batting was afflicted by *rigor mortis*. A gentleman in the pavilion spoke:

'Don't worry! They'll get the runs if only they play with straight bats.'

To which the lady at his side – and true love is not quenched by a day spent looking at gasometers – replied:

'Then, darling, can't you find them some straight bats?'

A single. Four more maidens. Spofforth's right arm gyrated against the dark background of the pavilion. A fierce breakback hit the top of Lyttelton's middle stump.

66–5–12.

Only 19 runs wanted. Lucas late-cut Boyle for 4. Steel, the new batsman (Studd still under his blanket), a fine legal brain in the making. Weighing the evidence presented by Spofforth's faster ball, he played an admirably fashioned forward stroke. It awaited the arrival of Spofforth's obscenely concealed *slower* ball. Steel caught and bowled.

70–6–0.

Read missed his second ball.

70–7–0.

Word had gone round the England dressing room: 'When you're walking to the wicket, DON'T look at Spofforth. He has the evil eye.'

A 2 to Barnes. Three byes! Blackham beaten by Spofforth's pace from the pitch. A Demon makes pace from *any* pitch. Lucas half-stopped Spofforth's next ball and watched it roll on to his stumps.

75–8–5.

Studd walked slowly to the wicket. He had removed his blanket and remembered his bat. In the pavilion the dosing of Peate with champagne had begun. As Lucas had fallen to the last ball of a Spofforth over, Studd was at the non-striker's end.

Boyle bowled to Barnes, the ball lifted from the bowler's follow-through and lobbed from the batsman's glove to silly point.

75–9–2.

Still 10 runs wanted. Studd concentrated, then wondered: would Peate bring instructions from Hornby? If so, would they advise Studd to shield Peate, or *command* Peate to shield Studd?

Peate, the taste of champagne on his lips, heaved at Boyle. The ball passed square-leg. Studd had the bowling. No, he insisted on running a 2. Studd was not selfish, he would let Peate have the glory. Peate's stroke to Boyle's next delivery summed up these moments of tension: it was the stroke of a man who has been dosed with too much champagne – or too little. Peate missed and grinned wildly. The last ball of the over was straight.

'Why, Ted, did you play a stroke like that?' men asked in the pavilion.

'Because I couldn't trust Maister Studd!'

The last six overs of the England innings may be transcribed:

Spofforth	Boyle	Spofforth	Boyle	Spofforth	Boyle
. W . .	4 . . .	W . W 2	. . . .	. . . W	W 2 . W

So ended 'Spofforth's Match'. Who now remembers Massie? A few days later the *Sporting Times* printed an obituary.

The inquest on George Eber Spendlove, aged forty-eight, was held in the Crown Tavern, Church Street, Lambeth – presumably with the bar closed. Mrs Spendlove identified her late husband. Edwin John Dyne gave evidence; the East Surrey coroner, Mr William Carter, reached a verdict of 'Natural causes', and referred to Dr W. G. Grace as 'the well-known cricketer'.

General Sir Garnet Wolseley – guns, camels and enemy in position – won a great victory at the Battle of Tel-el Kebir. He was rewarded with a peerage and £30,000, today's comparable purchasing power (had Lord Wolseley invested in property) over £2 million.

One thing remains to be said of 29 August 1882. While England could, and naturally would, have withstood Spofforth, they had no hope against Spofforth and Spendlove at the same end.

ENGLAND *v* AUSTRALIA
Played at the Oval 28, 29 August 1882

AUSTRALIA

A. C. Bannerman	c Grace b Peate	9	c Studd b Barnes	13
H. H. Massie	b Ulyett	1	b Steel	55
W. L. Murdoch	b Peate	13	run out	29
G. J. Bonnor	b Barlow	1	b Ulyett	2
T. Horan	b Barlow	3	c Grace b Peate	2
G. Giffen	b Peate	2	c Grace b Peate	0
J. McC. Blackham	c Grace b Barlow	17	c Lyttelton b Peate	7
T. W. Garrett	c Read b Peate	10	not out	2
H. F. Boyle	b Barlow	2	b Steel	0
S. P. Jones	c Barnes b Barlow	0	run out	6
F. R. Spofforth	not out	4	b Peate	0
Extras	(B1)	1	(B6)	6
Total		63		122

Fall of wickets: 1–6, 2–21, 3–22, 4–26, 5–30, 6–30, 7–48, 8–50, 9–59, 10–63.

2nd innings 1–66, 2–70, 3–70, 4–79, 5–79, 6–99, 7–114, 8–117, 9–122, 10–122.

ENGLAND BOWLING (4-ball overs)

	O.	M.	R.	W.	O.	M.	R.	W.
Peate	38	24	31	4	21	9	40	4
Ulyett	9	5	11	1	6	2	10	1
Barlow	31	22	19	5	13	5	27	0
Steel	–	–	–	–	7	0	15	2
Barnes	–	–	–	–	11	5	15	1
Studd	–	–	–	–	4	1	9	0

ENGLAND

R. G. Barlow	c Bannerman b Spofforth	11	(3) b Spofforth		0
W. G. Grace	b Spofforth	4	(2) c Bannerman b Boyle		32
G. Ulyett	st Blackham b Spofforth	26	(4) c Blackham b Spofforth		11
A. P. Lucas	c Blackham b Boyle	9	(5) b Spofforth		5
Hon A. Lyttelton	c Blackham b Spofforth	2	(6) b Spofforth		12
C. T. Studd	b Spofforth	0	(10) not out		0
J. M. Read	not out	19	(8) b Spofforth		0
W. Barnes	b Boyle	5	(9) c Murdoch b Boyle		2
A. G. Steel	b Garrett	14	(7) c & b Spofforth		0
A. N. Hornby	b Spofforth	2	(1) b Spofforth		9
E. Peate	c Boyle b Spofforth	0	(11) b Boyle		2
Extras	(B6, LB2, NB1)	9	(B3, NB1)		4
Total		101			77

Fall of wickets: 1–13, 2–18, 3–56, 4–59, 5–60, 6–63, 7–70, 8–96, 9–101, 10–101.

2nd innings   1–15, 2–15, 3–51, 4–53, 5–66, 6–70, 7–70, 8–75, 9–75, 10–77.

AUSTRALIA BOWLING (4-ball overs)

	O.	M.	R.	W.	O.	M.	R.	W.
Spofforth	36.3	18	46	7	28	15	44	7
Garrett	16	7	22	1	7	2	10	0
Boyle	19	7	24	2	20	11	19	3

AUSTRALIA WON BY 7 RUNS

Postscript to 1882

The authors have become cross-eyed trying to relate the runs from each Australian over to the runs credited to batsmen in England's second innings.

A.

England's 4th wicket (Grace) fell at 53.

Batsmen out		Bowling analysis	
Hornby	9	Spofforth	$13 - 3 - 34 - 3$
Barlow	9	Garrett	$17 - 2 - 10 - 0$
Ulyett	11	Boyle	$4\cdot3 - 1 - 9 - 1$
Grace	32		
	52		$24\cdot3 - 6 - 53 - 4$

How do we reconcile 52 runs from the bat with 53 runs scored off bowling? Hornby's 9 is readily confirmed, Barlow was out first ball; either Grace's or Ulyett's score is incorrect.

B.   Press reports account for England's last 11 runs thus:
Lucas 4 (1st ball of Boyle's 18th over, 51st of innings)
Barnes 2 (4th ball of Spofforth's 27th over, 52nd of innings)
Byes 3 (3rd ball of Spofforth's 28th over, 54th of innings)
Peate 2 (2nd ball of Boyle's 20th over, 55th of innings)
Therefore Spofforth's no-ball was bowled while England moved from 53 to 66, when Lyttelton was dismissed.

C.   England's 5th wicket (Lucas and Lyttelton) added 13. Lucas made 1 from the 1st ball of Spofforth's 14th over, 26th of the innings – see press reports. Since the no-ball was bowled at this time, Lyttelton made 11 and not 12.

'The scorer's hand shook so that he wrote Peate's name like "Geese".' – Horan. Perhaps the scorers were sharing a room with Spendlove?

CHAPTER TWO

The Romance of Ashes

If the inquest on Mr Spendlove was over briefly, that on England's defeat at the Oval lasted several months. Everyone agreed the fault lay with the MCC, a body which had grown increasingly conservative with the years. The authorities at Lord's really should make an effort to revolutionize cricket. For instance, the two sides taking part in a match should each bat on its own pitch. It was infamous to expect Englishmen to bat on the same pitch as Colonials. Again, would not cricket prove more popular if the side batting first was compelled to interrupt its innings on reaching 100 so that the opposition might have a turn – the first side resuming its occupation of the crease after the second had made 100. Meanwhile *The Times*, in an article of incomparable majesty, began with a dissertation on conditions in Ancient Athens, and ended with details of the seduction of schoolboys. Far too many English boys from the better public schools were being seduced by lawn tennis.

The Honourable Ivo Bligh now lent a hand. Approached by the Melbourne Cricket Club to take a side out, the Hon Ivo let it be known his men would play three matches against Murdoch's 1882 (Third) Australians. If victorious, he would bring back the Ashes. He would also play the State teams, XXIIs of Bendigo and Castlemaine, as well as a Combined Australian side. So saying, the Hon Ivo announced the names of his chosen; for brevity's sake, they were ten moustaches, one beard, and one clean-shaven. Here we should note – and the history of the Ashes pivots on this – that Bligh was a strikingly handsome man; in fact he bore a close resemblance to the young Laurence Olivier's

Sergius in Shaw's *Arms and the Man*, built-up nose and all, though more at ease in flannels and panama than in hussar's uniform.

The prelude to the encounters with Murdoch's team can best be set down in diary form.

14 September. North of England start game with Australians, winning by 10 wickets thanks mainly to their opening pair, Hornby and Barlow.

Advance guard of Bligh's side leave Gravesend in the P & O *Peshawar* – besides the captain, W. Barnes, F. Morley, W. W. Read, A. G. Steel, C. T. and G. B. Studd, E. S. F. Tylecote. All these players had moustaches, Bligh's by far the finest.

18 September. Alfred's Shaw's XI start game with Australians at the Oval. Tourists blanch on seeing R. G. Barlow and W. H. Scotton in partnership.* However, Barlow relatively frisky – 58 not out. Match drawn.

21 September. Remainder of Bligh's party leave England, crossing Channel en route for Brindisi: Barlow (beard), W. Bates and G. F. Vernon (moustaches), and CHARLES FREDERICK HENRY LESLIE – the last-named clean-shaven and the first English Demon bowler to get involved with the Ashes.

25 September. The four board the *Poonah* at Brindisi.

28 September. The four arrive at Alexandria where they inspect the ruins. Deeply impressed, also by the British Fleet anchored outside the harbour.

1 October. The four join their captain at Suez on the *Peshawar*. Leslie, chosen for his batting, announces that his bowling will remind Australians of Spofforth's. 'Not, mark you, the 1882 Spofforth but the Spofforth of 1878 who was very, *very* fast.'

13 October. Arrive Colombo, play XVII of the locals, several of whom bat without boots, pads or gloves.

15 October. Leave Colombo, the *Peshawar* soon in violent

---

* Barlow and Scotton were unrivalled masters of inactivity. Their six 'best' innings of over two hours' duration in first-class cricket (three by each) totalled 84 runs made in 16 hours 45 minutes – about 5 runs an hour.

TO BE OR NOT TO BE
17 FEB? 1883.

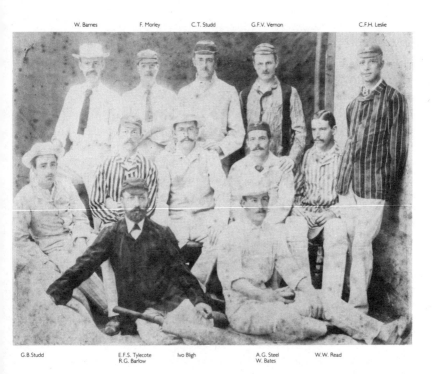

W. Barnes   F. Morley   C.T. Studd   G.F.V. Vernon   C.F.H. Leslie

G.B. Studd   E.F.S. Tylecote   Ivo Bligh   A.G. Steel   W.W. Read
R.G. Barlow   W. Bates

The Hon Ivo Bligh's team in Australia, 1882–3

collision with the *Glenroy*. Poor Fred Morley sustains fractured ribs, dies two years later aged only thirty-three, presumably from complications. The *Peshawar* limps back to port.

24 October. Leave Colombo a second time. The Hon Ivo, planning his campaign like the good general he is, says he cannot recall Mr Leslie ever having bowled for Oxford University or Middlesex.

'My dear Bligh! Forget about Oxford University and Middlesex. I can assure you I have bowled with no small success for the Gentlemen of Shropshire. Very fast, don't you know? Spofforth, '78.'

Soon the Hon Ivo badly injures a hand participating in a Tug of War. Will be out of action until the seventh match of the tour.

10 November. Eight weeks after leaving Gravesend, the *Peshawar* docks at Adelaide. The same day the Englishmen – bowlers listing heavily – play XV of Adelaide. Match drawn.

The train journey to Melbourne was remarkable for sundry stops when mayors and brass bands spoke and blew welcome. If once or twice a solitary figure shouted raucous greetings as the train slowed down – omitting the obligato through lack of a comb and paper, the Hon Ivo nevertheless appreciated the gesture. Already he liked Australia and felt ready to give his heart to the country. Even so, he kept in mind the purpose of his visit. When, on the evening of 14 November, he and his men supped with members of the Melbourne Cricket Club; when toasts flowed – to The Queen ('God Bless Her!'), to the Visitors, to Billy Murdoch's men now somewhere at sea on board *The City of New York* – then the Hon Ivo rose:

'We have come to beard the kangaroo in his den' – loud applause – 'and try to recover those Ashes.'

The second half of the Hon Ivo's sentence mystified.

'Ashes? What's the joker talking about?'

Clearly, members of the Melbourne Cricket Club were not – as the Hon Ivo Bligh was – avid readers of London's *Sporting Times*.

The Englishmen at practice impressed, none more so than

Charles Frederick Henry Leslie. First he measured out a long run.

'Spofforth is a master of length,' said Mr Leslie who then charged up and bowled. The striker under attack blinked, for the projectile launched by Mr Leslie made for another batsman practising some distance away.

'Length good,' announced Mr Leslie. 'I shall now concentrate on direction.'

Men watched in awe.

'Do you really think he's bowled with success for the Gentlemen of Shropshire?' asked one.

'Perhaps,' replied another, 'if the Gentlemen were playing the Ladies.'

Miss Florence Rose Morphy was not a lady of Shropshire. The daughter of Mr Stephen Morphy, her home was at Beechworth, Victoria. Where she was as Leslie tidied up his length and direction, history does not record. But at least she has been introduced to this story of the Ashes whose heroine she is.

The first major match of the tour, against Victoria, resulted in a handsome win for Bligh's men by 10 wickets. C. T. Studd made 56, Leslie 51 not out, Bates 48, and Barlow 44. Leslie was again in the runs at Sandhurst where XXII of Bendigo drew over two days. Here the Englishmen went underground at the Garden Gully United Mine but were not offered any gold. However, they were gratified on 25 November at not having been beaten by XXII of Castlemaine. In 1862 H. H. Stephenson's tourists had lost the corresponding encounter, though this may have been due in part to a diet of lobster washed down by gallons of champagne. Men who remember starting a match, but not finishing it, arouse envy but not sympathy. Which is another way of saying that Australian hospitality, though fabulous, may have a sinister aspect.

Back in Melbourne, the Englishmen attended a banquet given in honour of Murdoch's side. During the main course, Mr Leslie's neighbour remarked, 'How like a Demon Spofforth looks!' Mr Leslie nodded sagely; only as dessert was served did he permit himself – while holding an apple – to assume the manner of a Shropshire Demon. Little did the Australians know what was in store for them! Mr Leslie then ate his apple. For the present he was a batsman, and proved the point by making a brilliant 144 against New South Wales at Sydney. It was pleasant being his country's number three, it would be even more pleasant to supplant C. T. Studd, Steel, Barlow or Bates as the leading all-rounder.

The distance from Newcastle, New South Wales to Tamworth is about 200 miles. The nine hours it took Bligh's men to cover the distance did not add to their general gaiety, especially when the Tamworth cricket ground was flooded. But another banquet soothed ruffled feelings if adding to problems of weight. The question, 'Who's for tennis?' being unknown in the Tamworth of 1882, certain gullible Englishmen were taken in by its equivalent, 'Who's for a kangaroo hunt?' Rising at 4.30 a.m., the intrepid ones were led to some beady-eyed horses. Richard Barlow of Bolton, Lancs, was hoisted into the saddle, did the obvious thing with his arms (which was to place them round the horse's neck), and waited. In retrospect, he wished he had made arrangements to travel by kangaroo. After all, what use is an opening batsman and slow-medium bowler who can neither bend, run, walk nor sit?

During the week preceding Christmas, 1882 the Englishmen relaxed and ate normally. The Hon Ivo Bligh accepted an invitation to go shooting. It was then that his hostess introduced him to Miss Florence Morphy, a lady well versed in cricket lore. Conversation turned to the prowess of Australian and English heroes, especially that of the Demon Spofforth who had bowled so finely a few months earlier at the Oval. Miss Morphy could appreciate the presence of Bligh's men in her country; what made her feel slightly dizzy was the news that Bligh hoped to regain the Ashes which, of course, did not really exist. A day or so later, and undeterred by the cunning of XVII of Ballarat, the Hon Ivo struck many a blow to the boundary. Between blows, he twirled his moustache.

England's cricketers never make excuses, so no connection is claimed between the Melbourne banquet they attended on 29 December and a glut of dropped catches which afflicted them some hours later in their first arranged match with Murdoch's men. (The term 'Test Match' came into vogue only with A. E. Stoddart's tour of 1894–5.) Bligh lost the toss. (Apparently he had not heard of Dr Grace's method when calling: having made sure the Queen's head was on one side of the coin, and Britannia on the other, W. G. shouted 'The Lady!' before pocketing the evidence and hurrying away to put on his pads.) Bannerman and Massie opened for Australia. The latter did not last long – 5 for 1 – but Bannerman and Murdoch settled down with ominous ease. C. T. Studd and Barnes bowled, then Steel and Barlow, Studd again and Bates, even Walter Read. The permutations seemed without end. Captain the Hon Ivo meditated. Where one beard and five moustaches had failed, a razored face might possibly succeed.

'Leslie!' said Bligh.

'Bligh?' said Leslie.

'You may bowl,' went on Bligh.

'Indeed I will,' continued Leslie. 'And what is more, I shall bowl the off-theory.'

While Leslie's field is being set, we should note that Bannerman, Murdoch, and the next man in Horan, were the Woodfull, Bradman and McCabe of their day. To dismiss one of them was hard work, to dismiss all three something approaching (in the old legal sense) hard labour. With nine men strategically placed, and that fine wicketkeeper Tylecote standing up, Leslie spoke the incantation 'Spofforth, '78' in tones he sometimes used for a rare vintage, and strode off into the distance. Murdoch stood motionless at the crease, Tylecote jutted his posterior, and cover point glanced over his shoulder at the bowler apprehensive lest he receive the ball on the back of his neck. The Hon Ivo pondered the presence of Miss Morphy in the Ladies' Enclosure, then adjusted his thoughts: would Leslie concentrate first on length or direction?

The Hon Ivo Bligh,
later 8th Earl of Darnley

Miss Florence Rose Morphy,
later the Hon Mrs Ivo Bligh,
then Countess of Darnley

Leslie's initial delivery was very fast, only just short of a length had he been bowling from the other end. It passed Murdoch a yard outside his stumps and was acrobatically arrested by Tylecote.

'Off-theory,' said Leslie, whose second delivery was shorter still and finely taken by first slip. The bowler waved mid-off a little wider; Spofforth was always attentive to such matters. Leslie's third ball indicated he had put long-hops out of his system. It was a full-toss which exploded on Murdoch's middle stump.* 81 for 2.

'He's pretty quick,' said Murdoch to Horan as the batsmen crossed. 'And not as crooked as you'd think.'

Horan smiled grimly. He was acknowledged to be the most skilled player of fast bowling in all Australia. Long-hops he cut or hooked, full-tosses he forced back past the bowler. But he must be careful not to murder Leslie; Australia did not want him taken off yet.

Leslie began his long run, debating with himself as he travelled. He would skittle this Horan feller with another full-toss. As he swung into his final leap, he looked at the middle stump. There!

Horan's reflexes were sharp, his footwork exemplary. Leslie had contrived to bowl another of his very short wide balls. Horan cut savagely. Barlow at short third man clutched at his midriff, then looked at what he found there with acute distaste. 81 for 3.

Horan the batsman communed with his *alter ego*, 'Felix' the journalist-to-be. 'Fiercely scowling bowler – tremendous pace – unplayable length – heroic effort by striker – all to no avail – lesser men might have gnawed at their boots – dropped dead.'

Thus far Leslie had endangered, if not the off stump, the off-side field. Now this comparative accuracy deserted him. The stumps had contracted, the arena grown larger. Leslie began to

---

* The reader must not be censorious. In 1932–3 at Adelaide, D. G. Bradman bowled W. R. Hammond (85) with a full-toss. And whereas Bradman's bowling average against England was 51, Leslie's against Australia was 11. Bradman had the superior batting average.

spray his deliveries. True he had Bannerman superbly stumped off a wide fast half-volley to leg, but there was about this triumph (as about earlier ones) an element of fortune. Bligh's predicament was clear. He wished dearly to regain the Ashes – yet with honour. Leslie's method precluded honour. Bligh took him off. Australia lived again, the giant Bonnor heaved himself into hits of indecent velocity; George Palmer bowled straight, England succumbed by 9 wickets on the third day. The Hon Ivo's contribution was 0 and 3.

Miss Morphy did not comment on the purity of Bligh's first innings nor on the gay if brief abandon of his second; she was content with words of commiseration. The Hon Ivo assured her that there were still two matches to play, and that England would win them to regain the Ashes.

The next match against Murdoch's Australians began at Melbourne on 19 January 1883. By now Leslie was resigned; something told him his very fast, most effective bowling would not again be required this side of Shropshire. Very well! So when Bligh won the toss and England batted, Leslie entered like a lion at No. 3. Spofforth? Fie on mock Demons! Palmer and Giffen? Twice fie! Garrett? Not a bowler among them. Leslie attacked them all in turn. Unfortunately, seeking a run when his partner was at ease, Leslie ran himself out for 54. Hell and damnation! To reduce his self-esteem, William Bates from Huddersfield made 55, and then took 13 Australian wickets for 102, including a hat-trick. An innings victory for England, and all to play for.

The Hon Ivo Bligh again won the toss in the deciding game at Sydney. England 247 – Read and Tylecote 66 each; Leslie, having roused his rival's wrath, bowled Spofforth 0. Australia 218 – a splendid 94 by Bannerman, the maimed Fred Morley 4 for 47. Now twenty thousand turned up to watch the (Australian) Demon bowl out England. Spofforth 7 for 44, the tourists a paltry 123. The odds were on Australia. But no. Barlow accounted for Bannerman and Giffen, Morley for Murdoch and McDonnell; Horan was run out, and Barlow grabbed the rest. Australia 83 – Barlow 7 for 40, and a collection on the ground which saw him £25 the richer. The Ashes were back in English hands five months after a cremation.

Miss Morphy and Ivo Bligh discussed the outcome of the matches. Was it true that Mr Spofforth had the aspect of a demon? Most certainly, men trembled at his coming. Of course, England also had a kind of . . . demon. Miss Morphy still thought it strange Mr Bligh should be pleased to take home something which did not exist. The Hon Ivo smiled. Miss Morphy wondered if she might persuade Mr Bligh to accept a memento of the pleasure he and his side had given Australians. Ivo Bligh stared at the urn Miss Morphy held out to him: could it, did it, contain ashes? It did. Florence Morphy had incinerated some bails and placed their ashes inside the urn. The Hon Ivo Bligh asked Miss Morphy if he might call her Florence. He might. And would Miss Morphy call him Ivo? She would.

The Honourable Ivo Bligh and Miss Morphy were married on 9 February 1884. In due course, as the Earl and Countess of Darnley, they lived at Cobham Hall, Kent or at Clifton Lodge, Athboy, County Meath. Lord Darnley died on 10 April 1927, bequeathing his urn to the Marylebone Cricket Club. It is now in the Imperial Cricket Memorial Gallery at Lord's guarded by a bust of W. G. Grace.

Florence, Dowager Countess of Darnley lived until August 1944, a time of excitement when certain members of the Royal Australian Air Force (if not otherwise engaged flying sorties over Europe) played cricket at Lord's. One, Flying Officer K. R. Miller, later joined the great succession of Demon bowlers in a direct line from Spofforth. But being an all-rounder, Miller may prefer to be spoken of in the same breath as C. F. H. Leslie.

THE ASHES

...ice goes back with the urn, the ...
...r, Steel, Read and Tylecote retur...
...e welkin will ring loud,
...great crowd will feel proud,
...ulow and Bates with the urn,
...rest coming home with the urn

CHAPTER THREE

Waiting for Stoddart

The Ashes were back in England but, truth to tell, no one seemed to care where they were. After that fateful day at the Oval, and the mock obituary, few references to the Ashes can be traced until early in the twentieth century. Men were intent only on games in which touring Englishmen and Australians could show their skills, often in strange circumstances. Small wonder then that from 1884 to 1890 no fewer than seven teams set out to cross the world – eight if we remember 1887–8 when two English sides arrived in Australia. But since one of these was led by a man, C. Aubrey Smith, who more than fifty years later was better known in the English-speaking countries than any other cricketer *including* Bradman, we must refrain from smiling at the pioneers. After all, had they but known it, they were leading the way to a not-so-distant hill beyond which lay the Golden Age.

England won the three-match series of 1884 thanks to a superb century by A. G. Steel, and fine bowling by Peate and Ulyett, in an innings victory at Lord's. In command was Lord Harris, who played in a bow tie and is the only peer to have captained England against Australia. There followed a strange affair at the Oval. Two years previously, in 'Spofforth's Match', 40 wickets had fallen for 363 runs. Now, batting first in a heat wave, Australia reached 365 before the fall of their 3rd wicket. Percy McDonnell and Harry Scott made hundreds, and Murdoch 211 – the highest Test innings played in England until the advent of Bradman. As the score passed 500 and a baronial bow tie slipped for the umpteenth time, Lord Harris grew tired of Alfred Lyttelton's adverse comments on the bowling.

Remembering how Bligh had once turned to Leslie at Melbourne, his lordship invited – nay, *commanded* – Lyttelton to take off his gloves.

'Bowl!'

With W. G. in position behind the stumps, the still padded Alfred bowled. In retrospect it is clear that what unsettled the Australians was the new bowler's trajectory. In the words of one chronicler, he purveyed 'lady-like lobs'. W. E. Midwinter (the only man to play for both England and Australia against each other, and so meriting the fate which befell him) managed to snick one such lob into the Doctor's beard* from which it was rapidly retrieved and claimed as a catch, the Hon A. Lyttelton finishing with 4 for 19. As he never again bowled in Tests, his career average against Australia was 4·75, a figure unlikely to be equalled. For sheer effrontery, his observation that Dr Grace did not wash behind his ears is unlikely to be surpassed.

Late in the afternoon of the second day England began her reply to a hitherto unheard-of 551. The sun blazed as it had on Murdoch, and W. G. felt in the mood for runs. His partner Scotton may also have felt in the mood, though not for runs, it being his custom to take out squatter's rights and await the end of the season. Undismayed by the running out of Grace at 32, and by the fact that only two batsmen passed 20 – Steel 31 and *Debrett's* (in the combined persons of Harris and Lyttelton) 22 – the left-handed pride of Trent Bridge lingered. If few balls passed his bat, few balls from his bat passed the field; at one end was stalemate, at the other Australia made inroads.

Suddenly, at three o'clock on the third afternoon with England 181 for 8, Walter Read of Surrey came in. To say his brow was dark, his dudgeon high, is an understatement. He was fuming. He had watched Lord Harris write out the batting order with

---

* At Bath in 1905, after sharing in a third-wicket partnership of 320 for the Australians *v* Somerset, M. A. Noble (127) was caught behind by H. S. Poyntz off an S. M. J. Woods triple bouncer. This caused the non-striker W. W. Armstrong – on his way to 303 not out – to utter a coarse guffaw. But Poyntz did not have a beard.

growing disbelief. Was not he, Read, one of the very finest batsmen in England? W. G. said so. Then why was he going in last but one? Because Harris was a fool! So Read set about Spofforth, Palmer, Boyle and Giffen until they did not know where to pitch the ball. The scoreboard operator awoke, and Scotton blossomed like a rose – that is to say he increased his tempo from 15·14 runs an hour to 16·44. Read reached a century of devastating brilliance, the 9th wicket added 151. Alas, Scotton fell for 90, and vowed that one day he would show the Australians his full defensive powers. With time for only a score of overs, England followed on. Lyttelton opened, Harris was there at the close. His lordship had seen England through. He became Governor of Bombay.

Alfred Shaw's all professional side of 1884–5, captained by Shrewsbury, got off to a bad start in the entrepreneurial sense. Shortly before the first Test was due to begin in Adelaide, certain Australian players (all members of Murdoch's party to England) demanded half the takings from this and the Melbourne Test. As the Australians in question professed to be amateurs, their demand caused surprise. Offered thirty per cent they said, 'Not enough!' After much haggling — a twenty per cent offer, from Shaw, declined; a forty per cent demand, from which the Australians would pay their own expenses, refused – the South Australian Association stepped in with £450 for each side. The Englishmen were sorry they couldn't afford to be amateurs.

Troubles continued. Murdoch refused to allow James Lillywhite, one of the England managers, to stand as umpire. As there was no time to import men of experience from Melbourne and Sydney, two locals – Messrs I. Fisher and J. Travers – were recruited. Both performed admirably in counting the balls of an over, less so when asked to give a decision. Meanwhile four Australian batsmen had declined to practise. Not surprisingly, after Australia had won the toss at Adelaide, and McDonnell and Blackham (who had practised) made 124 and 66 respectively, the side crumpled to 243 all out. England's reply was forthright and circumspect; Ulyett (68) and Barnes (134) struck out like men who had enjoyed their practice, Scotton like one to whom 13·66 runs an hour represented profligacy.

Suddenly, after six hours' tenure, Scotton was given out stumped. Was this a good decision on the part of I. Fisher or J. Travers? At this distance of time, we can only say that had Dr Grace been present, and adjudged leg-before-wicket, he would surely have chased the offending umpire from the field and – having grabbed the kitty – continued his innings. Morality triumphed at Adelaide. McDonnell was run out for 83 in the Australian second innings, his partner Giffen having practised batting but not calling, and England won by 8 wickets. An even easier victory came to them at Melbourne after Murdoch's side had gone on strike, Australia being forced to play some men who were good on occasion, and some who had never been heard of before. The latter were never heard of again.

How Spofforth (absent at Adelaide due to a family bereavement) now returned to the fold and took 17 wickets in the third and fourth Tests; how in all five matches no fewer than twenty-eight men batted, and twenty bowled, for Australia; how the home side put their trust in four different captains – all these matters of academic interest, and England's win in the fifth Test to clinch the series, pale when set beside the events of 21 and 22 January 1885. The dates should be graven on the minds of all who seek the occasion of cricket's first excursion into the theatre of the absurd. For the moment let us no more than mention Moss Vale, a town in New South Wales, and return to that most pleasant theme – the defeat in Test matches of Australia. Being immortal, Moss Vale can wait.

Three Tests in 1886, three wins for England; two in 1886–7 both won by England who also conquered in the single match played at Sydney the following year. The Australians omitted Bannerman and McDonnell from their 1886 party; with Murdoch in temporary retirement, the loss did not improve matters. The sternly disciplined skills of Barlow – 38 not out and 30 in a tight four-wicket finish, and a match analysis of 75 overs 39 maidens 63 runs 8 wickets – put Old Trafford in festive mood, while at Lord's Shrewsbury played perhaps the century's greatest innings. With Garrett, Spofforth, Palmer and Giffen among the bowlers, and on a wicket that was at first fiery, and then (after rain) dead slow before becoming sticky, Shrewsbury batted 7 hours for 164. 'He played all the bowling as though it were as simple as A B C,' wrote an admiring George Giffen. To add point to a master batsman's genius, Briggs then took 11 for 74.

The Oval match found Australia overwhelmed by an innings and 217 runs, the most comprehensive margin in England until a Ponsford-Bradman duo took revenge in 1934. England's opening pair (at least one of them) advanced inexorably to 170, W. G. all massive authority, and the bowlers resigned. That the 170 – also Grace's eventual score – took three and three-quarter hours was due to a Nottinghamshire left-hander at the other end, his 34 oozing from the bat at 9 runs an hour. Walter Read, happy at second wicket down under A. G. Steel's leadership, made 94, Briggs hitting merrily for 53. Whereupon George Lohmann, supreme among medium-pace bowlers according to Grace and C. B. Fry, twice swept Australia aside. In this, and the three Tests of 1886–7 and 1887–8, his haul was 37 wickets at 7·91 each. Humiliation on the grand scale.

Yet if ever a pair of bowlers deserved backing from at least a competent batting side, it was C. T. B. Turner ('The Terror') and J. J. Ferris. The former – right-hand medium pace with extraordinary nip from the pitch – was clearly an Australian Maurice Tate of the eighties, Ferris left-hand fast-medium with an ability to make the ball go either way. In the first Sydney Test of 1886–7 they put England out for 45 and 184, in the second for 151 and 154, at Melbourne for 113 and 137; Australia lost all three. At Old Trafford in 1888 England managed 172, at the Oval 100; England won both. Eight times did Turner and Ferris open for Australia, between them taking 104 wickets at 13. Only at Lord's in 1888 did they finish on the winning side, and then after rain had fallen. Australia managed 116, the other innings realizing 53, 60 and 62. Turner and Ferris finished with 18 for

108; more, they were the only men to reach double figures in the victor's second innings, 32 out of 56 from the bat!

Cricket's first excursion into the theatre of the absurd had nothing to do with George Giffen's decision to sulk in his tent from 1886 until 1891, nor with an odd Australian selection. Seeking talent for the 1890 tour of England, a far-ranging eye noticed the Tasmanian K. E. Burn, the very man to act as Blackham's deputy behind the stumps and take Turner, Ferris and the young Hugh Trumble. When the party assembled at Adelaide, Burn announced he had never kept wicket previously, adding (so one hopes) 'Does it matter?' Rather as if, in 1926, the selectors had omitted Alan Kippax (which they unaccountably did) not on the grounds that he wasn't good enough but that he didn't like fish on Friday.

Here we must advise readers who regard the visit of an English side to Australia as altogether an occasion for high and grim seriousness to skip a page. During the early years of touring it was customary for Englishmen to play numerous games against odds, generally twenty-two. Matches against odds were good for Englishmen in more ways than one. They were obliged to adapt to local conditions, they were often rewarded for unusual deeds. If the pitch at Ballarat was not level, while at Gympie the tourists batted first on a pitch where cows normally took exercise, only to discover next day the men of Gympie laid down matting for their own use, then was not Scotton given mining shares for top scoring in this latter match? Two years previously at Brisbane, Walter Read had earned a plot of land; perhaps during George Parr's tour of 1864, Julius Caesar of Surrey was given the site of the present Sydney Opera House.

Shaw's men won the toss at Moss Vale and batted. For 50 minutes the bowlers toiled until, at 34, Shrewsbury contrived to get himself caught. With whoops of joy the fielders rushed from the middle to celebrate; that is to say, a lengthy lunch was taken. Misguided men of Moss Vale! Little did they know they had dismissed the wrong man, that undefeated was the maiden aunt of English cricket, William Scotton. Perhaps lunch robbed the faster bowlers of their sting and the slower of their pitch; certainly Ulyett now struck seven balls out of the ground, his share of a 60 partnership being 56. Bates came next and hit eleven balls even farther than had Ulyett. His 101 was enjoyed by spectators if not by the owners of nearby grazing cattle. At the close, after four and a quarter hours, Shaw's men were 248 for 3 – No. 2 44 not out.

On the second day Scotton applied himself. Lesser men came and went, he stayed. Last out at 432 (caught when forcing the pace), Scotton made 123 in 8 hours 15 minutes. No real estate came his way – not even enough to keep a hen – but he had shown the flag. His moral influence on Moss Vale was considerable. Just as in 1911–12 Australian mothers quelled their children with, 'If you're not good, Barnes will get you,' so in 1885 the threat was, 'I'll make you watch Scotton.'

The XXII of Moss Vale padded up. *Wisden* does not record the fate of individual batsmen, but if someone reached double figures, the other twenty-one must have failed.

England 432
Moss Vale 14*

Attewell and Peel bowled unchanged, the former singularly unsuccessful with only two wickets. Peel's analysis was remarkable: 24 overs 18 maidens 7 runs 18 wickets.

During the tour of 1884–5 Peel – against odds – took 321 wickets at 4·73 each. Facing stronger opposition, his 102 Australian Test wickets came in twenty games, his career extending into the Golden Age. He succeeded Peate, and preceded Rhodes and Verity, in a great quartet of Yorkshire slow left-handers. And now readers who skipped a page, and who alighted by chance on the 1932–3 season, come hastening back in search of humanity. Noting that in their second innings Moss

---

* Australian readers need not feel shame. At Winnipeg in 1913 the home side dismissed some Australian tourists with fast shooters, and obtained 4 byes from the first ball of their own innings. C. G. Macartney then took 6 for 0, J. N. Crawford 4 for 2. Total 6.

Vale made 19 for 4 (Peel being rested), we may continue our story.

By the end of 1890 Australian cricket was more prostrate than ever before or since. Eleven of the past twelve Tests had ended in defeat, and the cause was not hard to find. England's average innings in these matches – 182 – was far from impressive, but Australia's 111 verged on the deplorable. A great benefactor of the game in England, Lord Sheffield, decided there was only one thing to do. He must call in the Doctor. Would W. G. take a side to Australia? Zeus plucked at his beard, then began to tot up on his fingers. There would be the cost of a locum for his Bristol practice? Of course! And generous expenses? Naturally! In that case the Doctor would take a side to Australia. His fee: £3,000 – today's comparable purchasing power would be £400,000. (Great entertainers get what they ask: Noël Coward and Frank Sinatra at Las Vegas, Dame Edna anywhere.) Done! Lord Sheffield and W. G. were both satisfied, Australians waited anxiously lest they made fools of themselves.

But triumph! They won the three-match series of 1891–2 by the odd game. It was a new Australia. Hitherto their batsmen had often got out playing rash strokes, now they consolidated. The new Australia, 162 behind on the first innings at Sydney, and facing Lohmann, Attewell, Briggs and Peel, realized they were participating in a timeless Test (the first unaffected by rain to enter a fifth day): 1 for 1, 175 for 2, 254 for 3, 347 for 4. Throughout the series, Australia scored far more slowly than England, something not entirely due to three innings Bannerman played at Melbourne and Sydney and which totalled 177 runs made at 11 an hour. (Dare he have batted thus against Moss Vale?) Bobby Abel alone knew the answer to such tactics, carrying his bat for 132 in the second Test, a century which would have been denied him had not the last man, J. W. Sharpe, helped to raise the score from 235 to 307. Lord Sheffield and W. G. enjoyed the tour, Australians were unbearably ecstatic.

The cutting down to size of Australia – by an innings and 43 runs at the Oval in 1893 – was of less significance than the arrival of certain players destined to be numbered among the game's giants. If Hugh Trumble's debut for Australia was undistinguished, that of two England fast bowlers was not. W. H. Lockwood took 14 wickets in three innings, Tom Richardson's 10 for 156 at Old Trafford was the more remarkable in that he bowled unchanged during Australia's second innings for 44 overs. But overshadowing all, and counterpointing the serenity of Arthur Shrewsbury with an autocratic brilliance, a Cambridge undergraduate held sway. The Hon F. S. Jackson extended to his opponents the same benign firmness with which he had ruled his fag, Winston Churchill, at Harrow. At the Oval he was on 98 when the last man came in. So he hit a ball into the crowd. In his old age, the Rt Hon Sir Stanley Jackson – Privy Councillor, Knight Grand Commander of the Most Exalted Order of the Star of India, Knight Grand Commander of the Most Eminent Order of the Indian Empire – was asked if an attempt on his life in Bengal had not been . . . er, unnerving.

'Not as bad as facing Ernest Jones in '99. Deuced fast.'

We have climbed that not so distant hill beyond which lay the Golden Age. For the next twenty years until the Great War shattered its world for ever, Test cricket (indeed all cricket) basked in sun-lit innocence and technical bravura. It was an age of the amateur but one in which the greatest professionals rivalled – and surpassed – the achievements of their social masters. English public school coaching may have insisted on pupils learning the grammar of cricket; it was the age that insisted on pupils realizing their individual genius. The age was sometimes contrary. Who, in the Australia of 1887–8, could have guessed that one of the captains of the two English touring sides, C. A. Smith* would before long be a prop of the London and

---

* The movie-going public of the United States, as elsewhere, doted on the films of C. Aubrey Smith (knighted 1944) – among them *Lives of a Bengal Lancer*, *The Prisoner of Zenda* and *Rebecca*. His fellow bowler in the Hollywood C.C., Boris Karloff (once W. H. Pratt of Uppingham), was presumably less a Demon than a Monster.

Broadway theatre, later the essence of ducal grandeur in the then unknown wonder of American films, and captain of the Hollywood Cricket Club?

Statistics prove nothing, they illustrate. Greatly daring, we shall now let them illustrate the spirit of Test cricket in the Golden Age by comparing it with that of later times. The figures are based on the batting and bowling of both England and Australia, all series played in the latter country.

	Average total per completed innings	Runs per 100 balls	Balls per wicket
1894–5/ 1911–12 (30 Tests)	286	45·86	62·43
1920–1/ 1936–7 (25 Tests)	340	42·60	79·89
1958–9/ 1974–5 (27 Tests)	338	36·00	93·75

The fact that Australian pitches and outfields have changed over the years does not detract from the irony implicit in the above figures – that until the Second World War Tests in Australia were played to a finish (there was no need to hurry) – while since then they have been limited to thirty hours. Let us apply the figures quoted above to a Test in which four innings were completed; allowing for injured players unable to bat, and for rare declarations, there were twenty-seven matches between 1894 and 1937. Also proffered in our calculations are the five-hour day (in vogue until 1962–3) and the six-ball over (used until 1936–7 with the exception of 1924–5). The over rate is a matter for argument. When England scored 501 at a run a minute at Adelaide in 1911–12, Australia – with the very fast Cotter – managed 21·3 overs an hour. We have opted for a more modest

19 overs. Remembering three intervals between innings but not time lost for the consumption of drinks:

	TOTAL RUNS in four innings	TIME to finish a match
1894–5/ 1911–12	1,144	4 days 2 hours 24 minutes
1920–1/ 1936–7	1,360	5 days 40 minutes
1958–9/ 1974–5	in five days 1,230	44 per cent of Tests drawn

Statistics prove nothing, they merely suggest that spectators in the Golden Age had much to cheer.

CHAPTER FOUR

The Golden Age of Paradox

We must approach a myth with care. It is not enough to show Victor Trumper in the context of his time, to indicate wherein lay the nature of his greatness, to say he was himself the Golden Age. A myth must be approached with care, also obliquely and by stealth, uncontroversially. Thus: Victor Trumper was a batsman, Bert ('Dainty') Ironmonger was not. Ironmonger, who played against England five times between 1928 and 1933, was a fine left-arm spin bowler but a batsman so negligible he might as well have taken a table leg to the crease and sat on it. His least productive twenty Test innings realized an average of 1·50; Trumper's figures make an interesting comparison.

Opinions of Victor Trumper varied little. During MCC's tour of Australia in 1903–4, C. B. Fry rose at a London dinner to toast the 'world's greatest batsman'; England's captain, P. F. Warner, would one day write, 'He had grace, ease, style and power and a quickness of foot both in jumping out and in getting back to a ball that can surely never be surpassed.' B. J. T. Bosanquet, reviewing this same tour, declared Trumper 'by far the best bat on either side', the others including R. E. Foster, J. T. Tyldesley, Tom Hayward, Clem Hill, Duff, Noble and Armstrong. Asked by Warner how he would like his field placed, George Hirst shook his head: 'It doesn't much matter, sir, where we place 'em, Victor will still do as 'e likes.'

Some were less restrained in their praise. The brilliant Charlie Macartney for instance: 'I wasn't fit to tie up Vic's laces as a batsman'; A. C. MacLaren, a man not noted for his modesty, said with a snort: 'My best innings compared with one by Victor was shoddy – hack work!' H. L. Collins, among the wisest of Australian captains, summed up great batsmen simply: 'Put Trumper up there, and then talk of Bradman, Hobbs and George Headley.' Mrs C. B. Fry foresaw the day when someone would paint Trumper's portrait and have it hung in a National Gallery. 'He will be dressed in white, with his splendid neck bared to the wind, standing on short green grass against a blue sky; he will be waiting for the ball, the orchestra to strike up.' So, we must approach a myth with care, but noting that Trumper's least productive twenty Test innings against England averaged 1·65. But, the reader, will ask, surely that was not the whole of Trumper? Indeed not. Excluding two brief innings when he either retired injured or made a late token appearance sadly incapacitated, Trumper's least productive *sixty* innings against England averaged 17·40. How, then, shall we reconcile this form with the opinions of the batsmen quoted above? Have we alighted upon the paradox of both Trumper and of the Golden Age itself – that spectators crooned over a dozen perfectly executed strokes while today they take delight in (or pretend to) a five-hours' century laboriously compiled for the greater glory of England or Australia? Once batsmen were prepared to take chances and play their favourite strokes against bowlers who were willing to feed those strokes. Criminal risk-taking? Or playing cricket, even Test cricket, as a game?

It is 14 December 1894, Blackham and Stoddart have gone out to toss at Sydney. There is no Demon bowler on either side but England have a Titan, Tom Richardson. If ever a fast bowler was some elemental force of nature, it was he. Tall and of superb physique, he could bring the ball back sharply on any wicket. He never bowled short, and when he struck a batsman on an unprotected thigh (a most frequent occurrence) he would apologize and, if the blow was particularly painful, run down and rub the bruise. Throughout his career a fielding side had to be content with one ball to last an innings; throughout the Golden Age rather more than half of England's opening attacks included a slow bowler. This December day Australia won the toss in

perfect conditions, Richardson opening with the slow left-arm
Peel. (Larwood with Verity, Tyson with Wardle – as someone
would say in Oscar Wilde's new play due early in 1895, 'The idea
is grotesque and irreligious.') And Richardson is suffering from a
feverish chill.

The Titan attacks. In his 2nd over he bowls Lyons. 10 for 1.
The first two balls of his 5th over see Harry Trott and
Darling go in like fashion. 21 for 3 off 50 balls, 25 minutes
gone. Deduct 4 minutes for incoming batsmen: England, with
one slow bowler but the other using a long run, are completing
their overs too quickly – two and a half minutes each. A timeless
Test played by men who have yet to learn. So have the new pair,
Giffen and Iredale. If the Titan attacks, they will counter-
attack. At a run a minute 171 are added before Iredale is caught
for 81, giving Francis Ford his only wicket against Australia.
Poor Stoddart! Peel and Briggs are accurate but no more,
Brockwell commonplace; Lockwood manages three overs,
clearly unwell. Richardson, who likes to bowl all and every day,
has to be used in short bursts. At the close Australia are 346 for 5:
Giffen's great innings of 161 is ended but Gregory is well
established.

Shortly before 3.30 on Saturday, Australia are out for 586,
Gregory (201) and Blackham (74) having added 154 for the 9th
wicket. Since that disastrous start the batsmen have scored at 83
runs an hour, the bowlers responding with 24·2 overs. What shall
England do? With a Scotton in his Oval '86 mood – better still
with *two* Scottons – the target of 586 would be reached in just
over seven days, so disrupting the tour programme. But Scotton
is dead, doubtless welcomed by the Lord and commanded to bat
for ever against XXII of Hades. In this world at Sydney England
total 325, neither a poor score nor slowly made, just inadequate.
However, Blackham has sustained the injury that will make this
his last Test *and*, it is not too much to say, help England to 437
(Albert Ward 117) in her second innings.

On the sixth morning, with Australia needing only 64 to win
with 8 wickets standing, George Giffen, not out overnight,

rejoices as the sun pours through his window. In spite of batting for nearly five hours and then bowling 118 overs, George feels omnipotent.* So do Peel and Briggs, for different reasons.

'What a morning, Jack!' said Giffen to Blackham, whose face was 'as long as a coffee pot'.

'It has been pouring half the night, George.'

Australia are helpless on the 'sticky' and lose by 10 runs. The only man in Sydney who might conceivably have brought them victory – he would six years later – wasn't playing. The seventeen-year-old Victor Trumper had bowled at the nets against Stoddart's men – 'Not bad!' Invited to bat – 'One day that boy will be the best player in the world.' For Sydney Juniors he made 67 against the Englishmen.

So far Richardson's figures of 64·2–16–208–6 suggest only determination. Greatness will soon be his. In the second Test at Melbourne, Australia (with Giffen as captain) put England in on a wet wicket: 75 all out, Turner 5 for 32. With conditions easing – and the captains had agreed that at the close of play a heavy roller would be used to iron out the dents – it was clear that Australia had only to get through the day with minimum loss, and a big lead was likely on Monday. In the event the Australian loss was all 10 wickets, their lead 48. Richardson 5 for 57. After the feverish chill, white-hot passion. On a pitch now free from sin, England 'stonewall' (Giffen's word) at a soul-destroying 47 runs an hour. Everyone in double figures, Stoddart 173 – 'I had to buck up for England, home and beauty' – total 475. Iredale and Harry Trott fought well but England won by 94. Two-up with three to play.

A month later the series was all square, Australia winning by 382 at Adelaide and by an innings and 147 at Sydney. The latter game gave Australia ample revenge for that earlier disappointment. Put in after heavy rain, they were soon 51 for 6 before Harry Graham, the 'Little Dasher', marked his Test debut in

---

* Giffen liked to recall two matches South Australia played with Victoria in 1891, his personal contribution being 508 runs in two innings, and 28 wickets for 368.

Australia, as he had in England, with a century. Albert Trott, remembered now as the only man to hit a ball over the Lord's pavilion, drove mightily for 84 not out. On the second day a violent storm, on the third 68 overs from Harry Trott, Giffen and Turner were enough to rout England twice. The Adelaide match was purgatory for men used to getting their eight hours' sleep in Surbiton and points north; here they got none. The heat demoralized, Australian 10th-wicket stands of 81 and 64 confirmed England's need of a second penetrative bowler. Throughout the series Australian last pairs accounted for an astonishing one-eighth of the home side's runs. As Richardson took 8 wickets in 52 overs, the thermometer rose to 105, then dropped to 102. The thermometer was in the shade, Richardson was not.

All square. Expert opinion, and that of men pouring into Melbourne by train and steamer from up to two thousand miles away, held that the toss would mean the match. Stoddart called wrong. At the close on 1 March 1895 Australia were 282 for 4. Giffen, Gregory, Darling and Lyons all passed the half-century, the tenth pair performed as usual. Australia 414. Let England beat that! They finished a mere 29 short, thanks to a majestic 120 by MacLaren (hitherto a failure), and 73 by Peel, whose first run pleased him after 'spectacles' at Adelaide *and* Sydney. Australia ended the third day 98 ahead with 9 second-innings wickets in hand.

A high wind blew Melbourne inside out on March 5: the scoreboard held down by guy-ropes, ladies' hats often fielded, clouds of dust swirling. After Harry Trott had been bowled by Peel, Giffen and Iredale settled in with ominous authority. Then, at 105 for 2, Richardson was brought back. The game's climacteric: Australia 134 on with two men at the crease, and two to come, already centurions in the series. The wicket was still full of runs but how many could England hope to get in the fourth innings? The Titan bounded in – Iredale bowled for 18, Giffen for 51, and Gregory for 30. 179 for 5. Briggs intervened by foxing Lyons: 'Thanks Johnny, these are my wickets!' Graham trapped leg-before, Albert Trott comprehensively bowled. 'Mine!' Joe Darling presented a problem gratefully solved when Peel beat him through the air for 50. Richardson restricted the last pair to 19, Australia all out for 267, the Hero 6 for 104 off 45·2 overs. In nine innings, virtually eight, his haul was 32 wickets at 26·53, *26 of them bowled*. And Peel! 27 wickets at 26·70. Turn when possible – and flight, the seductive flight of implied innocence. Horan of *The Australasian* discovered he had run out of superlatives to use of Richardson; being the man he was, he looked around and found some more.

The 297 needed by England seemed an awesome target when Brockwell and Stoddart were out for 28. The captain looked glum: J. T. Brown in with Albert Ward, MacLaren next, then four men all averaging under 20 in the Tests, and two tail-enders. Conversation in the pavilion echoed disbelief:

'That can't be Jack Brown batting.'

'Well, Jack was the last to go in.'

'But he plays for Yorkshire.'

'If he goes on like this, he won't again.'

While Ward gleans a run here and a run there, Brown lays waste. Front foot, back foot; force square, drive straight; slash through the slips, hook, pull, leap to half-volley, lie back to ball just short of a length. 50 in 28 minutes. Giffen scratches his head: with the benefit of hindsight we may murmur, 'The young Hobbs off the front foot, the mature Hammond off the back.' The field disperses, Brown slows down; when he is caught off McKibbin, he has made 140 out of 210 in 2 hours 25 minutes. Ward goes placidly to 93, leaving MacLaren and Peel to put the finishing touches to an amazing 6 wickets victory. Stoddart beams as though he has planned it all. 'I had to buck up for England, home and beauty.' Had he used the royal 'We', he could have included Brown. And Richardson.

The constant star of Australia in 1894–5 was George Giffen – 475 runs at 52·77 and 34 wickets at 24·11. The end of his season was less successful, and more melodramatic, when South Australia played Stoddart's men on their way home and were hit for 609. Giffen took 5 for 309 off 87 overs; Giffen was the South Australian captain. But the sensation of the match was a youth only a few days past his eighteenth birthday who made 150 not out and 56, and played Richardson as he had scarcely ever been played before.

Clem Hill had arrived. Tom Richardson was approaching his finest hour.

The Golden Age was already rich in achievement; it now awaited its first genius. He duly appeared at Old Trafford in July 1896. Men marvelled, the Australians did not believe their eyes. 'Yes, he can play,' was one opinion, 'but he must have a lot of Satan in him.' And he wasn't even English but Kumar Shri Ranjitsinhji. His bat bemused bowlers, conjured runs by deft inscriptions on the air, was obedient to no laws save those of Ranji himself. Who, for instance, has successfully emulated his leg glide?

'I step across the wicket a little with my left foot, put my bat in front of my right leg behind my left calf and then just as the ball comes to the bat I pivot round on the toe of my right foot, turning the other part of my body towards the on side.'

There was a warning: 'But I would not recommend this method to anyone to whom it does not come naturally.'

England began the third and final day at Old Trafford perilously placed; following on, they were still 72 in arrears with 4 second-innings wickets already down. Ranji, 41 not out overnight, was at once assaulted by Ernest Jones with short-pitched deliveries. Now whereas Richardson and Lockwood were fast bowlers, Jones was very fast – probably as fast as anyone in history. A month earlier in the Lord's Test, he had sent the very first ball of the England innings through W. G.'s beard, a happening at which the Champion took umbrage before taking it out on Jones.

When a fast bowler pitched the ball up to Ranji, the batsman was apt to leap at it like some playful panther. But on this morning at Old Trafford Jones did not pitch the ball up, he sought to intimidate. The other batsmen took evasive action, two managing 19 runs and one 16; Ranji gave signs that he wished to become involved. Because Jones sometimes bowled on or outside the off stump, Ranji cut him to ribbons; because many balls were bowled on the leg stump, Ranji had to hook. The way was simple: move the body quickly so that the rising ball threatened the left temple. In no other way could the stroke be properly played. Then, at the precise moment – precision was of the essence – the bat swept across the line. Four behind square-leg.

Not that 154 not out made in 3 hours entirely satisfied Ranji. It was a flawed innings. He did not like flawed innings. A double century at Hove would be tarnished because one ball struck him on the pads: returning to the pavilion, he indicated the mark and asked the attendant to remove it forthwith. So at Old Trafford – feeling some liquid running down his neck, he sought the cause and discovered blood: a Jones bouncer had nicked his left ear. He, Ranji, had misjudged a hook; 154 should have been 158. The Prince was most displeased. If, as Fry said, Jessop raised rustic batting to a science, then Ranji used science to make dreams come true. His own, of course.

How Australia, requiring only 125 for victory, groped their way home by 3 wickets has been incomparably described by Neville Cardus. As the match ended, the players ran from the field, all save Richardson from whom the winning run had been scored:

> 'He stood at the bowling crease, dazed. *Could* the match have been lost? his spirit protested. Could it be that the gods had looked on and permitted so much painful striving to go by unrewarded? His body still shook from the violent motion. He stood there like some fine animal baffled at the uselessness of great strength and effort in this world . . . A companion led him to the pavilion, and there he fell wearily to a seat.'

Or was this one of Sir Neville's sublimer flights of fancy? The drama critic James Agate, twelve years Cardus's senior, professed to have been present that day at Old Trafford. He swore Richardson had legged it from the field far ahead of the others and been the first to down a pint. Let us settle for Cardus. The Titan who could bowl 42 overs and three balls *unrelieved* and take 6 for 76; who in the first two Tests of 1896 gathered 24 wickets at 17 to the 12 at 40 of such bowlers as Lohmann, J. T. Hearne, Briggs and F. S. Jackson – that man deserves to be immortalized in the mythology of cricket. In reality? S. F. Barnes gave best to only one bowler, Tom Richardson.

The Golden Age was rich in achievement and had produced its first genius. In 1897 an English cricketer began to practise an immoral act. He practised it the following winter while Stoddart took another side to Australia (and a four–one defeat), when MacLaren and Ranji both averaged over 50, only to see Darling, Hill and McLeod respond in unison and first contain, then collar the English attack. With no beard at the other end to inspire or inhibit him, Ernest Jones was magnificent, Trumble proclaimed himself as the greatest medium-pace off-spinner of all time, M. A. Noble emerged thoughtfully and with success. Richardson had diminished from a superb to a good bowler.* The series was well summed up in the final match at Sydney when Darling drove, hooked and cut 160 at a run a minute. His was the last wicket Tom Richardson took for England.

Practising an immoral act is fun if accessories are willing to participate. They were during the very hot summer of 1899. At Trent Bridge W. G.'s final Test coincided with Wilfred Rhodes's first, at Lord's – when Australia won by 10 wickets to retain the Ashes; Hill made 135, a score equalled by the not out No. 6. Of the latter innings men cooed, babbled, or just sighed with joy; those unaffected by aesthetic considerations approved of

---

* Richardson was willing, so Surrey guaranteed him a brief career. In each of the three years 1895–7 he averaged only six per cent fewer balls than Gregory and Macdonald bowled *together* in 1921, eleven per cent more than another prolific wicket-taker, the slow left-hander Lock, in 1955–7. In four years 1894–7 Richardson bowled 29,435 balls, in 1927–8 and 1931–2 Larwood 17,814.

Richardson   1,005 wkts at 14·08, balls per wkt 29·28
Larwood   529 wkts at 13·86, balls per wkt 33·82

Trumper but felt they would choose Clem Hill to play for their lives. The Trumper pattern was set in 1899: two innings averaged 198, seven 11·71. But who cared about runs when Victor showed he had at least three strokes for every ball? With a minimum of effort, he achieved perfection of style. The Golden Age worshipped style.

If a man practises an immoral act long enough – and, be it noted, on the lawns of country houses frequented by Old Etonians – the outcome deserves to be imperfect. So it was at Lord's on 20 July 1900. Samuel Coe, a Leicestershire left-hander, was stumped for 98 off a ball that bounced four times, though whether he was beaten through the air or off the pitch, and if the latter by which bounce, is not recorded. The bowler concerned was Bernard James Tindall Bosanquet who, in this same match, opened for Middlesex (captained by P. F. Warner) and scored 136 and 139 at a brisk 59 runs an hour. His innings gave him pleasure, his wicket even more, for it was the first he had taken in county cricket with a . . . 'What shall we call it? A googly.' In due course Arthur Shrewsbury also fell victim to the species.

'That new ball of yours, Mr Bosanquet, is unfair.'

'Not at all, Arthur. Merely immoral.'

As the fate of the Ashes over the next sixty years was sometimes to be decided by the exploitation of Bosanquet's discovery, a tentative history is in order:

1897–1900: B. J. T. places a young cousin Louise at far end of lawn and experiments with a tennis ball (or so insists Nigel Dennis, novelist and critic, son of Louise, *née* Bosanquet).

20 July 1900: Lord's. S. Coe baffled.

15 August 1902: Trent Bridge. William Gunn, local figure of Victorian rectitude, is stumped more than halfway down the wicket seeking to destroy a googly. Bosanquet 7 for 57.

26 November 1902: San Francisco. First googly bowled

outside England. Bosanquet 11 for 37, Lord Hawke's side *v* XVIII of California.

15 January 1903: Wellington, New Zealand. Bosanquet offers his assorted lures. (Round the corner at Mount Cook Boys' School, an eleven-year-old fast bowler, Clarrie Grimmett, is unaware of his destiny.)

21 March 1903: Sydney. Playing for New South Wales *v* Lord Hawke's side, Victor Trumper has made 37 in 20 minutes. Bosanquet says a silent prayer and bowls the first googly to be sent down in Australia. Trumper plays for the leg-break, his middle stump is hit.

3 March 1904: Sydney. Bosanquet takes 6 for 51, so winning the fourth Test for England who regain the Ashes. (Watching are Herbert Hordern, aged twenty, and Arthur Mailey, sixteen. Both leave the ground pondering deeply.)

Little more than twenty-one months later at White Cliffs, New South Wales, William Joseph O'Reilly entered this world, doubtless appealing lustily and bowling – the breeze behind him – nothing but googlies at an indecency of left-handers.

Sydney Francis Barnes did not bowl the googly. 'I never needed it.' His natural ball was a fast-medium *spun* leg-break. He also swerved. So evolved the 'Barnes ball' which moved late in the air before reversing direction off the pitch. Taken by MacLaren to Australia in 1901–2 with an English first-class record of 13 wickets at 37·38 runs each, he rewarded a prescient captain by dismissing nineteen Australians in two Tests before withdrawing from the remainder of the tour with a knee injury. Oddly, his balls per wicket in the Tests was exactly the same, 41, as that against XXII of New England and XVIIIs of Bendigo and Ballarat, perhaps proving that Barnes welcomed strong opposition. Less oddly, in view of the bowler's intractable temperament, MacLaren fell out with his genius; at sea in rough weather he mused, 'There's one comfort, if we go down that bugger Barnes will go down with us.'

SYDNEY FRANCIS BARNES, 1901–12
The Bowler

Barnes did not require a captain – 'There's only one captain of a side when I'm bowling – me!' – He required an impresario.

'Ladies and gentlemen! It is my proud privilege to present to you the most stupendous, the colossal, the one and only – BARNES! We have assembled as supporting cast the finest fielders the world has ever seen, or ever will see. Godfrey Evans to keep wicket; Wally Hammond, Jack Gregory and Bobby Simpson in slips; Percy Chapman in gully; Jack Hobbs at cover; Gilbert Jessop at extra-cover; Tony Lock at short-leg; and to make sure that no snick reaches the boundary, "Nip" Pellew and Don Bradman. Pray silence while Barnes inspects his field.'

Five minutes pass. Barnes *appears* satisfied.

'Ladies and gentlemen. Watch now as I hand Barnes this ball. Not, as you will observe, a new ball, but the newest ball ever made. With this ball Barnes will earn £1,000 a wicket.'

A drum-roll.

'Ladies and gentlemen, I give you – BARNES!'

Richie Benaud could doubtless have handled Barnes.

1902

1902 was Trumper. At Edgbaston Hirst and Rhodes skittled Australia for 36 on a rain-damaged pitch, at Sheffield Barnes took 6 for 49. But 1902 was Trumper. Trumble wrought devastation with 26 wickets in three Tests – F. S. Jackson's perfect back foot technique often subjugated even him. But 1902 was Trumper. At the Oval England were set 263 in the fourth innings on a bowlers' pitch and lost MacLaren, Palairet, J. T. Tyldesley, Tom Hayward and Braund for 48. Jessop joined the imperturbable Jackson. 50 in an hour to the great hitter. Because this was the Golden Age, the Australians continued to attack – *they wanted to win the match.* On 92 Jessop lifted Trumble high above the pavilion balcony (only 4 in those days), then cut the slow trundling Armstrong so hard the ball might have been bowled as fast as light – or by Ernest Jones. Jessop's second 50 took a quarter of an hour. Hysteria. Jessop out. The rest of the game was 'a crescendo of excitement' according to *Wisden*.

Perhaps to twenty thousand spectators, possibly to the Australians – not to Hirst and Rhodes, who came together at 248 for 9. This was the moment for a Yorkshire *adagio*; whatever George said (or did not say) to Wilfred about 'getting 'em in ones', that was how the pair took England to victory. But 1902 was Trumper.

The Golden Age of paradox. Trumper played in eight series against England, heading the batting averages once (1903–4) to Hill's four times. A. G. ('Johnnie') Moyes, a good enough cricketer to be selected for the aborted 1914–15 tour of South Africa and later Australia's historian of the game, worshipped Hill, who knew his own worth. 'Ah! but just you wait till you see Victor.' In 1902 Trumper marched processionally through England; on pudding wickets, on drying, even on sticky wickets, he conquered with 2,570 runs, cruising at 45 to 50 an hour, with eleven centuries – top score 128.* Five other Australians either equalled or vastly surpassed 128, but Trumper's aggregate was 900 more than the next man's. Yet in five Test innings (the Lord's game was abandoned after less than 2 hours' play) he made only 18, 15, 1, 4 and 2 run out.

It was hinted earlier that whereas Bert Ironmonger could not bat, Victor Trumper could. And although Ranji, Fry, Jessop, Hirst and Barnes were dropped, and Hobbs omitted, from England sides, Trumper was always chosen for Australia. Were the selectors justified in persevering with a man of whose 71 innings against England 60 averaged only 17·40? Presumably so in the Golden Age when, leaving such matters as style out of the argument, certain batsmen were match-winners. Trumper was one, so after him were Macartney, McCabe and Harvey. Converting (unforgivably to aesthetes) the achievements of master batsmen into mere runs, the eleven most productive

---

* When Trumper reached 100, the next man made sure his bat was handy. In 1902 Trumper's eleven hundreds in three-day games averaged 115; in 1930 Bradman's six hundreds in three-day games averaged 395. Figures prove nothing, they illustrate.

innings of the above named averaged Macartney 108, McCabe 120, Harvey 121, and Trumper 131.

Trumper won the series of 1902 – that is, he created the conditions which permitted Australia's bowlers to dismiss England without having to perform miracles – by batting for 2 hours and 45 minutes: between 11.55 a.m. and 12.45 p.m. on 4 July at Sheffield, and for just under 2 hours on 24 July at Old Trafford. The former was the more remarkable, if less famous, innings. Australia had made 194 (Barnes 6 for 49) and England 145 (Saunders 5 for 50, Noble 5 for 51), the ball moving sharply, the light sometimes poor. Just before noon on the second day Hirst and Rhodes bowled to Trumper and Duff. Twenty were scored at a run a minute before Duff was caught for 1. Hill came in, seemingly to hold one end – Hill whose 119 struck men afterwards as an eclipsed masterpiece. Trumper was on fire. 'Spoil a bowler's length and you've got him.' Hirst's dreaded swerve was treated like a child's plaything, Rhodes found himself driven by a batsman yards down the wicket. Hirst retired before the storm, Barnes took over, only to find good length balls on the off stump played late with a straight bat wide of mid-on to the boundary. Braund's leg-breaks were consumed. Trumper 62 in 50 minutes, his side 129 ahead with 8 wickets to fall (remember Hill?) – the game was Australia's.

The Old Trafford Test was deservedly England's. To take 9 Australian wickets for 126, reply with 262, and then to dismiss the enemy for 86 (wonderful Lockwood with 11 wickets for 70! disdainful Jackson's finest hundred!): what more could partisans hope for? Why, with only 70 or 80 Australian runs made before lunch on the first day, England could send in Lilley and Rhodes to knock off the few needed for victory. The Old Trafford Test was deservedly England's – from two o'clock on the first day. Yet shortly before five in the afternoon two days later, Fred Tate left the ground a broken man. Chosen to play because Lord Hawke (President and captain of Yorkshire, chairman of the England Selectors) refused to release Schofield Haigh from his county obligations, and also in place of Hirst and Barnes, poor Tate missed a vital catch and then, last man in, was bowled with England only four short of victory.*

Australia did not make a good start of 70 or 80 runs to the Old Trafford Test, they made such a wonderful start that they won the game before lunch, taken at 173 for 1. The wicket was dead, the sun hidden and not yet roused to cook the turf. When it was, 9 wickets fell for 126. MacLaren instructed his bowlers to contain the Australians until lunch, and set his fields accordingly. And? Not to quote Cardus on Trumper is as though we were to ignore Bernard Darwin on Bobby Jones – the devotion of the lover to the beloved: 'Over his play was cast a robe of purple; underneath were the cannons of battle.' Victor Trumper advanced against England's bowlers. He drove and pulled, cut, then drove and pulled again. When the field was adjusted, as it was repeatedly, he hit the ball through the gaps newly created. Soon after the start of play he twice drove Rhodes far beyond the prescribed confines of Old Trafford into the practice ground. Years later MacLaren expostulated: 'Now I couldn't place my long-on in the practice ground . . . could I?' With Duff employing his customary short-arm savagery, the pair devoured all bowlers. *Wisden* insisted everyone bowled too short, but what is length when a Trumper has the practice ground in his sights? Wet foot-holds prevented the introduction of Lockwood until just before lunch, but who would back Lockwood – or Barnes or Spofforth – against an inspired Trumper? When Duff was caught for 54, the total was *135 made in 80 minutes*. Hill watched until veal and ham pie broke the spell: Australia 173 for 1, Trumper not out 103.

England recovered her pride after two o'clock on the first day. By then, thanks to Trumper, 1902's battle for the Ashes had been decided.

---

* Consolation for Tate came some time later in the person of his son Maurice, but in those days he was a seven-year-old with big feet and no aptitude for cricket.

VICTOR THOMAS TRUMPER, 1899–1912
Prince of the Golden Age

1903–4

The sayings of wise men are the result of thought and observation. When Victor Trumper played what he termed a 'back-cut' at an outswinger from Ted Arnold and was brilliantly caught in the slips, Wilfred Rhodes noted that the Australian score was 2, and clicked his tongue. When Duff did exactly the same thing 7 runs later, Rhodes again clicked his tongue. Indeed, his tongue was still in the clicking position when Clem Hill decided to back-cut Hirst: Australia 12 for 3. 'Cut never were business stroke,' said Rhodes to himself, then, for the rest of his life, to all mankind.

Pelham Francis Warner blinked with joy. So this was what Test matches were like! He had not previously played against Australia, now (F. S. Jackson being unavailable) he was captain of the first side sent out by the MCC. Passengers on the *Orantes* had included the Countess of Darnley, Warner's fiancée Miss Agnes Blyth, and Bishop Welldon, the last named being asked if it was wrong to pray to beat Australians.

'My dear Warner, anything which tends to the prestige of England is worth praying for.' And Albert Knight, one of Warner's party not appearing in the current Sydney match – was he praying? Possibly, it being his custom to take guard at the crease before bowing his head for a few moments. Walter Brearley of Lancashire was outraged by public prayer and vowed he would report Knight to the MCC.

Whether from prayers answered or strokes injudicious, Australia were 12 for 3. But Noble and Armstrong both eschewed the cut and lived chastely, batted in fact as men determined to last out the day until, in mid-afternoon, Armstrong was bowled. Not only was he bowled, he had become Test cricket's first victim of the googly. Bosanquet had struck. Just before the close he struck again as Gregory played for the leg-break which turned inside out. 259 for 7 was a good recovery owing almost everything to Noble's undefeated 131. Next day

Australia were out for 285, England at once losing Warner for 0 and Tom Hayward for 15.

Hereabouts the game became eccentric. Arnold, normally a tail-ender, persuaded Warner to send him in early, arguing he couldn't do worse at four than he had been doing at nine. But no sooner had Arnold gone in than John Tyldesley got out, his response to a timeless Test being 53 in 56 minutes. R. E. Foster (the most glorious of seven brothers, all of whom played for Worcestershire and one, Basil, became a star of Daly's Theatre) proved ill at ease and was unable to time the ball. Braund succeeded Arnold, still Foster's bat refused to obey his brain; for him, 71 in 3 hours was appalling. England 243 for 4 at the close on Saturday – damn it, they should have been at least 300!

On Monday inspiration. Was Foster a greater master of the cut than Ranji? He was. Could his on-drive surpass that of Fry? It could. Did his feet move as rapidly as Tyldesley's? They did. Were the Australian fielders made to feel as useless as Trumper had rendered Englishmen in 1902? They were. Foster and Braund (102) 192 for the 5th wicket; three men went cheaply, then Foster and Relf* 115 for the 9th wicket. Wilfred Rhodes came forth – 'He will make runs in Australia,' said Ranji to Warner, 'but take few wickets.' In 66 minutes Foster and Rhodes made 130. Then, quite exhausted, Foster was caught for 287, his first Test innings. On Monday he had travelled serenely at 50 runs an hour. Rhodes, left high and dry on 40, murmured, 'Ah like battin'.' With England's 577 looming on the scoreboard, Noble sent in Gregory and Kelly to play out time. 'Please! no back-cuts.' Australia 16 without loss – only 276 behind.

Counter-attack. The exclamation mark is omitted because Noble was a wise leader. None wiser has led Australia.

---

* Relf, batting at No. 10 in this match, did the 'double' of 1,000 runs and 100 wickets in an English season eight times. By the end of their careers, eight of the men playing at Sydney in 1903 had totalled 50 'doubles': Rhodes 16, Hirst 14, Relf 8, Arnold 4, Braund and the Australian Armstrong 3 each, Bosanquet and Hayward 1 apiece. Lilley, a great wicketkeeper, three times topped 1,000 runs in a season.

Consolidate – *then* counter-attack. When Kelly was bowled by Arnold at 36, Duff joined Gregory who fell to Rhodes in the last over before lunch. 108 for 2: only 92 had been added in an hour and a half. Consolidate. Duff and Hill obeyed orders, though the former was sorely tempted to penetrate Rhodes's packed off-side field. Not a risk was taken, only a canny three runs an over. 120, 130 . . . If things were not getting out of control, they were not under control. 150, 160 . . . Did Warner recall writing to MacLaren in late summer, asking if he advised taking Barnes to Australia?

'God, no! If he doesn't break down, he'll . . .' MacLaren had supplied details of Barnes's alleged temperamental failings.

170, 180 . . .

Warner was stuck with Bosanquet's blend of long-hops and full-tosses . . . 190. Clem Hill seemed unlikely to follow the example of S. Coe of Leicestershire and be stumped off a four-bouncer even if, on the faster Australian wickets, such a delivery would achieve only three bounces.

Duff was out! The tempter had trapped him, Relf taking a mis-hit in the covers. 191 for 3, last man 84. As the crowd stretched itself, a mighty roar came from the Hill. Here he was at last! With 20 minutes to go before tea, Victor would . . . Trumper scored 7 before tea, playing carefully down the line. Australia 207 for 3, Clem Hill 46.

Minutes after the resumption a drive passed mid-off who sensed rather than saw the ball.

'Mr Warner,' said Rhodes, 'I want a long-on, a long-off *and* a deep extra-cover.'

This did not prevent the batsmen scoring freely at the other end. 234 for 3, Braund with his leg-breaks from the Randwick end. His first ball was elegantly cut to the boundary, so was the next, only finer. Trumper's wrists were in order. The third ball went for four byes, the fourth stroked effortlessly past cover. The fifth – and this showed Trumper's mood – was played back to the bowler, the sixth driven wide of Hirst at mid-off. The batsmen ran one, two, three; as Hirst threw, they went for a fourth. The ball slipped from the fielder's hand and Trumper called Hill, who had overrun by some ten yards on the fourth run, for a fifth. Relf now threw – *perfectly* – at the far end towards which Hill was running. Lilley whipped off the bails and umpire Bob Crockett raised a finger. Foster at short-leg, and Hayward deep at point, agreed later that Hill was out by at least a foot. But on his return to the crease (again he had overrun, this time by fifteen yards), Hill refused to believe he was out. The crowd turned on their enemy, Crockett.

'Crock-Crock-Crock-Crock.' The noise was like an amplification of frogs. Warner walked to the Members' Stand but the response was deafening. He decided to take his side off but was dissuaded by the new batsman, Noble. Trumper came to the rescue by taking four successive 4s from Braund's next over. His stroke play was incandescent, his confidence supreme; on 90, he hit 4,4,2 off Relf and the crowd forgot about Crockett. Most incredible was Trumper's ability to force balls just short of a length anywhere between mid-on and square-leg. At the close, with Australia 367 for 5, he was 119 not out; in 100 minutes after tea, Trumper had scored 112, in the final 40 minutes 64. Next day he continued in like vein, carrying his score to 185. Lilley held this innings to be not only Trumper's masterpiece but the finest he had ever kept to.

'If Trumper had remained to double his score – which he might well have done had he not run out of partners – I should never have tired of watching him.'

Five England bowlers with 4 wickets for 363 did not enjoy Australia's second innings; the slow left-hander who, according to Ranji, would be useless in Australia, finished with 40·2 overs 10 maidens 94 runs 5 wickets. Rhodes liked bowling to Trumper, who was accorded the accolade of being 'a good bat'. England deserved to win this first Test though it might have been a close thing, even defeat. Needing 194 to win, they lost Warner, Tyldesley, Foster and Braund for 82. Then George Hirst, on a 'pair', pushed his first ball into short-leg's hands. Laver, normally the safest of catchers, dropped it. As it turned out,

England's victory meant the Ashes, for the remaining Tests went with the toss, the second and the fifth being settled by rain. Both were played at Melbourne, and a sticky there demanded super-human skill.

The second Test saw England move from 277 for 2 to 315 for 9 (Foster retired ill for 49 and could not bat in the second innings), whereupon Rhodes demoralized all the Australian batsmen save one. Pitching on the middle and off stumps of mere mortals, Rhodes paid Trumper the compliment of bowling outside the off stump. When England batted again, Trumble broke back more than a foot and made the ball rise chest high. Johnny Tyldesley's answer put even Trumper's in the shade; where the Australian leaped to kill everything, the Englishman treated the conditions as though they were an everyday occurrence. The quality of the two innings may be seen by noting the runs made by the bemused:

Trumper 74: 10, 5, 0, 1, 18, 2, 1, 8, 0, 2 not out

Tyldesley 62: 3, 0, 3, 0, 4, 9, 0, 10 not out, 4

Rhodes's match figures of 15 for 124 off 30·2 overs suffered through 8 catches being missed off him, some extremely simple. Australia's revenge for these humiliations came in the final Test (victory by 218 runs, England's totals 61 and 101) but then the series had been settled.

Not in the third match at Adelaide, when Australia were 129 for 1 at lunch with Duff outshining his partner and 200 for 1 made in 135 minutes, but in the return encounter at Sydney. At last Warner's oddity, the seducer of S. Coe and Arthur Shrewsbury, found his length. Three Australians were stumped (one, Clem Hill, said Bosanquet had himself won back the Ashes), none having the smallest idea of the ball's turn. When the 9th Australian second-innings wicket fell – and before some rustic heaves from 'Tibby' Cotter – Bose had taken 6 for 12. It was ironical that Warner, who later became identified with the maintenance of cricket's traditions, should have encouraged the game's greatest revolutionary outrage.

AUSTRALIA *v* ENGLAND
Played at Sydney 11, 12, 14, 15, 16, 17 December 1903

AUSTRALIA

R. A. Duff	c Lilley b Arnold	3	(3) c Relf b Rhodes	84
V. T. Trumper	c Foster b Arnold	1	(5) not out	185
C. Hill	c Lilley b Hirst	5	(4) run out	51
M. A. Noble	c Foster b Arnold	133	(6) st Lilley b Bosanquet	22
W. W. Armstrong	b Bosanquet	48	(7) c Bosanquet b Rhodes	27
A. J. Hopkins	b Hirst	39	(8) c Arnold b Rhodes	20
W. P. Howell	c Relf b Arnold	5	(9) c Lilley b Arnold	4
S. E. Gregory	b Bosanquet	23	(1) c Lilley b Rhodes	43
F. Laver	lbw b Rhodes	4	(10) c Relf b Rhodes	6
J. J. Kelly	c Braund b Rhodes	10	(2) b Arnold	13
J. V. Saunders	not out	11	(11) run out	2
Extras	(NB3)	3	(B10, LB15, W2, NB1)	28
Total		285		485

Fall of wickets: 1–2, 2–9, 3–12, 4–118, 5–200, 6–207, 7–259, 8–263, 9–266, 10–285.

2nd innings   1–36, 2–108, 3–191, 4–254, 5–334, 6–393, 7–441, 8–468, 9–473, 10–485.

ENGLAND BOWLING (6-ball overs)

	O.	M.	R.	W.	O.	M.	R.	W.
Hirst	24	8	47	2	29	1	79	0
Arnold	32	7	76	4	28	3	93	2
Braund	26	9	39	0	12	2	56	0
Bosanquet	13	0	52	2	24	1	100	1
Rhodes	17·2	3	41	2	40·2	10	94	5
Relf	6	1	27	0	13	5	35	0

ENGLAND

P. F. Warner	c Kelly b Laver	0	(1) b Howell	8
T. Hayward	b Howell	15	(2) st Kelly b Saunders	91
J. T. Tyldesley	b Noble	53	(3) c Noble b Saunders	9
E. G. Arnold	c Laver b Armstrong	27		
R. E. Foster	c Noble b Saunders	287	(4) st Kelly b Armstrong	19
L. C. Braund	b Howell	102	(5) c Noble b Howell	0
G. H. Hirst	b Howell	0	(6) not out	60
B. J. T. Bosanquet	c Howell b Noble	2	(7) not out	1
A. A. Lilley	c Hill b Noble	4		
A. E. Relf	c Armstrong b Saunders	31		
W. Rhodes	not out	40		
Extras	(B6, LB7, W1, NB 2)	16	(B4, W2)	6
Total		577	(5 wkts)	194

Fall of wickets: 1–0, 2–49, 3–73, 4–117, 5–309, 6–311, 7–318, 8–332, 9–447, 10–577.

2nd innings   1–21, 2–39, 3–81, 4–82, 5–181.

AUSTRALIA BOWLING (6-ball overs)

	O.	M.	R.	W.	O.	M.	R.	W.
Saunders	36·2	8	126	2	18·5	3	51	2
Laver	37	12	116	1	16	4	37	0
Howell	31	7	113	3	31	18	35	2
Noble	34	8	99	3	12	2	37	0
Armstrong	23	3	47	1	18	6	28	1
Hopkins	11	1	40	0				
Trumper	7	1	12	0				
Gregory	2	0	8	0				

ENGLAND WON BY 5 WICKETS

An Australian lady acknowledged MCC's victory of 1903–4 by presenting Warner with an urn:

> The Ashes of Australian Cricket
> Won by Captain Warner:
> assisted by Captain Weather.

As the recipient of the urn was about to be married to an English lady, there was no repetition of an earlier courtship. Besides, the Australian lady had forgotten the proprieties observed at Lord's: . . . Won by Captain Warner: assisted by *Private* Weather.

In the first two Tests of 1905 Ted Arnold went in last for England; in 1905 Arnold not only performed the 'double' but had a batting average of 37. It was F. S. Jackson's year. Allowing City interests to fend for themselves, the Honourable accepted the leadership of England. So be it. What should a captain of England do? Win the toss. Jackson did so – all five times. What next? Make runs. Jackson headed the England averages with 70·28, including two hundreds. Were the Australians reluctant to get out? At the right moment Jackson would take the ball and make great batsmen play dreadful strokes. Who headed the England bowling averages? Jackson with 15·46. With two wins and three draws, and the Ashes retained, Jackson retired from Test cricket. Did he agree he had talent to lead in 1905? A. C. MacLaren, T. Hayward, J. T. Tyldesley, C. B. Fry, Himself, R. H. Spooner, G. H. Hirst . . . Yes, there was talent. And something else.

Style? Character? Pedigree? On his retirement from first-class cricket Frank Woolley contributed to the 1939 *Wisden*. 'Before 1914' (Woolley began his career in 1906) 'there were something like thirty players up to his [Hammond's] standard and he would have been in the England team only if at the top of his form.' Few, if any, of those who saw Hammond will agree with Woolley's conclusion; what they may concede, under pressure, is that thirty players in the Golden Age may, in their different ways, have *looked* as good as Hammond. Style? Character? Pedigree? We have Warner's word that prior to 1914 Hobbs batted as freely as any amateur. By 1914 Hobbs was incontestably the world's finest batsman.

Australia's wins by four matches to one in the series of 1907–8, and by two to one in 1909, even now evoke much bewilderment among Englishmen. How could a team including J. N. Crawford (only twenty at the start of the 1907–8 tour, and able to bring the ball back on the most pitiless Australian wicket), Arthur Fielder and Barnes who, between them, took 79 wickets at 25; and George Gunn reminding men of Shrewsbury, with Hobbs suggesting greatness – how could such a team lose? Possibly because the MCC side was not truly representative, because those selected as batsmen had finished the 1907 English season as 8th, 21st, 29th . . . in the averages! However, readers who wish to find some fault with the spirit of the Golden Age shall be reminded of H. S. Altham's strictures on 1907–8: 'The rate of scoring in the five Test matches averaged no more than 43 runs per hour, perhaps the first unmistakable evidence of the logical implications of matches without time-limit.' Not at all – those 43 runs per hour may be translated into 48 runs per 100 balls. In 1907–8 Australia and England were content to bowl *fifteen six-ball overs an hour*.

1909 was generally low-scoring – with compensations. Vernon Ransford, who scored 143 not out at Lord's, and Warren Bardsley (136 and 130 at the Oval) were left-hand batsmen of the highest class, Macartney came in No. 8 at Leeds before taking 7 for 58 and 4 for 27, Hobbs was brilliant in his first Test innings at home, Trumper serenely masterful in a valedictory appearance at the Oval. The England selectors excelled themselves by naming twenty-five men during the summer but should be forgiven everything for one choice. Douglas Ward Carr, born 1872, had played club cricket. Aged thirty-two, he began to practise the googly; the next year he lost his leg-break. In 1909 aged thirty-seven, he made his debut for Kent *v* Oxford University, took 15 wickets in two Gentlemen *v* Players games,

and 51 in seven county championship matches. He was chosen
for England.

Australia arrived at the Oval one up. As the wicket was hard
and fast, the England selectors 'touched the confines of lunacy'
(*Wisden*) by omitting their fast bowler. MacLaren lost the toss
and opened the bowling with Carr and Barnes. At 9 Carr bowled
Gregory, whereupon MacLaren took Barnes off and replaced
him by Jack Sharp, whose tally of wickets for the season would
be 26. Carr soon had Noble and Armstrong lbw and so was kept
on. Barnes sulked, various men turned their arms over. The
game was drawn, Carr's figures for both Australian innings 69
overs 3 maidens 282 runs 7 wickets. MacLaren was a great
batsman; his record as a captain against Australia was four wins
and eleven losses.

1911–12

The captaincy of the MCC side was offered to C. B. Fry who
hummed and hawed, then hummed again – and said, 'No, I have
my work at the Training Ship *Mercury*.' This was surely the
most honourable excuse ever given for declining the leadership
of England or Australia. Warner, who had already been offered
and accepted the vice-captaincy, was accordingly promoted.
There were two other amateurs in the party to tour, J. W. H. T.
Douglas of Essex and F. R. Foster of Warwickshire – both all-
rounders and captains of their respective counties, Douglas the
senior. This, as it turned out, was a matter of significance
because Warner, after scoring 151 in the opening match of the
tour at Adelaide, was taken seriously ill and removed to a nursing
home. From there he decided that Douglas should assume
command.

At Adelaide Warner had entrusted the new ball to Foster and
Barnes; against New South Wales and Queensland, Douglas –
with Foster and Barnes also playing – opened the bowling with
Foster and himself.

When Clem Hill beat Douglas in the toss at Sydney on 15
December 1911, Foster bowled the first over. Two or three

steps, a graceful skip, then a short run, Foster was left-arm round the wicket; his field consisted of four short-legs (three behind the wicket and one in front), a long-leg and a mid-on, with only a mid-off, cover and deep third man on the off side. Foster was medium-pace through the air – at least when seen from the pavilion – whose deliveries came from the pitch with trebled velocity. The wicketkeeper stood up; when the ball eluded him, it reached the boundary as quickly as a thunderbolt by Ernest Jones. Barnes approved of Foster's ability to make the batsman play at almost every ball. That 'almost' was of course important; without it Foster would have been a left-arm Barnes. There was only one Barnes – 'Me!'

As Douglas himself prepared to bowl the second over of the innings, Barnes's rage was terrible to behold. Hobbs tried to placate him, so did Woolley; both failed. Trumper, batting at five, made 100, Armstrong 60 and Roy Minnett 90. 'Ranji' Hordern (he bore a striking facial resemblance to the Indian prince) took 5 for 85 and 7 for 90 in his first Test against England, bowling leg-breaks and googlies at brisk pace. Oh, Bosanquet! What did you start? Australia won by 146 runs and all the world knew why – Barnes had not been given the new ball. A fortnight later Warner received Douglas at his sick bed. Diplomatic words were spoken, Douglas nodded and said he understood.

The morning of the second Test at Melbourne was overcast. A band played light music. Hill again won the toss. Foster started with a maiden to Kelleway; Barnes and Douglas (that is to say Barnes) then set the field for a medium-pace bowler. Bardsley the striker waited. At last Barnes was satisfied. He glowered. An easy, controlled approach, at the crease both feet momentarily off the ground, right arm high in its final swing. His first ball swung in late and hit Bardsley on the pad before sliding on to the stumps. The batsman who would have been lbw, was bowled. Barnes looked at Douglas: 'I told you so!' Two overs later Kelleway prepared to let an inswinger go down the leg side; at the last moment it straightened. Kelleway lbw. For Hill was reserved the 'Barnes ball'. It swung in to pitch on the leg stump, then hit the top of the off. Armstrong at once snicked one to the keeper standing up. At 12.45 p.m. the players left the field for a brief shower of rain.

AUSTRALIA

C. E. Kelleway	lbw b Barnes	2
W. Bardsley	b Barnes	0
C. Hill	b Barnes	4
W. W. Armstrong	c Smith b Barnes	4 4
V. Trumper	not out	2
V. S. Ransford	not out	1
Extras		1
Total (4 wkts)		14

Barnes 5 overs 4 maidens 1 run 4 wickets. By lunch Australia had recovered to 38 for 6 wickets: Barnes 11 overs 7 maidens 6 runs 5 wickets.

England's side of 1911–12 was certainly one of her very greatest: J. B. Hobbs, W. Rhodes, G. Gunn, J. W. Hearne, F. R. Foster, J. W. H. T. Douglas, F. E. Woolley, C. P. Mead, E. J. Smith, S. F. Barnes, J. W. Hitch. In the third Test they totalled 501, in the fourth 589 – Hobbs and Rhodes opening with 323 in the latter game. The young Hobbs was indeed as glorious a stroke-maker as Trumper had been years earlier. He played spin bowling in the safest of all ways – right back or right out. Foster (32), Barnes (34) and Douglas (15) accounted for 79 of the 93 Australian wickets to fall to bowlers; the fielding throughout was excellent. The home side was overwhelmed, only Hordern with 32 wickets at 24·37 rivalling the individual prowess of certain Englishmen. This being the Golden Age of paradox, Macartney played in one Test for Australia as a left-arm bowler; the selectors held he might also be useful as a stonewalling batsman.

We must bid farewell to a myth with gratitude. The vintage Trumper, or so Warner believed, would have despatched Foster's leg-stump deliveries over the heads of the close-in fielders. But by 1911–12 the great man was a mere shadow of his former self. Yet he made a good end, his last Test innings of 50 revealing touches of the old genius. He was miraculously caught by Woolley off Barnes. What better pair to succumb to – the

BARNES'S FIELD AT MELBOURNE
30 December 1911

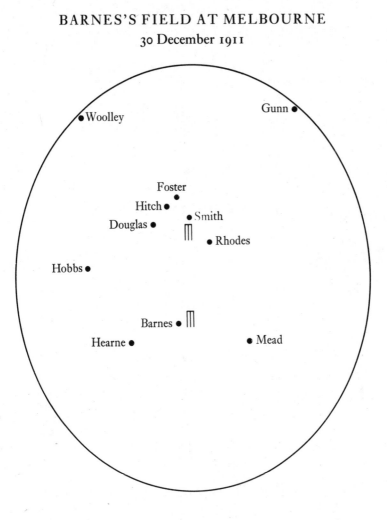

English Demon, and a cricketer whose felicitous runs would delight crowds the world over for another quarter of a century? Woolley was his own Golden Age, his last innings against the old enemy a handsome trifle of 81 made in an hour at Canterbury in 1938. Woolley was then caught by Bradman. Trumper-Barnes-Woolley-Bradman. Immortals all.

VICTOR TRUMPER
Died 28 June 1915, aged thirty-seven

The pall-bearers at Waverley Cemetery were all Test cricketers whose careers against England spanned more than forty years:

> W. Bardsley
> A. Cotter
> S. E. Gregory
> Dr H. V. Hordern
> F. A. Iredale
> C. E. Kelleway
> C. G. Macartney
> M. A. Noble
> J. A. O'Connor
> C. T. B. Turner

Cotter, of the Australian Imperial Forces, was killed in action before Beersheba on 20 October 1917, aged thirty-three.

In the Imperial Cricket Memorial Gallery at Lord's are a cap and blazer worn by Trumper, and presented by his widow, Sarah Ann. A note on him ends: 'He remains a legendary figure in Australia, one whose fame rests not only on his greatness as a batsman but also on his qualities as a man.'

DR WILLIAM GILBERT GRACE
Died 23 October 1915, aged sixty-seven

At Elmer's End Cemetery the family mourners were accompanied by C. L. Townsend. Lord Hawke (President) and Lord Harris represented the Marylebone Cricket Club. Among those present in uniform were The Jam Saheb of Nawanagar (Ranjitsinhji), Captain P. F. Warner and Captain H. D. G. Leveson-Gower.

Lord Hawke received the following cablegram: 'Kindly convey condolences of the club to the Grace family – Trumble, Melbourne Cricket Club.' A message was also received from King George V.

Lord Harris later wrote of Grace: 'He was always a most genial, even-tempered, considerate companion, and, of all the many cricketers I have known, the kindest as well as the best. He was ever ready with an encouraging word for the novice, and a compassionate one for the man who made a mistake.'

When, in 1923, the Grace Memorial gates were erected at the members' entrance to Lord's, three words (suggested by Sir Stanley Jackson) identified W. G.:

THE GREAT CRICKETER

CHAPTER FIVE

The Twenties

Warwick Windridge Armstrong was a colossus. He captained Australia in ten Tests against England, winning eight in a row and losing none. He scored more first-class runs than Macartney or Ponsford, and took more wickets than O'Reilly or Lindwall. On three tours of England, as noted, he performed the 'double' of 1,000 runs and 100 wickets.* In the Trent Bridge Test of 1905, he hit a day's last ball out of the ground, presumably as a gesture. Armstrong was always making gestures which were rarely appreciated by the other side and sometimes not by his own administrators. A survivor from the Golden Age (born only eighteen months after Trumper), he ended his career as ringmaster of one of the two greatest teams ever to perform in England. When Armstrong couldn't find trouble, he made it. The method of the colossus was to trample on anyone who got in his way. He weighed twenty-two stone.

In November 1920 the colossus awaited an MCC side led by Lieutenant-Colonel J. W. H. T. Douglas, late of the Bedfordshires. Had the Englishman spent the season playing against South Australia and Victoria, the Ashes would most certainly have been retained. Both State teams were twice thrashed, although Victoria were on each occasion without Armstrong. Once he was dropped in spite of being captain of

---

* The only other touring cricketers to perform this feat in the present century were G. A. Faulkner (South Africans) 1907, H. L. Collins (AIF) 1919, J. M. Gregory (Australians) 1921, L. N. Constantine (West Indians) 1928, and V. Mankad (Indians) 1946.

Australia. However, the Victorian authorities soon capitulated, perhaps disappointed that Armstrong's leg-spinning replacement had been murdered by Hendren. The poor man had already tried his luck in Sydney; soon he would leave Melbourne for Adelaide where – aged thirty-three, and with only 9 first-class wickets to his credit – he began to prosper. His name was Grimmett.

Unfortunately for Douglas and his men, there remained New South Wales, with perhaps as powerful an array of batsmen ever found in a non-national side: H. L. Collins, W. Bardsley, C. G. Macartney, T. J. E. Andrews, C. E. Kelleway, J. M. Taylor, J. M. Gregory and H. L. Hendry. All save Andrews, and he was to manage a 94, would make hundreds against England before the decade was over. Gregory was also a tremendous fast bowler and superb slip fielder; as a batsman, incidentally, he scorned the use of gloves even when, in 1926, facing Larwood. Carter and Oldfield took it in turns to keep wicket, both outrageously great. So the Australian selectors did not have a difficult task: Armstrong, Ryder, and later Macdonald, from Victoria; Pellew from South Australia; and a posse of New South Welshmen. Should further proof be needed of Australia's run-scoring potential, Ryder – who four years later would make 201 not out against England – now strengthened the tail at nine.

The key to the series was the poverty of England's bowling – Fender and Parkin between them taking 28 wickets at 38, the others 37 wickets at 59. Because the England bowling was so weak, Australia's batting prospered inordinately. Only twice, in the first and third Tests, did the home side play two completed innings, and then the totals were 848 and 936. In the second match Australia made 499 and won by an innings, in the fourth and fifth victory was by 8 and 9 wickets respectively, Australia's runs 600 and 485. Inevitably in the circumstances, the English batting (and Hobbs, Woolley, Hendren, A. C. Russell, Makepeace, Fender and Rhodes were not, on paper, a negligible force) became an irrelevant factor;

WARWICK WINDRIDGE ARMSTRONG, 1901–21
The Big Ship

however many runs it achieved in timeless Tests, the outcome was a formality. Which explained why the 1920–1 series was unique, why Armstrong could use with impunity a bowler who never paused to count the cost – who would have regarded any counting of cost a matter for base arithmeticians. Arthur Mailey was an artist.

Born in a slum and visited on his deathbed by his friend Sir Robert Menzies, Prime Minister of Australia, a cartoonist of distinction and the greatest player never to have been chosen by *Wisden* as one of its Five Cricketers of the Year, Mailey was a dilettante of the googly. His aim was to draw batsmen down the wicket, his means of destruction apparent to all. Or so it seemed. But Mailey knew that a ball delivered with *his* spin (and no one, except perhaps the left-handed Fleetwood-Smith, has spun the ball more) would curve deviously through the air, that a promised half-volley was often a perfect length, that a viciously spun ball would often swerve late. Hence Mailey's relish when he more than once bowled Hobbs with a succulent full-toss. He also, in a Shield game, bowled a man with a polyhop shorter than Bosanquet's Coe-destroying masterpiece. Mailey's victims in 1920–1 included Hobbs and Hendren three times each, Woolley and Russell twice, Hearne and Rhodes. The dogged Douglas, who was ensnared on six occasions, conducted a personal battle with Mailey; thrusting forward and sometimes finding the ball strike the middle of the bat, England's captain would be rewarded with a quiet, 'Well played, Colonel.'

As we note with resignation the ten Australian hundreds – Armstrong's three (one came when the colossus was weak from malaria; a couple of waterless whiskies did the trick), two each from Collins and Pellew, with Gregory, Kelleway and Macartney adding their mite – it is tempting to telescope time and compare the Mailey of 1920–1 with the Laker of 1956. Both averaged 9 wickets a match, Laker from 56 overs, Mailey from 61. But while Laker conceded a mere and unbelievable 88 runs, a bartering Mailey conceded 237. Mailey always finished on the winning side in 1920–1, Laker in 1956 did not. And since most Englishmen still insist that Armstrong won his two series after the Great War by launching Gregory and Macdonald with their unfair bouncers, the last three Tests of 1920–1 (when the fast bowlers first came together) should be recalled:

	GREGORY & MACDONALD	MAILEY
Adelaide	8 wkts for 331	10 wkts for 302
Melbourne	2 wkts for 215	13 wkts for 236
Sydney	5 wkts for 175	7 wkts for 208
	15 wkts for 721	30 wkts for 746
	av. 48·06	av. 24·86

Mailey last played in first-class cricket at Melbourne in November 1930, appearing for the Rest of Australia *v* Australia in Jack Ryder's benefit. 'Got a couple of rabbits,' mused Mailey in later years.

D. G. Bradman	b Mailey	73
D. G. Bradman	c & b Mailey	29

On 18 March 1921 the defeated Englishmen boarded the *Osterley* at Adelaide. So, too, did fourteen Australians intent on relaxation before starting *their* tour at Leicester. A fifteenth Australian, Armstrong, was intent less on relaxation than on work. He paid daily visits to the bowels of the ship where he shovelled coal. Twenty-two stone was his fighting weight; he did not wish to carry surplus poundage round England. That Armstrong appeared to grow in stature during 1921 was, of course, an illusion fostered by his supermen. The Ashes had been retained by the end of the third Test, England's six innings averaging 4 hours each. Gregory and Macdonald generally pulverized the opposition, though Woolley's 95 and 93 at Lord's were heroic efforts – the former ended by a Mailey full-toss, the latter by a ball that 'stuck in Mailey's

MAILEY'S FIELD IN AUSTRALIA 1920–1

He played in all five Tests but did not bowl in the second.

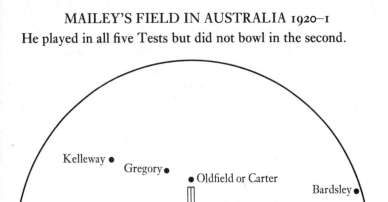

In four Tests:

Mailey 36 wkts at 26.27
Others 40 wkts at 33.62
Mailey 40.50 balls/wkt;
64 runs/100 balls
Others 81.15 balls/wkt;
41 runs/100 balls

Mailey's 36 wkts

3 bowled
3 lbw
9 stumped

21 caught

3 caught and bowled
1 wicketkeeper
8 slip
3 cover
2 mid-off
2 long-on
1 deep square-leg
1 deep extra-cover

hand and dropped halfway on the leg side' (Woolley's description). The batsman pulled it hard and Hendry at mid-wicket jumped high. 'The ball hit him, I think, on the wrist, and he lost his balance. The ball went up ten feet and as he was lying on the ground it fell in his lap and he caught it. A marvellous catch.'

England's only excuse for the debacle of 1921 was the absence, through injury and then illness, of Hobbs. However, readers of *The Times* probably wondered if his loss meant much as the paper regarded Gregory, Macdonald, Mailey and Armstrong as almost the weakest attack ever sent from Australia. Throughout the summer various cries were heard: that Armstrong was fortunate in being able to keep Gregory and Macdonald fresh for the Tests, though in games *exclusive* of the Tests the pair bowled 1,148 overs; that Mailey was a purveyor of rubbish, even if batsmen who tried to knock him off his length were soon caught; that Armstrong was – and let us choose the mildest epithet – a bully. The Australian Board of Control had insisted, prior to the tour, on restricted hours for the county matches – noon till six. But if Armstrong was in a dark mood he would bark, 'TWO till six!'

Oddly, the best way of determining how good the 1921 Australians were is to examine their record in twenty-one county games. First innings averaged 445 scored at 85 runs an hour; the opposition was then dismissed in 3 hours for 160. Individual Australians scored well though one, Bardsley – 'as fine a left-hander as Hill' of the 1902 side – was often reproached for crawling: 80 not out in 2 hours on the first day at Leicester, 127 in two and a half hours against Gloucestershire, 209 at a run a minute against Hampshire. Macartney was less restricted: 140 not out in 2 hours at Leicester, 105 in 85 minutes at Southampton, 193 in two and a half hours against Northants, 345 in under 4 hours at Trent Bridge. Ah! but the bowling must have been pathetic.

Was it? Hitch of Surrey was a very good fast bowler, Fender a master of variations; Parker of Gloucestershire a great slow

WHAT IS 'INTIMIDATORY' BOWLING?

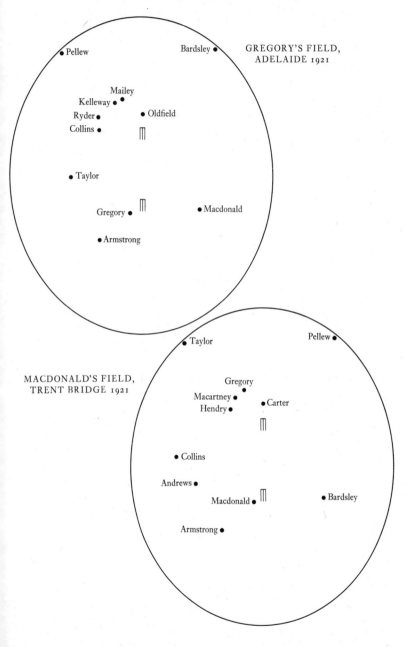

left-hander, Kennedy and Newman of Hampshire a legendary pair; Astill of Leicestershire a length bowler, Freeman of Kent the scourge of English batsmen, J. C. White a left-hander of such accuracy that in Australia he would one day contain everyone save Archie Jackson – playing in county games against Armstrong's men these bowlers collected 9 wickets at 104 runs each. And was English batting also pathetic? George Gunn, Hendren and Hearne of Middlesex, D. J. Knight and Sandham of Surrey, Makepeace, Watson and Ernest Tyldesley of Lancashire, Holmes and Sutcliffe of Yorkshire, Russell and Woolley – they were good enough to score twenty centuries against Australia. But in eighteen innings for their counties in 1921 against almost the weakest attack ever sent from Australia, they averaged 6·83.

When the Australians next toured in 1926, they were greeted by a new Golden Age (see Warner, Altham, Cardus, etc.). Hobbs, Sutcliffe, Woolley, Hendren and Chapman batted, Tate, Larwood, Geary and Root bowled – a worthy bunch of players. By 1926 Macartney was forty, and Macdonald playing for Lancashire. In the Tests of that year Macartney scored three centuries (including one before lunch at Headingley) and averaged 94; during the four seasons 1925–8 Macdonald took 720 wickets and bowled his side to three championships. So if in 1926 English cricket was as good as men claimed, if Macdonald (*without Gregory at the other end*) could still wreak havoc in his mid-thirties, and unless Macartney could do at forty what he couldn't five years previously – then Armstrong's rampage was due less to the feebleness of English cricket than to the superlative quality of Australia's.

What enraged the patriots in 1921 was the ease with which the tourists conquered. Admittedly Macdonald was a beautiful sight with an action that suggested 'silk running off a spool' (Sir Robert Menzies), Gregory's bounding run up and kangaroo hop were enough to terrify the most stout-hearted, Mailey's bland deceits must have been more difficult than they looked from the ring, Pellew and Taylor did skirt the boundary like deer, turning presumed fours into hard-run singles. If such greatness was bearable, the nimble elephant looming inexorably at mid-off was not. What was it the bully said after he'd drifted to the outfield during the Oval Test and picked up – *and read* – a stray newspaper? 'Wanted to see who we're playing.'

The poet Edmund Blunden shall have the last word on the sun-drenched summer of 1921.*

'Armstrong made a bat look like a tea-spoon, and the bowling weak tea . . . If I were to write a Dictionary of Cricket, I would enter in the Index: Armstrong, W. W., *see* Grace, W. G., and Grace, W. G., *see* Armstrong, W. W.'

The colossus spent the rest of his life making a lot of money and growling that Tate and O'Reilly couldn't bowl, and Bradman couldn't bat.

1924-5

Jack Hobbs was at first reluctant to tour Australia with Arthur Gilligan's side of 1924–5. When the Sydney Test began it would be seventeen years since his debut in international cricket. He was still capable of making runs, even though he was aware he made them increasingly off the back foot. In the past he had played against, and overcome, such bowlers as Cotter and Hordern, Noble, Armstrong and Macartney (a very good slow left-hander), Kelleway, Gregory, Macdonald and Mailey. His old partner Rhodes was no longer a Test batsman, but Hobbs had recently become professionally acquainted with another Yorkshireman, Herbert Sutcliffe, whose attitude to crisis would soon be made clear: 'We shall do very well today – if Jack doesn't

---

* When the Australian tourists were statistically impressive. Macartney and Bardsley topped 2,000 runs, six others 1,000. Armstrong took 106 wickets, Macdonald 150, Gregory 120, Mailey 146 – their collective average was 16·85, a wicket every 36 balls. No bowler suffered injury from April till September; Armstrong did not permit pulled muscles or, come to that, psychological upsets.

JOHN BERRY HOBBS, 1907–30
The Master when young

get out.' So Jack agreed to a fourth tour of Australia; in his forty-third year, having played 37 innings against Australia averaging 53·60, he was about to embark on another 34 – at a higher average. The new visiting card was engraved:

HOBBS & SUTCLIFFE Ltd.
Bowlers rebuked and chastised

Maurice Tate, alas, was to be alone in his finest hour. Perhaps the outcome of the series had been determined at the Oval on 3 July 1924 when Arthur Gilligan, England's finest fast bowler and Tate's Sussex fellow-opener, was struck an awful blow over the heart during the Gentlemen and Players match. Never again could Gilligan bowl fast; had he been able to, England might have worked their way through Australia's batting which (and here was the key to the series) had abnormal depth – the last 3 wickets adding 171 in the second innings at Sydney, the last 5 301 in the first innings at Melbourne, and last 4 370 in the first innings at Adelaide. Tate in sole magnificence proclaimed himself the equal of Barnes, but this was not enough. At Adelaide he bowled comparatively little as the big toe of his left foot was a bloody pulp; in each of the other eight Australian innings he averaged the equivalent of 48 six-ball overs. In five Tests Tate took 38 wickets at 23·18 while the shade of Tom Richardson looked on approvingly.

At Sydney on 19 December 1924, Tate's field placings said everything: one man on the leg side at mid-on – then mid-off, short square cover, deep third man, four slips and a gully positioned as for a fast bowler, with the wicketkeeper standing up. The approach – a couple of walking steps and six accelerating running strides; and the action – left arm thrown high, the right completing a straight line through the body, a final leap and swing of the massive shoulders – were perfect for their purpose. Tate bowled every ball to take a wicket; perfect length, his delivery stride not too close to the stumps so that the ball veered from off to middle before moving late away with increased pace from the pitch. (Scientifically impossible but believed by all who faced Tate.) Occasionally one was brought back sharply from the off to be stopped by Collins's willing pads. Collins not only made a century this day, he also made one for Ponsford.

The Victorian's first over from Tate was a nightmare as the ball went through him. 'The first swung a little, hit the pitch and fizzed through like a flat pebble off a millpond,' Ponsford recalled years later. So did the second. 'The third came off the pitch like a Larwood bouncer . . .' Then Collins got a single and took Tate for what seemed an eternity, Ponsford making 110 in his first Test innings. And so throughout the series – Tate *v* Australia. To go back to him on the vulcanite pitches was suicide, the forward players Taylor and Arthur Richardson seeming the most secure. Of Tate's 38 wickets 16 were bowled, 4 lbw, 17 caught (8 by the wicketkeeper) and 1 stumped; they were identified as Collins and Taylor six times each, Kelleway four times, Ponsford and Bardsley three times each, Hendry and Gregory twice each, Arthur and Victor Richardson, Ryder and Andrews once each. With a fit Gilligan at the other end . . .

The firm of Hobbs and Sutcliffe was at once profitably in business. 157 and 110 for the 1st wicket at Sydney (individual hundreds to both men) in a match when England were set 605 to win and reached 411 – the highest total yet made in the fourth innings of a Test. Woolley's 123 in two and a half hours was the most delectable knock of the series, its strategic worth put into perspective by an earlier Australian 10th-wicket stand of 127 by Taylor and Mailey. Australia again won the toss at Melbourne (Collins lost it only twice in ten games against England) and batted two days for 600 – Arthur Richardson, Taylor and Victor Richardson all run out. Undismayed, Hobbs and Sutcliffe scored 283 on the third day, a superb partnership broken in the opening over of the fourth when Hobbs missed a Mailey full-toss. The batsman expected interrogation by googly and received a custard pie. In spite of a century in both innings by Sutcliffe, Australia won by 81 runs. But the gap was closing.

England's misfortunes, and near triumph, at Adelaide were unbelievable. Australia 22 for 3, a half-pace Tate dismissing

MAURICE WILLIAM TATE, 1924–30
Indomitably great

Collins and Taylor. After lunch he was unable to take the field, yet Roy Kilner, Gilligan and Freeman reduced Australia to 119 for 6. Perhaps 150 all out. Gilligan then suffered a strain and had to go off, soon followed by Freeman with an injured wrist. Two slow left-handers, Kilner and Woolley, bowled 99 overs, assisted by a few from Hobbs, Hendren and Whysall, the tour's reserve wicketkeeper. England fought back, Hobbs 119; in Australia's second innings a rain-affected pitch helped Kilner and Woolley. 373 to win and keep the series alive, England's last wicket fell at 363. The Ashes were still Australia's.

In the return game at Melbourne, Gilligan at last won the toss. 126 for the 1st wicket – Hobbs 66, Sutcliffe 143: England marched determinedly to 548 and won by an innings and 29, Tate a revived giant, if without a nail to his left big toe. The tourists approached the fifth Test with confidence. They knew they had the measure of Gregory and Mailey, that the Australians dreaded an almost fit Tate who, if he required an incentive which he most certainly did not, was only 8 wickets short of beating Mailey's record 36 in a series. In six opening partnerships Hobbs and Sutcliffe averaged 129, Sutcliffe himself over 100 and Hobbs 80.

Tate beat Mailey's record, England had the measure of Gregory, and Mailey bowled no more than 5 fruitless overs in the match. With moderate scores of 295 and 320 Australia won handsomely by over 300 runs, England crumbling twice before a spare little man, new to Test cricket but clearly as ancient as the hills, who tripped up to the wicket and bowled leg-breaks, top spinners and the occasional googly. Four men played back and perished lbw, four were sucked out and stumped. 5 for 45 and 6 for 37 – the victims Hobbs, Sandham, Woolley, Hendren, Hearne twice, Whysall twice, Kilner . . . all confounded by flight and balls that turned two or three inches.

Clarence Victor Grimmett had arrived.

1926

If the decision to send three googly bowlers to Australia in 1924–5 suggested optimism, the way the Australian Board of Control chose the 1926 side for England bordered on lunacy. Early in December 1925, almost before the Sheffield Shield season had begun, a trial match was held in which The Rest easily beat Australia. Soon twelve names were announced as 'certainties' for England; they did not include Kippax or Kelleway (the latter finished the season with a first-class average of 97), Blackie the best off-spinner available, Ironmonger or Hornibrook, two left-handers whose methods seemed suited to English conditions. In the Tests of 1926 Australia's openers would be Gregory, a shadow of his former self and plagued by injury, and Macartney or Grimmett.

The charm of 1926 may be stated simply: with half a dozen great batsmen on display, the matches were of three days' duration – except the last which would be played to a finish if the sides were level. After the Trent Bridge Test had been washed out with England 32 for none, that at Lord's proved almost frolicsome. True Australia scored 393 at only a run a minute (Bardsley carried his bat for 193), but with Kilner the sole spinner to support Tate and Root at medium pace, and Larwood who was exceeding fast, England's over rate settled for 23·3 an hour. Australia could manage only 21, the boredom offset by England making 475 for 3 declared: Hobbs 119, Sutcliffe 82, Woolley 87, Hendren 127 not out, Chapman 50 not out. Allowed a few hours for their second innings, six Australians scraped 44 runs and not a person left the ground. Macartney was at his magical best, cutting Larwood from the leg stump and glancing good length balls on the off – 133 not out. King George V, who watched Bardsley, was less fortunate than the future King George VI who turned up for Macartney.

The Headingley Test was immortal. Carr won the toss and, suspecting a helpful wicket, put Australia in. (Charles Parker, the man most likely to use such a wicket, had previously been omitted from the England side.) From the first ball of the game Bardsley was caught at slip, from the fifth Macartney missed at slip by Carr. Let the massacre begin! Macartney shattered Macaulay's length in a couple of overs, the accurate Kilner soon had four men on the boundary: Macartney 51 out of 64 in 54 minutes. Tate, of course, did not bowl anything but a perfect length; successive and identical deliveries on the middle stump being forced past square-leg and driven late through the covers. Geary tried, found he had insufficient fielders, and withdrew. Macartney 100 out of 131 (William Woodfull, admiring greatly, at the other end) in 105 minutes.

This Headingley Test was drawn – so, too, the one at Old Trafford where the first day's play consisted of ten balls, Woodfull and Macartney again made hundreds, Greville Stevens had Bardsley caught off a long-hopping leg-break, and the Australian manager, Sydney Smith, expressed thanks that three-day Tests were doomed. Of small interest to Mr Smith in 1926, and of no concern to anyone now, the two teams had maintained a scoring rate of about a run a minute and bowled between 22 and 23 overs an hour. However, all gaiety was about to be put aside for the Oval match which, being played to a finish, might cause the cancellation of Australian journeys to Taunton, Canterbury and Brighton, even of the Scarborough Festival itself.

On Sunday, 8 August 1926 the England selectors (Warner, Percy Perrin and Arthur Gilligan) met to choose the Oval side. Co-opted were Jack Hobbs and Wilfred Rhodes, the latter having played in the Oval Test of 1899 when he caught and bowled Trumper. The first thing to do was drop Carr from the captaincy and appoint Percy Chapman. Next the vital question:

'How are you bowling, Wilfred?'

'Ah'm still dropping 'em there' – and Rhodes being a cautious man – 'or thereabouts.'

So Wilfred had better play for England again, hadn't he? To which the sage, about to enter his fiftieth year, replied, 'Ay.'

What the selectors apparently forgot to include in the

invitations they sent out was a reminder that the match had no time-limit. Rhodes knew, and he reminded Sutcliffe of the other Yorkshireman chosen. For the rest . . .

Chapman won the toss and Hobbs started to play the innings of the season, toying with the bowling as though Gregory, Grimmett and Mailey were so many small girls compelled to use the wrong hand. 50 were made in less than an hour before a full-toss from Mailey landed on Hobbs's stumps. The batsman expressed surprise, then laughed; Mailey laughed, spectators did not. Woolley came in, waved his wand for a while and was bowled by Mailey. Hendren fell to Gregory – lunch being taken at 108 for 3; Chapman treated the Australian masters of spin as though, or so Cardus swore, they were the Devon Dumplings. He and Sutcliffe added 81 in even time, Stevens's innings consisted of 4.3.4.6 out, and Rhodes appeared. Cheered all the way to the wicket ('His first Test was W. G.'s last!'), Wilfred responded with a cow shot against Mailey's spin. Sutcliffe, whose dignity was monumental, mistimed a pull to Mailey and was hit in the eye, being bowled next ball. Tate heaved, Rhodes forgot a lifetime's chastity and late-cut pleasantly; England were out for 280, the last 6 wickets having fallen for 91 *in an hour*!

How Australia ended the first day at 60 for 4, how Macartney threatened a repeat of Headingley and was bowled by a Stevens long-hop; how on the Monday Rhodes persuaded Woodfull to play on, and after an hour his figures were 10–9–3–1; how Collins and Gregory added 107, and Grimmett and Oldfield 67, taking Australia to a first-innings lead of 22 before Hobbs and Sutcliffe played out the second day with 49 – all this, and the admiration Cardus felt for Woodfull who, like tomatoes and Marcel Proust, was an acquired taste, no more than a prelude to Monday night when a thunderstorm broke over London. Next day at noon the sun blazed down, the ball turned and popped extravagantly. Collins ordered Arthur Richardson to bowl round the wicket, and set four short-legs.

10 overs Richardson completed in this spell, and Hobbs took 8 of them. His guard a foot outside the leg stump, he moved

CHARLES GEORGE MACARTNEY, 1907–26
The Governor-General

quickly into position when he had discerned the pace and direction of the ball. M. A. Noble insisted that Hobbs fooled Collins by *pretending* Richardson was difficult, that Macartney's break-away deliveries must have presented greater problems. (Ironmonger was asleep in Melbourne.) But Richardson, poor man, was bowling at *Hobbs*, at one who Douglas Jardine would soon hail as 'the Master'. Hobbs on a sticky wicket had the footwork, the ability to delay his strokes, to take all pace from the ball, then lean on anything slightly overpitched or be right back to the short ball, that made mockery of the spinner's craft. Sutcliffe had felt at the start of play that all would be well if Jack didn't get out, so there they were at lunch with England 161 for none – Hobbs 97 and Sutcliffe 53. The pair had taken countless short singles without a word being spoken; it was all pre-ordained by the Almighty who, in earthly guise, was Herbert Sutcliffe.

Hobbs made 100 exactly, the final run a gentle tap to point from a Gregory thunderbolt, and Sutcliffe succumbed to the day's last ball for 161. The third highest score in England's 436 was Extras 37, the peerless Oldfield unable to prevent nineteen byes on a vile pitch. No one thought Australia had any chance of making 415, but no one thought they would collapse for 125. Larwood bowled faster than any Englishman had since N. A. Knox in the summer of 1906, and Bardsley, Ponsford, Collins and Arthur Richardson were lured to destruction by Rhodes* whose match figures were 45 overs 24 maidens 79 runs 6 wickets. The Ashes were once more England's. Collins was gracious in defeat, and wise: 'Jack Hobbs's century was the finest piece of batting I have ever seen. England owe nearly everything to him.'

---

* Rhodes retired from first-class cricket in 1930 aged fifty-two, Yorkshire having found a replacement, Hedley Verity. The previous winter in West Indies, Rhodes had contained a useful array of batsmen; at Kingston 20.5–12–17–1 when West Indies made 286; in the second innings, as 408 for 5 (George Headley 223) were scored, 24–13–22–1.

1928-9

The decade ended as it had begun, with one side's bowling so lacking in penetration on Australian wickets that the outcome was inevitable. This time England held the cards, and when in the second Test Australia's attack was opened by Grimmett and Dr Otto Nothling (whose medium-pace brought him 36 wickets at 41 in first-class cricket), it was clear fate had given Chapman several fistfuls of trumps. What the England selectors had given him merits discussion.

The MCC party of 1928-9 consisted of seventeen players – nine batsmen, one of whom was an all-rounder, two wicket-keepers and six bowlers. Any modern captain would settle for four of the batsmen and guarantee to win a series. BUT although Chapman, Hammond, Jardine and Leyland were still in their twenties, and Sutcliffe thirty-four, Hobbs (the Master had agreed to a fifth tour of Australia), Hendren, Mead and Ernest Tyldesley were all over forty and therefore more likely to suffer from aches and pains. So with the bowlers of whom only Larwood (twenty-four) was young. Freeman (forty) was included presumably because he had just taken 304 wickets in an English season, White (thirty-eight during the tour), an almost spinless slow left-hander who kept an impeccable length, Tate (thirty-three), Geary (thirty-five) and Sam Staples (thirty-six) as medium-pace stock bowlers who gave nothing away. Staples returned home, debilitated by rheumatic fever, before the tour began, Geary had his nose broken in a match at Perth and would not be available for serious purposes until the second Test at Sydney. And lest men of Sussex resent Tate being described as a 'stock' bowler, he had during the past six years (including tours of Australia and India) averaged annually 1,748 overs. If he wasn't feeling jaded, he should have been.

So Chapman found himself with Larwood, Tate, Geary when fit, White and Freeman to bowl throughout the tour. There was, of course, Hammond, but as he was to score 905 runs in the Tests, no captain would think of using him save as a very occasional change bowler. Freeman had been quite innocuous at the highest level with Gilligan's team, so he wasn't considered for the Tests. A very hot Australian summer, a touring side with four bowlers and the knowledge it would take a couple of months to ship out and acclimatize a replacement. The die was cast: England's monolithic batting to occupy the crease for as long as possible, Australia to be blasted by Larwood and then challenged by the perfect length of Tate, Geary and White. In the last four Tests White would average 100 (six-ball) overs a game, Tate 85, Geary and Larwood 60. Between them the four bowled more balls than any England-Australia side *in toto* before or since, save Gilligan's of 1924–5 and the dozen bowlers chosen by Australia in 1928–9. They were magnificent.

And the series – whatever its individual achievements, which were numerous – was a bore. The second Test went into six days, the third and fourth into seven, and the last into eight. For the first time in the present century, both teams scored at less than 40 runs per 100 balls. Initially, the Australian selectors put their faith in the old guard – five Armstrong men appearing at Brisbane; by the final match, only Ryder (the captain) and Oldfield survived. The final game was the one won by Australia, Larwood's sole wicket costing 168.

If the innings of the series was played by the ill-fated Archie Jackson – 164 at Adelaide – who died four years later, Hammond's disciplined majesty subdued Australia. 251 at Sydney, 200 at Melbourne, and then 119 not out and 177 at Adelaide – his scoring rate often dropped to below 30 an hour in spite of Ryder's tactical blunder of not placing a man on the boundary at cover. In 1928–9 Hammond's method was to go down the wicket to Grimmett in defence, and then hit like fury off the back foot. The noblest sight ever seen on a cricket field would one day score more valuable runs for England in harsher circumstances. Not so Sutcliffe who, with help from Hobbs, Jardine and others, won an unlikely triumph in the third Test at Melbourne.

On the sixth afternoon England needed 332 to win; Hugh

Trumble gave them 100, if they were lucky, for the pitch was an infamous Melbourne sticky. Sutcliffe let it be known that he had the matter under control, that if Jack . . . Hobbs obliged with 49, the pair making 105 while suffering innumerable bruises and feeling glad Ironmonger had been dropped for this match. On the seventh day the pitch was too far gone for rolling, but Sutcliffe tended it lovingly. His 135 took six and a half hours, and England won by 3 wickets. Hobbs delighted all Australia in the fifth Test when Sutcliffe was absent through injury. He had begun at Melbourne in 1908 with 83 bowled Cotter, and 28 bowled Noble; now in 1929 142 bowled Ryder, and 65 caught Fairfax bowled Grimmett. A vast crowd roared the Master into immortality.

The improbable hero of MCC in 1928–9 was Jack White, a Somerset farmer whose pace Jack Fingleton saw as 'slow to stationary'. The purpose of White was obvious: when Larwood or Tate or Geary was being rested, batsmen would wish to score off the amiable replacement. But the fast Australian wickets allowed White to bowl a yard short of his English length, so 38–10–79–0 and 30–5–83–0 at Sydney, 57–30–64–1 and 56·5–20–107–5 at Melbourne, 60–16–130–5 and 64·5–21–126–8 in the stifling heat of Adelaide. Among the batsmen he dismissed were Kippax and Hendry three times each, Ryder twice, and Woodfull, Jackson and Bradman.

The twenties began with Warwick Armstrong who not only looked but was ruthless, and ended with Percy Chapman of the cherubic countenance whose domestic background was Uppingham, Cambridge University and Kent. Chapman could never be Armstrong. Or could he? In the first Test at Brisbane England made 521, Gregory's knee giving way so that he did not bowl again. Larwood then destroyed Australia for 122. This was a timeless match so England, leading by 399, batted again. By now Kelleway, Australia's other opening bowler, was laid low by ptomaine poisoning. When England were 518 ahead, Jardine let 65 runs accrue to him in 3 hours. A declaration was made – but only that Australia might have half an hour's batting before the close on the fourth day. Overnight rain, then hot sun produced a sticky wicket. Requiring 742 for victory, Australia made 66.

The Brisbane Test was Donald George Bradman's tenth first-class game. He scored 18 lbw to Tate, and 1 caught by Chapman at silly point off White. Dropped for the second Test at Sydney, Bradman fielded as substitute for Ponsford whose hand had been broken by Larwood. So at the close of this match, Bradman's contribution to Test cricket was 19 runs and some fine fielding as the opposition made 1,515. There was a large deficit to be made up.

CHAPTER SIX

The Thirties

The Inevitability of Bodyline

On 11 July 1930, the first day of the Headingley Test, Bradman made 309 not out. *The Times* praised this feat in its news columns but devoted more space to a match at Lord's where Eton's Atkinson-Clark was balanced by Harrow's Stewart-Brown, where Princess Imeretinsky dazzled in black romaine, Viscountess Plumer – the Field Marshal's lady – was suitably camouflaged, and dukes nodded distantly to barons. (The reader will observe that, more than half a century after the event, we are using facts to put Bradman in his place.) A former captain of England, C. Aubrey Smith, had his name in lights outside the Duke of York's Theatre, Winston Churchill deplored Conservative disunity, thirty-seven-year-old William T. Tilden had just won the Gentlemen's Singles title at Wimbledon, while far away at Interlachen Bobby Jones was about to triumph in the US Open, the third step in his season's Grand Slam. But whereas Tilden and Jones would now retire, and Churchill languished in the political wilderness, Bradman had only just arrived.

During the next eighteen years he did not know what a wilderness was. Himself an Everest, he awaited the assault of various bowlers and generally rewarded them with an off-putting avalanche. R. C. Robertson-Glasgow would one day write, 'Next to Mr Winston Churchill, Bradman was the most celebrated man in England during the summer of 1948.' Between Headingley 1930 and Bradman's retirement, Australia rejoiced in many great cricketers – Ponsford, McCabe, Oldfield, Grimmett, O'Reilly, Hassett, Tallon, Lindwall and Miller, to name but some – yet one was to dominate each series either as

DONALD GEORGE BRADMAN, 1928–48
'The greatest batsman' – Wilfred Rhodes

batsman, captain, or as the main target of a controversial bowling style. The day after Headingley 1930, *The Times* summed up the future in a leading article: '*England v Bradman*'. Wilfred Rhodes put it another way: 'The greatest batsman the world has ever seen.'

Bradman's Australian season of 1929–30 had been successful: 1,586 first-class runs at 113·28, with 124 and 225 in the Test Trial at Sydney. His 452 not out for New South Wales *v* Queensland saw the first 400 made at 65 runs an hour; thereafter the batsman scored rapidly, his last 52 in 29 minutes. Chosen to tour England with Woodfull's seventeenth Australians, Bradman at once got the pace of the slower wickets with 236 at Worcester, followed by 185 not out at Leicester, and reached 1,000 runs by the end of May. On the eve of the third Test at Headingley he had played in sixteen matches and averaged 93·94. But even more remarkable from his team's point of view was the progress of Grimmett – in thirteen matches 102 wickets at 13·65, including a first-innings haul at Sheffield of 10 Yorkshire wickets for 37.

In 1930 Tests in England were, for the first time, played over four days. Hitherto a side which batted the first day and made upwards of 350 had been immune from defeat; now the extra day turned earlier calculations upside down. After Trent Bridge, where they lost by 93 runs in spite of a Bradman hundred and 10 wickets by Grimmett, Australia went to Lord's and perfect conditions. The match was a joy from start to finish, in the opinion of many the 'ideal' Test. One reason why England lost was that they played three-day cricket in a four-day context; 405 for 9 in 6 hours – Duleepsinhji 173 on his debut against Australia, after Woolley going in first had made 41 from 46 balls – was a spectacle for the gods. But Bradman was on the other side; coming in at 3.30 (162 for 1 in reply to England's 425) after Woodfull and Ponsford had blunted the attack, he had made 155 from 171 balls at the close – Australia 404 for 2.

On Monday the butcher became fasting friar, that is to say in a little over 3 hours Bradman scored only 99. Then at 585 for 2, he lofted a ball – something he had not done before. Chapman at extra-cover made the catch of anyone else's lifetime. Woodfull declared at tea – Australia 729 for 6 – which meant that England had to bat for at least 6 hours to avoid defeat while scoring at over 60 runs an hour. They lost by 7 wickets but only after Chapman had hit with a sublime disregard for logic, 121 in two and a half hours. The lesson was plain: it was no use a side making 800 runs in a match of four days with Bradman in opposition. However, with a glance at an imperishable scoresheet, we must remember that at Lord's England's greatest fast bowler, as well as one of her most accurate medium-pacers, had been absent. Moreover, Bradman had come in when the bowling was tired.

Exultant Yorkshiremen bayed. It was 11.36 on the morning of 11 July 1930. From the ninth ball of the Australian innings Jackson steered an inswinger from Tate into the hands of short-leg. 2–1–1. The ball was new, the bowlers fresh, as Bradman took guard. The temperature was 64°F, the sun shone. Bradman wore no sweater. Within minutes he faced Larwood. 4 – an off-drive. 4 – a ferocious pull which said much for the shock-absorbent qualities of someone's bat. 2 – a force to leg. 1 – near the end of an over Bradman liked to take one.

Percy Chapman decided Larwood must be rested in favour of Geary who bowled – or so county batsmen insisted – an undriveable length. At once he tested Bradman with a ball just outside the off stump. The matrons of Headingley nodded approval as Bradman played *their* stroke. Batting to a four-year-old at Scarborough, the matrons achieved a convulsive jerk at balls of Geary's undriveable length, sending them past the sandcastle on the left – that is wide of mid-on's right hand. Whether Bradman played forward or back to Geary, and whether his bat was straight or crooked, none knew; the fielder glimpsed a blur, then trotted off like a retriever.

As Bradman's 50 came in 49 minutes, William Woodfull reflected he had been there before. Of course! Four years ago – Macartney. Then the total had been 64, now it was 63. Then

ENGLAND *v* AUSTRALIA

Played at Lord's 27, 28, 30 June, 1 July 1930

ENGLAND

	First Innings			Second Innings	
J. B. Hobbs	c Oldfield b Fairfax	1		b Grimmett	19
F. E. Woolley	c Wall b Fairfax	41		hit wkt b Grimmett	28
W. R. Hammond	b Grimmett	38		c Fairfax b Grimmett	32
K. S. Duleepsinhji	c Bradman b Grimmett	173		c Oldfield bHornibrook	48
E. Hendren	c McCabe b Fairfax	48		c Richardson b Grimmett	9
A. P. F. Chapman	c Oldfield b Wall	11		c Oldfield b Fairfax	121
G. O. Allen	b Fairfax	3		lbw b Grimmett	
M. W. Tate	c McCabe b Wall	54		c Ponsford b Grimmett	57 / 10
R. W. V. Robins	c Oldfield b Hornibrook	5		not out	11
J. C. White	not out	23		run out	10
G. Duckworth	c Oldfield b Wall	18		lbw b Fairfax	0
Extras	(B2, LB7, NB1)	10		(B16, LB13, W1)	30
Total		**425**			**375**

Fall of wickets: 1–13, 2–53, 3–105, 4–209, 5–236, 6–239, 7–337, 8–363, 9–387, 10–425.

2nd innings   1–45, 2–58, 3–129, 4–141, 5–147, 6–272, 7–329, 8–354, 9–372, 10–375.

AUSTRALIA BOWLING (6-ball overs)

	O.	M.	R.	W.	O.	M.	R.	W.
Wall	29·4	2	118	3	25	2	80	0
Fairfax	31	3	101	4	12·4	2	37	2
Grimmett	33	4	105	2	53	13	167	6
Hornibrook	26	6	62	1	22	6	49	1
McCabe	9	1	29	0	3	1	11	0
Bradman	–	–	–	–	1	0	1	0

AUSTRALIA

W. M. Woodfull	st Duckworth b Robins	155	not out	26
W. H. Ponsford	c Hammond b White	81	b Robins	14
D. G. Bradman	c Chapman b White	254	c Chapman b Tate	1
A. F. Kippax	b White	83	c Duckworth b Robins	3
S. J. McCabe	c Woolley b Hammond	44	not out	25
V. Y. Richardson	c Hobbs b Tate	30		
W. A. Oldfield	not out	43		
A. G. Fairfax	not out	20		
C. V. Grimmett				
P. M. Hornibrook	did not bat			
T. W. Wall				
Extras	(B6, LB8, W5)	19	(B1, LB2)	3
Total	(6 wkts declared)	729	(3 wickets)	72

Fall of wickets: 1–162, 2–393, 3–585, 4–588, 5–643, 6–672.

2nd innings   1–16, 2–17, 3–22.

ENGLAND BOWLING (6-ball overs)

	O.	M.	R.	W.	O.	M.	R.	W.
Allen	34	7	115	0	–	–	–	–
Tate	64	16	148	1	13	6	21	1
White	51	7	158	3	2	0	8	0
Robins	42	1	172	1	9	1	34	2
Hammond	35		82	1	4·2	1	6	0

AUSTRALIA WON BY 7 WICKETS

Cardus had likened Woodfull's bat to a sort of 'pom-pom-pom accompaniment in the bass to Macartney's sparkling *valse caprice*', now 'Woodfull was as much a man to be noticed in conjunction with Bradman as Kreisler's conscientious accompanist'. But while Macartney had lived dangerously, Bradman was playing two out of three deliveries as though bolting a door. 'A forcing defensive batsman,' thought Cardus.

Chapman recalled the theory that Bradman was fallible against flighted leg spin. Very well, Dick Tyldesley's accuracy of pitch was undoubted; he would make Bradman think. As the ball left the bowler's hand, Bradman thought; having thought, he advanced a couple of yards down the wicket. Two Tyldesley overs produced 4.4.1.2.4.1. Much time was wasted as Master Leonard Hutton and other boys sought to handle the ball. Tyldesley bowled, Hammond bowled; Tate and Larwood returned, Geary came and went. Bradman's 100 arrived in 99 minutes; on his lunch-time report schoolmaster Woodfull wrote: 'Most promising start, on no occasion did he take the slightest risk.'

Australia: 136 for 1* (Woodfull not out 29, Bradman not out 105).

The reader already tired of Bradman's name may seek temporary refuge in the match at Lord's where by lunch Harrow had lost 7 wickets. One reason advanced for this unsatisfactory (to non-Etonians) state of affairs was the absence through lack of form of a Harrow batsman. Terence Rattigan was working for an Oxford scholarship and, it was said, scribbling dialogue when he should have been fashioning cuts.

At three o'clock Woodfull was bowled by Hammond for 50; with Kippax in, Bradman scored 3.2.4 to reach 151 out of a total of 203 for 2. Here was a moment of truth; the new ball was taken and entrusted to Larwood and Tate. Very soon the ball ceased to be new save by pedantic definition, for Bradman swatted it to all parts of the field. Leaving the batsman on 186 (something he would not permit the bowlers to do), we may consider a myth

* During the morning's two hours, England – using mainly fast or fast-medium bowlers – managed 46 overs.

long connected with Headingley 1930 – that Bradman scored as fast as he did because Chapman persisted with attacking fields throughout the day. P. G. H. Fender was in the press box, and later published *The Tests of 1930*. Larwood, with the second and third new balls, had, it seems, only one slip and a gully because an extra man was required in the covers and also at deepish mid-wicket. Geary – the Hendrick of 1930 – soon dispensed with any slip at all, and at one period had a man straight behind him on the boundary as well as a long-on and a long-off. Tyldesley's field was likewise far flung.

With Bradman on 186, mourners were leaving the funeral of Sir Arthur Conan Doyle, who had once dismissed W. G., though admittedly after the Doctor had made 100 and was about to declare. Seeking a new Watson to question Bradman's Holmes, Chapman summoned up Maurice Leyland from the deep. Five balls of the left-hander's initial over were struck for 2.2.4.4.1 and Chapman stroked his chin. However, things quietened down until the 4.30 tea interval when Australia were 305 for 2 – Bradman 220 and Kippax 33. Could Bradman pass R. E. Foster's record Test score of 287 made at Sydney in 1903–4? Foster not being a Yorkshireman, and Bradman having been an honorary one since lunch (since 1948 for the remainder of his life), the crowd willed the deed to be done. It was – at six o'clock with a single off Tate who had told Bradman at the end of 1928–9 that he would have to play with a straighter bat in England. The day's scoresheet was unusual:

AUSTRALIA

W. M. Woodfull	b Hammond	50
A. A. Jackson	c Larwood b Tate	1
D. G. Bradman	not out	309
A. F. Kippax	c Chapman b Tate	77
S. J. McCabe	not out	12
Extras (B1, LB8)		9
Total (3 wkts)		458

Fall of wickets: 1–2, 2–194, 3–423.

Next day P. F. Warner, who had fielded to several Trumper masterpieces and watched Macartney with something approaching ecstasy, wrote that Bradman's footwork permitted him to force any ball *whatever its length*. When Bradman was finally caught at the wicket off Tate for 334, scored out of 506, he had hit forty-six 4s – *forty-two on the first day*. Australia's 566 were made in 460 minutes, and owed much to the bowling in more senses than one. Larwood 33, Tate, Geary and Hammond between them 91, Tyldesley and Leyland 44, together bowled 168 overs. How was this done?

Today a bowler of Larwood's pace would take at least four and a quarter minutes to complete an over (14 an hour), his 33 occupying 140 minutes. Assuming Tate, Geary and Hammond got through an over in three and a quarter minutes (18·3 overs an hour), then their 91 overs would take 295 minutes. In which case Tyldesley and Leyland bowled 44 overs in 25 minutes. O happy men of Headingley! A day in the sun watching Bradman at his most magnoperative, with Tyldesley and Leyland each bowling an over in 34 seconds. Superman chased by two Keystone Cops.

England's trials were not yet over. The series level at one-all, the Oval Test was played to a finish. Facing an England total of 405, and ignoring a brilliant 110 by Ponsford, Bradman made 232 in a stay of over seven hours, with many interruptions by rain. Although still short of his twenty-second birthday, Bradman had done much to help Australia regain the Ashes, adding a new dimension to cricket. Scoring as fast as Trumper, Macartney or Woolley, Bradman seemed to take as few risks as Scotton* had long ago. He showed the need for a new law, that a batsman should be compulsorily retired on reaching 100; had such a law existed then Bradman's fifteen Test innings against England averaged 61, in itself an indecent figure. Unimpeded by a compulsorily retired law, Bradman's average was 103.

---

* Who, it will be recalled, had batted for over eight hours in scoring 123 *v* Moss Vale in 1885. In May 1926 and May 1927 Bradman played innings of 300 and 320 not out for Bowral *v* Moss Vale, thus proving how pointless it is to change one's bowlers.

BRADMAN AT HEADINGLEY 1930

c G. Duckworth b M. W. Tate 334

Made out of 506 in 6 hours 23 minutes

52·32 runs an hour   74·55 runs/100 balls

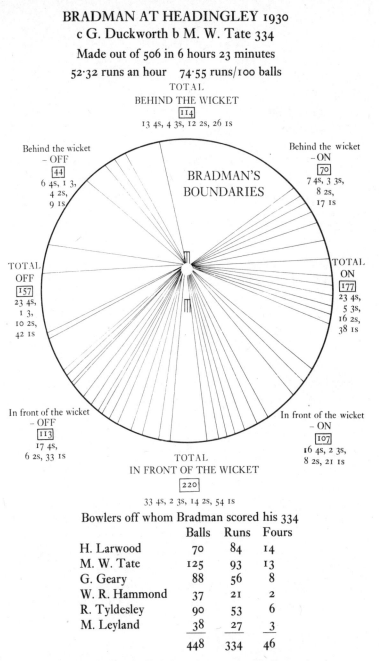

TOTAL
BEHIND THE WICKET
114
13 4s, 4 3s, 12 2s, 26 1s

Behind the wicket
– OFF
44
6 4s, 1 3,
4 2s,
9 1s

BRADMAN'S
BOUNDARIES

Behind the wicket
– ON
70
7 4s, 3 3s,
8 2s,
17 1s

TOTAL
OFF
157
23 4s,
1 3,
10 2s,
42 1s

TOTAL
ON
177
23 4s,
5 3s,
16 2s,
38 1s

In front of the wicket
– OFF
113
17 4s,
6 2s, 33 1s

In front of the wicket
– ON
107
16 4s, 2 3s,
8 2s, 21 1s

TOTAL
IN FRONT OF THE WICKET
220
33 4s, 2 3s, 14 2s, 54 1s

Bowlers off whom Bradman scored his 334

	Balls	Runs	Fours
H. Larwood	70	84	14
M. W. Tate	125	93	13
G. Geary	88	56	8
W. R. Hammond	37	21	2
R. Tyldesley	90	53	6
M. Leyland	38	27	3
	448	334	46

Bradman scored off 158 (35 per cent) of balls received

England's future appeared bleak. By the next MCC tour of Australia, Tate would be nearing thirty-eight; Larwood alone was in the highest class. Yet in the last three Tests of 1928–9, and in three of 1930, Larwood's 10 wickets had each cost 77 runs. His pace and accuracy had restricted the Woodfull, Ponsford, Kippax, Jackson, McCabe and Richardson of 1930 to a mere 33 runs every 100 balls; from the same number of balls Bradman had made 93. Australians had good reason to believe the Ashes would remain in their custody for many years to come. They needed to augment their bowling for, as Woodfull had pointed out at the close of 1930, whereas Australia could have got by without Bradman, the loss of Grimmett must have proved fatal. But there was Bradman.

MCC's captain of 1932–3, Douglas Jardine, had no intention of contributing to the Bradman legend. He would destroy it. Chapman's side had included one fast bowler, Larwood; his, when chosen, had four – Larwood, Voce (left-handed), Allen and Bowes, the first named by far the fastest. Their task was to lower Bradman's average by reducing the number of strokes he could play to one, and that one when under acute physical and mental pressure – the hook. A decade earlier Gregory and Macdonald had caused English howls by their occasional short-pitched deliveries which, with a couple or at most three men on the on side, could hardly have been bowled too frequently to batsmen capable of the hook stroke for fear of giving away runs. As Armstrong wrote after 1921, English batsmen could not play rising deliveries on, or outside, the off stump. Jardine had a bowler of phenomenal pace and accuracy in his side; he meant to encourage, compel, *yet restrict command over*, the hook stroke by setting five or six short-legs (for the mis-hit or self-protective prod), with two men out deep behind them for the stroke that connected. The essence of Larwood's accuracy was that he could, at will, pitch a length from which the ball would reach the batsman at 90 mph somewhere between the waist and the head. Englishmen termed this form of attack 'leg-theory', Australians preferred to call it 'bodyline'.

Bearing in mind the customary length of Larwood and Voce, it will be seen that the great South African batsman H. W. Taylor was wrong when, asked by an agency man in January 1933 what he thought of the Australian response to 'bodyline', he stated that, 'There is no danger if the batsmen play forward.' The only other joke to emerge from 1932–3 was the refusal of G. O. Allen to bowl to a leg field. Had he been a professional and refused, Jardine would certainly have booked a passage on the next boat home; but Allen was an amateur. Jardine had been educated at Winchester, Allen at Eton – Wykehamists do *not* tell Etonians what to do. Had Jardine persisted, he might well have suffered a moral rebuke:

'I must remind you, Douglas, that when Eton play at Lord's, *The Times* devotes at least half a column to a detailed description of ladies' dresses. Winchester do not play at Lord's, nor are their ladies' dresses noticed anywhere.'

No one was killed during 1932–3 but the 'Battle of Adelaide' was decidedly unpleasant. From the last ball of Larwood's third over – and *before* the leg field had been set, Woodfull was hit over the heart. For Larwood's next over, Jardine switched to the full battery of short-legs, the still groggy Australian captain taking blow after blow on his body. The crowd resented this. Later in the innings Oldfield mistimed a hook at an *off stump* bouncer and snicked the ball on to his head. As he was assisted from the field forty mounted troopers were ready to ride forth if the enraged crowd swarmed over the fences. When Warner, MCC's joint manager, who had denounced Bowes's bumper attack on Hobbs the previous English summer and was now standing uneasily on one leg, visited the Australian dressing room to express regret for the odd fractured skull, he was rebuked by Woodfull: 'I don't want to see you, Mr Warner. There are two sides out there. One is playing cricket; the other is not. The game is too good to be spoilt.' Warner admitted he could do nothing with Jardine; perhaps the only manager who might have (had Jardine been a Catholic) was the Duke of Norfolk, with a threat of excommunication.

Douglas Jardine was a most determined man; the adversary he deserved was Warwick Armstrong – or one who came to power as Chancellor of Germany a few days after Adelaide, Adolf Hitler. Whether the *Führer* would have reacted to Jardine's Oxford Harlequins cap as Australians did will never be known.

Much of the cricket played in 1932–3 was superb. When not tending their bruises, Woodfull, Ponsford, Fingleton, Victor Richardson, O'Brien and Darling all played at least one brave innings for Australia. In normal conditions the bowler of the series might well have been O'Reilly, whose medium-pace leg-breaks and googlies brought him 27 wickets at 26·81, a first indication that here was one of the half-dozen masters of all time. His immediate adversaries were an impressive bunch: Sutcliffe, Hammond and the Nawab of Pataudi who scored hundreds (on one occasion, after the Indian had refused to enter the leg-trap, Jardine observed 'I see His Highness is a conscientious objector' – and thereafter purged the offender), Ames and Allen who might come in at nine, and Larwood at eleven, with Jardine, Wyatt and Leyland to add stiffening. Brisbane in February is no place for a cricketer with a high temperature and tonsillitis. 'What of those fellows who marched to Kandahar with the fever on them?' queried Jardine. So little Eddie Paynter tottered from his nursing home bed to 83 runs and immortality.

The greatest innings in history was played at Sydney in 1932 when McCabe stood up and hooked 'bodyline' into oblivion – or so it seemed – and even Jardine gazed in wonder. 187 not out in 4 hours, 55 out of 60 for the last wicket in half an hour: it was an innings that Ranji or Trumper might have conjured, as McCabe did, *once*. 'I was lucky,' said McCabe. 'Don't expect me to do it again.' Meanwhile the person for whom 'bodyline' had been devised, Bradman, missed the first Test through illness. Having no intention of being hit, he relied on his twinkling feet and unorthodoxy; sometimes a hook, sometimes (if the ball was delivered from the edge of the return crease) a backwards movement and slash into the vacant covers. A not out 103 – after

LARWOOD'S FIELD WHEN BOWLING
TO WOODFULL
Brisbane 1933

Mr Leslie Ames points out that Woodfull was not looked upon as a hooker; when McCabe, Bradman and others were batting, Verity moved across to make a second long-leg.

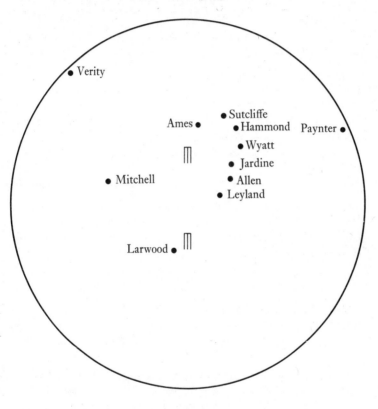

AUSTRALIA

V. Y. Richardson	E. H. Bromley
W. M. Woodfull	H. S. Love
D. G. Bradman	T. W. Wall
S. J. McCabe	W. J. O'Reilly
W. H. Ponsford	H. Ironmonger
L. S. Darling	

ENGLAND

D. R. Jardine	G. O. Allen
H. Sutcliffe	E. Paynter
W. R. Hammond	H. Larwood
R. E. S. Wyatt	H. Verity
M. Leyland	T. B. Mitchell
L. E. G. Ames	

a first ball 'duck' – in the second Test at Melbourne enabled
O'Reilly with 10 for 129 to win that game for Australia. The rest
of Bradman was, by his standards, feverish brilliance or failure.
An average of 56·57, though higher than that of Sutcliffe and
Hammond, saw him reduced to human stature. 'Bodyline' had
fulfilled its purpose.

Larwood, hailed by Australian batsmen as a truly great
bowler, never played for England again. Jardine took an MCC
side to India, then notified Lord's he would not be available for
the Tests of 1934.

And After – 1934

Cricket now proceeded in proper fashion; Bradman re-ascended
his throne and ruled over English wickets doped with cow dung.
But this was a new Bradman: recovering from shell shock,
Trumper-esque in brilliance and an ability to get out when none
expected it. The Tests at Trent Bridge, Lord's, and Old
Trafford where he suffered from a throat infection, went by: five
Bradman innings totalled 133. Bowlers took heart and rejoiced.
Then glancing inside the Australian throne room, they were
shocked; not only was the king still there but on a second throne
sat an emperor by the name of Ponsford. The law of probabilities
was consulted. Ponsford had twice, and Bradman once, topped
400 in first-class innings, yet playing together in the same
Australian side against England on nine occasions they had come
together only twice – and then in minor partnerships of 81 and
32. What if king and emperor should form a dual alliance?

The best fairy stories begin 'Once upon a time'. Once upon a
time, in 1934, Australia used three different opening bowlers –
Wall, Ebeling and McCabe. Their haul in five Tests was 13
wickets at 60 runs each, each wicket requiring 136 balls. Gregory
and Macdonald had done better than this; Lindwall and Miller,
Davidson, and Lillee would do better. But in 1934 Australia won
the series handsomely – by three matches to one, had not rain
saved England at Headingley. Over after over, hour after hour,
day by day and week by week, home batsmen were put on the

rack and kept there by two bowlers who conceded fewer than two runs an over – Grimmett and O'Reilly, leg-spinners both. To continue, and conclude, our fairy story analogy, Grimmett looked like Old Mother Hubbard and O'Reilly a tiger in wolf's clothing.

Judged from afar, Australia's campaign consisted of a holding operation until the king should be himself once more. At Trent Bridge Bill Brown batted at three with blade as straight as a guardsman's, McCabe's 65 and 88 were the connoisseur's memory of the match, unhappy Arthur Chipperfield perished for 99 in his first Test. Kenneth Farnes strove heroically to take 10 for 179, and everyone criticized Woodfull for an absurdly late declaration – England 380 to win in four and three-quarter hours. The sort of closure which gives cricket a bad name unless a captain has faith in two wonderful bowlers. In England's first innings Grimmett had conducted sapping means (58·3–24–81–5) while O'Reilly cursed each run scored off him and, indeed, suffered heavy punishment (37–16–75–4). With England intent on saving the game, and ignoring the 380 needed for victory, the terrible pair did better – the last wicket falling at 6.20. Grimmett 47–28–39–3, and O'Reilly 41·4–24–54–7.

At the close on the second day at Lord's, the match was evenly poised – possibly in the visitors' favour: England 440, Australia 192 for 2 with Brown 103 not out. Leyland and Ames both made centuries, which was as well, for England's early batting had held off Grimmett and O'Reilly only to fall to the leg-breaks of Chipperfield. Cardus opined that, 'Mr G. K. Chesterton or Mr Bernard Shaw would, with leg-spin, bring lines of concern to the faces of England batsmen at the present time.' A match evenly poised suffered revolutionary change over the weekend; rain fell, and on Monday Verity took 14 wickets with exquisitely poised and directed left-arm spin. Woodfull fought gallantly, Bradman played a hideous slash, and England won by an innings and 38. At Melbourne in 1904 Rhodes's 15 wickets had cost 124, at Lord's Verity did better with 15 for 104 from 58·3 overs.

Old Trafford belied its reputation: instead of rain and hard grafting, a heatwave and 1,307 runs for 20 wickets, with sore throats (at one time suspected diphtheria) in the Australian camp. The forty-five-year-old Hendren, Leyland and McCabe scored hundreds, O'Reilly dismissed Walters, Wyatt and Hammond in four deliveries, then finished with 7 for 189. England batted for ten hours, so did Australia; Allen's opening over included three wides, four no-balls, and self-recriminatory oaths in profusion. Perhaps the sweetest joy of the match was the 52 in an hour with which Cyril Walters launched England's innings. If only . . . If only Walters had stayed in cricket after 1935, if Duleepsinhji's health had not broken down, then by the end of the decade the selectors would have used a pin to choose from Walters, Hutton, Charles Barnett, Duleep, Hammond, Compton and Paynter – with Ames as a bulwark at seven.

And so to Headingley and what the England captain termed a 'feather bed' on which Grimmett and O'Reilly toiled (7 for 103 from 65·4 overs) while batsmen slept. By 5.25 England had settled for a prim 200, 10 minutes before the close Australia were coasting at 37 for none. Bowes changed to the pavilion end and in ten balls accounted for Brown, a nightwatchman Oldfield, and Woodfull. Australia 39 for 3, Ponsford 22 not out – an over to be completed. Next morning it was. Bowes bowled two balls just short of a length; the first was driven off the back foot straight for 4, the second to the on for 4. As the umpire called 'Over', Bowes looked at the striker of boundaries. A cold, merciless expression spoke louder than words – 'I've got you.' On the Australian balcony eyes lit up, not at the 4s but at the manner of their making; Bradman was playing as correctly as H. L. Collins sober to produce results which would never for one moment have been contemplated by H. L. Collins drunk.

As Verity bowled seven consecutive maidens, it became clear that diplomacy had failed – that the dual alliance of Ponsford and Bradman was at last a fact. For an hour both batsmen did little, in two and a half hours before lunch they managed only 129. Apart from those initial boundaries, Bradman's 76 had come at only 27 runs an hour. During the afternoon Bradman still crawled (41 runs an hour); so, too, did Ponsford. 329 for 3 at tea represented nothing more than steady going. Alas, the partnership ended at 427 when Ponsford pulled Verity massively to the on boundary, his left foot swinging back to dislodge a bail. So somewhat aggrieved that a personal flaw rather than England's bowlers had dismissed him, Ponsford departed for 181. The dual monarchs had added 388 at 68 an hour. Ponsford was a very great batsman save to the fastest of bowling: a superb technique, mastery of every stroke, worn with an air of utter impregnability, persuaded some international bowlers they preferred attacking Bradman. But on 21 July 1934 Bradman had not finished: with McCabe in, he ravished the tired trundlers, finishing 271 not out (58 an hour since tea). 39 for 3 to 494 for 4 was a good recovery.

A thunderstorm washed out the Headingley Test with England requiring 155 to avoid an innings defeat with only 4 wickets standing. A Yorkshire crowd brought up to despise googly bowling did their sums and concluded that the match figures of Grimmett and O'Reilly were 173·3 overs 76 maidens 263 runs 12 wickets. A month later at the Oval Australia beat England by 562 runs, the second time Woodfull had regained the Ashes on his birthday – 22 August. As a variant on Headingley, Grimmett and O'Reilly finished with 135–42–318–12, so turning a timeless Test into an intimate four-day affair.

The climax occurred on the first day, rather as if Act 1 of *Hamlet* consisted of corpses, leaving the rest of the play to Gravediggers and hangers-on. On the fourth day 17 wickets (8 Australian and 9 England) fell for 286, and no one cared; for on the third day England had declined from 90 for none to 321 – Leyland's 110 in the best 'Let's have some fun' style, with Australia tripping gaily to 186 for 2. And the second day hadn't been very interesting as Australia collapsed to 701.

What jarred on local susceptibilities was Saturday, 18 August. Impossible, ridiculous, dull: the accepted verdict was 'boring'. Between noon and 6.23 p.m. the dual alliance had improved on Headingley, raising the hourly rate from 68 to 85, though *only 100 overs* were bowled during the day. If the emperor was not at his very best, the king played one of his masterpieces – however, 'I think Bill should have taken more of the new ball at 400.' England passed a bad weekend looking at

AUSTRALIA

W. A. Brown	b Clark	10
W. H. Ponsford	not out	205
D. G. Bradman	c Ames b Bowes	244
S. J. McCabe	not out	1
Extras (B1, LB8, W2, NB4)		15
Total (2 wkts)		475

Fall of wickets: 1–21, 2–472.

Ponsford soon announced his retirement from cricket to go fishing. Bradman* gave the impression he would go on treating England bowlers as minnows.

1936–7 and 1938

History repeats itself. In his first five innings of 1936–7, as of 1934, Bradman scored 133 runs. Return to normal (or shall we say abnormal?) normalcy in England had been represented by 304, 244 and 77, now in Australia by 270, 26, 212 and 169. One aspect of Bradman's genius may be expressed in figures; the sheer and abiding wonder of his batting over twenty years is now only a cherished memory of those who saw him. In 1936–7 the side he captained won the series after recovering from two down; each game went with the toss, yet of the first four it might be asked – who deserved to lose? Certainly the England selectors who had omitted from G. O. Allen's party a rare fighter, Eddie Paynter. A success with Jardine's side, and in 1938 at home, he had topped 2,000 runs in the preceding English season

---

* Bradman's health was not good in 1934. On 24 September he was taken seriously ill and within hours had been operated on by the Melbourne surgeon Sir Douglas Shields at the latter's Park Lane nursing home. Bradman's appendix was practically gangrenous.

and was equally at ease anywhere in the order. In 1936–7 only three English batsmen – Hammond 58, Leyland 55, and Barnett 43 – averaged more than 30 in the Tests. In seven matches against Australia when the selectors did notice Paynter, he averaged 84!

Australia required 381 to win at Brisbane: rain, 58 all out. Bradman 0, second ball. England occupied the middle interminably at Sydney: 426 for 6 declared – Hammond's 231 not out a reminder of his methods eight years previously. Rain, the pitch damp rather than sticky: Australia 1 for 3, 31 for 7, 80 all out. Bradman 0, first ball. Things improved but not enough to avert an innings defeat. So England went to Melbourne two-up. Soon after tea on the first day Australia were 130 for 6 (HE had played a slack stroke when 13), with the Englishmen thinking how simple it was to regain the Ashes. Then rain and a wet ball, Australia 181 for 6 at the close.

What is – or rather was – a Melbourne 'glue-pot'? A wicket on which the ball will stand up from a good length. So! When play *could* start on 2 January 1937 . . . Australia 200 for 9 declared; England 76 for 9 declared; Australia 3 for 1. Hammond 32 and Leyland 17 somehow achieved rational batting until both were out to incredible short-leg catches by Darling. How, men asked, had Johnny Tyldesley and Trumper relished performing on such a pig against Trumble and Saunders, Rhodes and Hirst? The question abides till Judgement Day. Bradman showed much sense at the day's end when Allen (too late!) closed England's innings. He sent in Fleetwood-Smith who, generally unable to hit the ball on a good wicket, had only to play his normal game.

A rainless weekend, and answered Australian prayers, reformed the pitch. Fingleton came in sixth at 74, Bradman seventh at 97; 6 hours and 346 runs later Fingleton was out for 136. Amen. England went to Adelaide one-up with two to play, somehow they persuaded Australia to be content with 288 in perfect conditions. A lead of 150, and England might be able to dictate terms. But the lead was a mere 42, Ames's half-century the only true support for Barnett's 129. Quite inexplicable until we recall that this was the first England-Australia series to be played under the new lbw law whereby a batsman could be out to a ball pitched outside the off stump. It was not that Fleetwood-Smith's 'chinaman' stock deliveries were getting batsmen lbw but that such balls could no longer be played *with impunity* off the back foot by pads. Techniques were having to be adjusted; Fleetwood-Smith at Adelaide took 10 for 239: in three innings this southpaw Mailey had caused bewilderment with 97·2 overs 13 maidens 363 runs 15 wickets. England's answer was a great finger-spinner, Verity; in two of the three innings he defied even Bradman to play strokes. 3 for 133 from 74·7 overs was superb but not match-winning bowling. The series would be decided in the fifth Test at Melbourne.

It was – in the first couple of hours. Allen missed Fingleton when that batsman was 1, which did not matter, and McCabe when 11, which did. Both chances were off Farnes who hurled himself at the enemy. And Bradman? He was in a relentless mood, hitting only seven boundaries in his century which nonetheless came in 125 minutes. He and the aristocratic McCabe, 112, added 249 for the 3rd wicket in only 2 hours 43 minutes. Next day Badcock made a century and young Ross Gregory 80; Farnes's 6 for 96 was a fist brandished at the gods who permitted Australia to reach 604, who had seemed to offer Allen everything – and then quirkishly changed their minds.

1938 was a season of four Tests (not a ball was bowled at Old Trafford), individual greatness, some triumphant debuts, one superb match at Headingley and a farce at the Oval – and two Australian omissions from the chosen party. Grimmett, the perfect foil to O'Reilly, was ignored. Now forty-six but in fine physical trim, he had always been a more dangerous bowler in England than in Australia; for the next two seasons he would be the most successful Shield bowler *in* Australia. Also omitted was Tallon, commonly regarded as the finest wicketkeeper in Australia, and certainly in 1946–7 the finest in the world. Errors behind the stumps did not affect the destination of the Ashes –

Australia retained them by going to the Oval one-up – only the visitors' pride.

Barnett at Trent Bridge reached his century from the first ball after lunch, one ball too late to place him in the select company of Trumper, Macartney and Bradman who reached three figures before the interval. Hutton and Compton both made hundreds on their debut, a restored-to-favour Paynter 216 not out. Bill Brown followed a second-innings century at Trent Bridge with an undefeated 206 at Lord's, Bradman made a hundred in each of the three Tests in which he batted. At the Oval he did not bat, perhaps the outcome of his outrageous gamble. Knowing the match would be played to a finish, Bradman and Hammond both gambled on winning the toss: England's front-line attack was Farnes, Bowes and Verity – very fine as far as it went which, if the opposition took root on the 1938 Oval wicket, wasn't very far. Australia chose *two* bowlers of Test class – O'Reilly and Fleetwood-Smith; and then lost the toss!

Hammond ordered his batsmen not to get out. Hutton did get out, but after 13 hours 20 minutes for 364. Of this martyrdom O'Reilly said, 'The greatest innings ever played against my bowling' – praise enough for any man. A second-wicket partnership with Leyland (187 *run out*) produced 382 runs, but this was merely a stepping stone to later extravagances. Hammond did finally declare at 903 for 7* after learning that Bradman, who had put his left foot in the pit made by O'Reilly and broken a bone, would take no further part in the match. By this time Fingleton had also retired with a pulled muscle. The records say that England won by an innings and 579; Yorkshiremen, ever lusting after ultimate truth, prefer to remember that Hutton, Leyland, Arthur Wood (53) and Verity (8 not out) contributed 612 runs, and Bowes, Verity and Leyland took 10 of the 16 Australian wickets to fall.

Postscript: while Yorkshire in England caps were beating

---

* During England's marathon, a wicket fell every 288 balls. Six months later at Durban, South Africa and England played an unfinished ten-day Test when 1,981 runs were scored for 35 wickets – a dismissal every 363 balls.

Australia at the Oval, Sutcliffe – Hutton's mentor – made a century *v* Notts at Trent Bridge. Herbert said he knew that Leonard would do well, meaning of course when Herbert was no longer at the other end.

The Australian selectors doubtless noted that when 40 Hutton should have been stumped off Fleetwood-Smith. As a non-wicketkeeper once observed: 'All stumpings are difficult, and none should be missed.'

Masters

Monday, 13 June 1938. At the start of the day Australia were 520 behind England's 658 for 8 declared, with Fingleton, Brown and Bradman already out, and McCabe on 19. 6 runs were added before Farnes bowled the nightwatchman Ward, at 151 Hassett touched a Wright leg-break to Hammond at slip. 43 more runs and Badcock, the last recognized Australian batsman, found his stumps wrecked by a Wright googly. 194 for 6, with McCabe easing into his 60s. He did little that was extraordinary save score with effortless ease, hooking Farnes and making ground to Wright's medium-pace – Wright who was to be hailed by Bradman as 'the discovery of the year'. Ben Barnett, the Australian wicketkeeper, now played safely until lunch taken at 261 for 6: Barnett 20 and McCabe 107, the latter having made 88 out of 120 from the bat since play began.

Immediately after lunch, Barnett was caught off Farnes for 22. 263 for 7. The three remaining batsmen were O'Reilly, the fast bowler McCormick, and Fleetwood-Smith. On those occasions when they played together for Victoria, Fleetwood-Smith went in above Ironmonger. As O'Reilly reduced his tour average by only 0·2 in making 9, his effort was commendable. McCormick, alas, discovered his limit to be 2. At the other end there was no limit to the England bowlers' humiliation. Stanley Joseph McCabe was a classical batsman; every stroke he made would have served to illustrate the drive, cut and hook in a manual of instruction. Twice he whipped Hammond off his toes to the square-leg boundary; having forced Farnes past extra-cover, he

WALTER REGINALD HAMMOND, 1928–47
'The Elgin Marbles' according to Cardus

replied to the inevitable bouncer by hooking it high into the eastern stand. The fielders were so many sentinels, demanding in vain the password as the ball flashed by. In 47 minutes McCabe made 53 out of 66 from the bat. So far he had struck one 6 and eighteen 4s – 160 since he came in 202 minutes earlier.

The sight of Fleetwood-Smith (who bore a striking resemblance to a British Guards officer impersonating Hitler – or the other way about) concentrated McCabe's mind. Boundaries were called for, and a single at the end of every over. Two mighty straight drives off Wright boomed against the sight screen; three times in one over McCabe waited indulgently for Farnes's outswinger and then cut it beyond the range of third-man. Fleetwood-Smith applauded each such wonder as though it had been fashioned from his own bowling; inspired, he also held his bat in the right place. McCabe passed his second hundred during four consecutive balls from Wright: 4 past mid-on, 4 over square-leg, 4 off the back foot past extra-cover, 4 over mid-wicket. The tapestry completed, Compton (the only other man present who might one day play such an innings) held a lofted drive. With Fleetwood-Smith as partner, McCabe had scored 72 out of 77 in 28 minutes; in three and a quarter hours on 13 June 1938 seven Australians made 50, McCabe 213. The thirty-four boundaries struck in McCabe's innings would have been as many with a wicket marked in the centre of Salisbury Plain.

Bradman later held this to be the finest innings he had ever seen. We may, of course, prefer McCabe's 187 at Sydney where 'bodyline' so restricted him that only 16 runs were scored in front of the wicket on the off side. It depends whether you admire moral and physical heroism more than divine inspiration.

Friday, 24 June 1938. His Majesty would come to Lord's this day; unless he hastened, he would watch the England tail and the start of Australia's reply. To a very fast McCormick, Hutton and Barnett had prodded and prayed, the former soon caught at short-leg. Bill Edrich did not prod; he hooked, missed – and survived. He pulled – and did not survive. 20 for 2. In the Long

Room (where stroke-play was already fluent) members nudged one another, some shrank from the passing figure whose expression denoted black fury. Down the pavilion steps and on to the field he strode – silk shirt rustling, blue handkerchief protruding from right hip pocket. He took guard, and surveyed with disdain eleven rampant Australians.

'This is Lord's! MY KINGDOM!'

Walter Hammond, captain of England, was ready to work the fury out of his system. Or he would be after Barnett had departed, also caught at short-leg off McCormick. 31 for 3. Paynter pattered in.

The spectator appeal of some batsmen is in proportion to the runs they score; that of Hammond was related to a manner somewhat more than grand. He was not only a great cricketer, he looked as men thought a great cricketer should: athletic, powerful of build, serene and relaxed, who when the mood was on him could bowl at medium-pace and summon up memories of Barnes, whose slip fielding seemed infallible, whose batting was opulent. He had known failure against Australians (just before and after his eighteenth birthday in 1921 he had been brushed aside by Armstrong's giants: b Hendry 1, b Gregory 0, b Mailey 1), but for every Test dismissal in single figures he had made amends with a hundred.

A few regal blows and McCormick faded. Fleetwood-Smith's first over conceded two boundaries driven from good length balls. O'Reilly found Hammond's bat – 2 lb 3 oz, though on a badly damaged pitch he sometimes used a boy's 'Harrow' – an impenetrable barrier. Most of the Australians directed their attack at the leg stump, Hammond being weak on that side. Put another way, Hammond was the greatest off-side player in cricket history, the point never to be agreed upon whether he hit harder and more surely off the front foot than the back. By lunch England were 134 for 3, the partnership with Paynter worth 103 in 80 minutes. When presented to King George VI by Earl Baldwin, Hammond was as sartorially perfect (the blue handkerchief absent) as Savile Row expected of him.

The exquisite symmetry of this day at Lord's emphasized Hammond's unhurried command. Of 134 runs before lunch, he made 70; of 137 between lunch and tea, 70; of 138 between tea and the close, 70. He cruised; nothing incredible, only mellow inevitability. Paynter supplied the brilliance before falling to O'Reilly one short of his century: Compton might have added to it had he not tried, too early, to get after O'Reilly. 271 for 5 at tea – a fine recovery wasted. Perhaps not, for No. 7 was England's wicketkeeper, Leslie Ames, whose on-drive had the splendour of Hammond through the covers. Six seasons later – mighty men in a mighty age! – Ames would make his hundredth first-class century. At Lord's in 1938 he spent the evening modestly, answering his captain's calls, and contenting himself with 50 not out.

Just before 6.30, with England 409 for 5, Hammond faced the day's last over. The fury worked from his system, he permitted a maiden. Not a chanceless innings – a tremendous straight drive had split Chipperfield's finger – but one worthy of his Sovereign's inspection. 210 and undefeated, Walter Hammond strode from the field. He had made his point.

Monday, 25 July 1938. 'Why don't they play at the *ball?*' Wilfred Rhodes was sorely perturbed in the press box at Headingley. 'They're all playing at his *action.*' The action of William Joseph O'Reilly might more readily *not* have been played at had batsmen been able to ignore it. The sight of a gangling 6 ft 3 ins giant lumbering seven great paces to the wicket with arms whirling, and face contorted, was off-putting. The fact that one was being assaulted by a perambulating pump-handle (as R. C. Robertson-Glasgow saw him), with the bowling hand encouraging the would-be striker's eyes to follow, as it were, a shifting horizon, did not make for confidence. Had the ball that emerged to pitch on a perfect length been a rolled leg-break and nothing more, O'Reilly must have ranked as the best stock bowler of the decade. But the rolled leg-break was sometimes medium-pace, sometimes slower and flighted; even so, the top batsmen could have coped.

WILLIAM JOSEPH O'REILLY, 1932–8
The Tiger

O'Reilly also commanded a top spinner of some velocity, so adding to his value as a stock bowler. What made him the greatest attacking bowler of his age (when English pitches were lifeless and plumb) was his googly. This bounced like a tennis ball, lifting to hit the bat's splice and then balloon into the waiting hands of Brown and Fingleton squatting close in at short-leg. Controlling these spins was the most hostile temper since Barnes. O'Reilly did not get cross when hit for 4; already cross at the sight of a batsman, he became livid. The Australian writer, Ray Robinson, thought the only thing missing from O'Reilly's make-up was that he was not born a minotaur, half-man, half-bull, so that he could have a tail to lash. Batsmen did not believe O'Reilly needed a tail.

The England side chosen for Headingley in 1938 lacked Hutton and Ames, both injured; the absence of the latter was perhaps more vital, for it meant that the specialist batsmen (Ames was good enough to be so considered) numbered six instead of seven. Winning the toss and batting first on an *un*-doped pitch – the groundsman had been hampered by rain and changed strips at a late hour – England found the ball turning. Edrich was bowled by an O'Reilly googly; Hammond, after promising a large score, played forward to O'Reilly's leg-break and was bowled for 76. 142 for 4; 29 runs later, Paynter was stumped off Fleetwood-Smith, and Compton bowled by O'Reilly. That Australia topped England's first-innings total of 223 by 19 was due to a stolid 57 by nightwatchman Ben Barnett, and an incredible 103 out of 153 by Bradman who refused to appeal against hours of semi-darkness because he preferred batting when only he could see than on a rain-affected pitch. Even so, at the close of the second day England were 30 ahead with their openers still in possession.

Monday, 25 July belonged to O'Reilly. Its final moments – with Australia requiring 105 to win on a wearing pitch – saw gay stroke-making by Hassett and Hammond's decision to gamble on logic, the length of Farnes, Bowes and Verity. Wright, who could have won, *or lost*, the match in a handful of overs, was not brought on until Australia were 48 for 2, and then took 3 for 26 off 5 overs. Whether or not Hammond was right, Australia's target must have been far greater, maybe unreachable, but for O'Reilly. Years ago at Melbourne in his second Test against England, he had won the match by bowling Sutcliffe with a ball that pitched on the leg stump and hit the top of the off – his ninth England wicket. Now at Headingley in his eighteenth Test he would win another match by taking his 95th and 96th wickets.

England were 65 for 1 – 46 ahead – with Edrich and Hardstaff together. Hardstaff made a psychological blunder, he hooked O'Reilly for 4. Inevitably there followed a faster delivery, a no-ball. Another 4. O'Reilly re-paced his run, the minotaur's tail he did not possess visibly thrashing. Up he bounded to bowl, not a faster but a very fast ball. It pitched on the leg stump and took Hardstaff's off bail. 73 for 2. At a sign from Bradman, Brown and Fingleton (the Horan and Boyle of Spofforth's age) closed in at short-leg. To Hammond O'Reilly sent a googly on the off and middle stumps which had to be played. Hammond – the bat handle well forward – offered a half-cock stroke guaranteed to anaesthetize any ordinary googly. But this was O'Reilly's. As it turned, it bounced to the top of the blade. Brown swooped. The hope of England was out.

Somewhere – in Australia, England or South Africa – a batsman who played against 'Tiger' O'Reilly may deny he was the supreme bowler of the thirties. This batsman has yet to be traced.

1939–45

The scoresheet of Australia's innings in the fifth Test at Melbourne, 1936–7, contained this entry:

R. G. Gregory c Verity b Farnes 80

Neville Cardus wrote: 'Gregory welcomed Oldfield with a gloriously upright straight drive. Heaven bless us! We have again witnessed strokes in a Test match, gay and handsome and cultured strokes.' Cardus saw Gregory's innings as 'most promising in its defence, composure, and judgement'.

Pilot Officer Kenneth Farnes played for Cambridge University and Essex; he had trained as a pilot and was killed in a flying accident on 20 October 1941. He was thirty.

Sergeant Observer Ross Gerald Gregory, RAAF, who had played for Victoria while still at school, died on active service in Assam in June 1942. He was twenty-six.

Captain Hedley Verity played for Yorkshire from 1930 to 1939. Leading a company of the Green Howards during the invasion of Sicily, he was severely wounded and died on 31 July 1943 at the age of thirty-eight. Verity's last words were 'Keep going.'

CHAPTER SEVEN

Swan-Song

The toast throughout England in 1948 was – or should have been – 'Borwick!' Who? Not one Englishman in ten thousand had heard of this Australian. Yet it was he who, perhaps more than any other man, had made their dreams come true. He might have said 'Yes'; he preferred to say 'No'. The date 29 November 1946, the time 1.28 p.m., the location the Woolloogabba ground at Brisbane: in the first post-war Test against England, Australia were 74 for 2 (S. G. Barnes and A. R. Morris out) with Bradman on 28 and recovering from a start which would have embarrassed a Tasmanian No. 8. Deprived of its middle, the Bradman bat had acquired half a dozen edges. Suddenly, to a ball of full length from Voce, Bradman tried a placement through gully. At second slip Ikin caught the miscue chest-high: exuding disbelief then ecstasy, he received congratulatory beams if not kisses – this was 1946 – from the other close fielders. Bradman did not budge. A belated appeal to Umpire George Borwick met with 'Not out', both umpire and Bradman deciding the catch had been made from a bump ball.

Instead of being 74 for 3 and shaken by Bradman's dismissal, Australia went to lunch emotionally intact. At the day's end they were 292 for 2, Bradman 162 not out; at lunch on the third day they were out for 645, a total Bradman could have observed to be satisfactory but well short of the 903 compiled by England at the Oval some years previously. It is safe to say that had Bradman been given out for 28, *and had England held their catches*, Australia must have been caught on the rain-damaged pitch which twice scuttled England. And had Bradman played his

second innings on a rain-damaged pitch in 1946 as he had in 1936
. . . Bradman's sternest critic was, and always had been,
Bradman. A double failure at Brisbane may have persuaded him
to withdraw from the subsequent Tests, in which case there
would most surely have been no announcement on 5 February
1948 that, 'I have today advised my co-selectors that I am
available for the Australian tour of England.' A consensus of
opinion suggested Borwick's fateful decision was indeed a wrong
one, cruelly handicapping eleven Englishmen at Brisbane.
Eighteen months later hundreds of thousands of Englishmen
were thrilled to count every run of Bradman's last triumphant
journey.

Even to mention Bradman's victorious sides of 1946–7 and
1948 is to provoke comparisons with Armstrong's of the early
post-Great War years. The task is made the more difficult
because like is not compared with like. Armstrong played his
Tests in Australia to a finish, Bradman's were confined to six
five-hour days. Armstrong won every game, Bradman only
three. However, Armstrong's wins were all obtained within the
time-limit imposed on Bradman – one in six days, two in five
days, and two in four days. Some will argue the Australian
bowlers of 1920–1 had a simpler problem to solve, that Hobbs,
Rhodes, Makepeace, Hendren, Woolley and Russell were
together less an obstacle than Hutton, Washbrook, Hammond,
Compton and W. J. Edrich. For the moment we shall evade the
issue by imagining Armstrong's and Bradman's sides engaged
(as Bligh's travellers of 1882 did) in a Tug of War. With
Armstrong as anchor man . . .

When one team overwhelms the other it is customary to
denigrate the losers rather than praise the winners. So it was in
1946–7. Bradman the supreme realist saw matters differently:
give England a fast bowler – say the Farnes of 1936–7, and a
staunch middle-order batsman – the Jardine of 1928–9, and
Australia would really have had a fight on their hands. Bradman
was fortunate to possess two cricketers who loved batting but
were also devastating fast bowlers. Yet was there any reason –

save the whim of fate – why Lindwall, who had served for two and half years in the South-West Pacific and contracted malaria, and Miller, whose back was injured during a forced landing in Norfolk ('Very flat, Norfolk,' observed a Noël Coward character), should have been Australians and not Englishmen? Bradman was fortunate. In the first Test after 1914–18 Armstrong had Ryder to bat at nine, in 1946–7 at Brisbane Bradman had the left-arm googly bowler George Tribe at ten. Playing for Northamptonshire in the next decade, Tribe performed the 'double' seven times.

England's defeat by an innings and 332 runs at Brisbane meant little, the most torrential thunderstorm in living memory rendering the pitch unplayable in spite of some fine defensive batting by Edrich, Compton, Hammond and Yardley. Miller took the first 4 wickets with quick-medium break-backs while at the other end Toshack bowled his normal length and did nothing but hit the batsmen 'twixt waist and head. On the fifth morning Bradman took his perplexed left-hander by the arm, pointed to spot 'X' and said *'That's* the danger length. Bowl at it!' Whereupon Toshack took nine of the last fifteen wickets to fall. If the match had a hero, it was Miller: 9 for 77, and a golden innings of 79. And so to Sydney, where England won the toss and batted first on the plumbest of pitches against an Australian attack without Lindwall, laid low by chicken-pox.

He was not needed. His replacement, Freer, bowled Washbrook for 1; thereafter Hutton and Edrich batted gravely, parsing each delivery from the flighty off-spinner, Ian Johnson. His initial spell of 11 overs brought him Hutton's wicket, 88 balls being struck for 3 runs. The equally flighty leg-spinner McCool now joined in the fun and accounted for Compton, Hammond and Edrich. The joke for those who knew and cherished their Compton as a chaser after spin bowling lay in Hammond's advice that the slow bowlers should be played from the crease. So Johnson, with two short-legs and no man out, tossed the ball ever higher. England's 219 for 8 on the first day challenged the senses: all out for 255, small effort had been made to disturb the length of Johnson (6 for 42 off 30·1 overs) and McCool whose 9 wickets cost only 115 runs made off 425 balls. Doubtless the tourists were consoled by Bradman's absence, caused by a torn muscle in his left thigh.

Soon after Australia had started batting on the second afternoon, rain fell. The rest of the day produced 27 runs for the loss of Morris, and innumerable appeals by Barnes against the light, spectators moving or perhaps not moving, and the state of the universe in general. Worn down, the umpires surrendered, so saving Australia from the perils of a drying wicket. During the weekend Bradman was afflicted by gastritis. Wan and heavily strapped, he did not come in until 3.50 on the Monday afternoon when Australia were 159 for 4, Barnes on 71 and – if there is any justice in this world – hoarse. Playing entirely off the back foot, Bradman lasted for six and a half hours and made 234. His summary of the situation – 'There's runs out there, if only a man had legs' – was not addressed to the England side, and so was not construed as actionable by the Society for the Prevention of Cruelty to Dumb Cricketers. With Barnes also falling for 234 (ten and three-quarter hours), Bradman eventually declared at 659 for 8. England had to bat for nine hours and score over 400 to save the game.

The winning margin was an innings and 33 runs. Although Edrich made a magnificent 5 hours' hundred (piloting a bomber and gaining a DFC had transformed this often flashy fox-terrier into a formidable small mastiff), the glory of England's second innings was contained in 20 minutes before lunch on the fifth day. In the context of the match, this was the most pointless effort of Hutton's whole career; it was also his most perfect innings, a sublime miniature worthy of Trumper. Cuts and drives reduced Miller and Freer with the new ball to panting futility; it was the young Hobbs facing schoolboys or an amateur of the Golden Age inspired beyond all reason. 37 in 20 minutes: Hutton forced the last ball before lunch off the back foot but the bat slipped from his hand in the follow-through, dropping over his shoulder to disturb the bails. Beauty from Hutton, yes; but beauty

LEONARD HUTTON, 1938–55
Classic

for its own sake . . . Sydney marvels yet; so perhaps does Hutton.

The battle for the Ashes was over unless England could reverse the design of 1936–7 and win the last three games. Impossible in theory, there was a hint of something in practice when Australia lost 6 wickets for 192 at Melbourne. Then a hundred by McCool helped almost to double the score. Yet England at 155 for the loss of Hutton were riding high before Edrich was adjudged lbw to a ball he had snicked on to his pad. Righteous cries rent the air, though wise men recalled Bradman's reply when once asked if he did not agree it is generally the losing side which complains of bad umpiring: 'I don't agree, it's *always* the losing side.' Only 14 ahead on the first innings, Australia were not all that impressive when they batted again, in spite of 155 by Morris. Poor England! Tallon (92) and Lindwall (100) added 154 in an hour and a half as Hammond palpably lost control. Aloof, out of form with the bat though several times out to marvellous catches, then stricken by fibrositis, the great cricketer had only the trappings of majesty to console him.

Hundreds galore at Adelaide followed the draw at Melbourne: two each by Morris and Compton, six for various partnerships including 137 and 116 for England's 1st wicket from Hutton and Washbrook, and six days with the temperature exceeding 100°F. Bradman bowled Bedser 0: the ball started on the off stump, pitched on the leg, then hit the off. By the end of the tour Bradman placed Bedser above Tate, a verdict which caused Ponsford – who recalled the Tate of 1924–5 – to raise all available eyebrows. Australia won the final Test at Sydney by 5 wickets after trailing by 27 on the first innings. Hutton's 122 retired was noble as Lindwall finished with 7 for 63, especially as the batsman was suffering from tonsillitis and spent the rest of the match in hospital. Wright's 7 for 105 (when Mailey had a match analysis like 51–5–198–9 he finished on the winning side) was cancelled out by McCool's 5 for 44, only Compton (76) managing more than 24 in England's second innings. Set 214 for victory, Australia lost Barnes and Morris for 51; then Bradman was missed at slip off Wright when 2.

The series of 1946–7 may be summarized thus. England had Bedser and Wright to bowl, Australia – in the third and fourth Tests – Lindwall, Miller, Toshack, McCool, Dooland and Ian Johnson. The reader with an eclectic eye will note the highest scores achieved by individual Australians: in batting order, though Bradman's double century was made at six – Barnes 234, Morris 155, Bradman 234, Hassett 128, Miller 141, not out, McCool 104, not out, Johnson 52, Tallon 92, Lindwall 100.

A fine side in the making.

1948

'We are going to do our best to make sure this is one of the greatest tours ever made by an Australian cricket team.'

Don Bradman.

When the nineteenth Australians left the *Strathaird* at Tilbury on 16 April 1948, their early arrival was duly noted. The 1930 party had arrived a full week later, that of 1934 nine days: had Generalissimo Bradman informed the shipping line he wished to have a long period of acclimatization for his men? No one put it beyond him. And had he commanded the ship's barber to shear the locks of all save Miller so that they resembled convicted prisoners about to begin long sentences? Perhaps the schoolboy present had been let off with a caution, but he looked suitably grim. Not a schoolboy – the nineteen-year-old Neil Harvey, doubtless brought along to help W. H. Ferguson with the baggage. In 1921 the ringmaster Armstrong had whipped his circus into action; 1948 saw Bradman's Grand Army embark on a long campaign. A couple of skirmishes, at Bradford and Southampton when Marshal Hassett was in command, inflicted bloody noses on the invader before he pulled through, but by September the major battles had been won and England lay prostrate under Bradman's heel.

Armstrong or Bradman: who led the greater side? Judged by their success at the highest level, the answer must for ever be inconclusive. The Tests of 1921 were limited to three days, those of 1948 sprawled over five; the summer of 1921 was one of almost unbroken sunshine and bone-hard pitches, 1948 saw four of the Tests interrupted by rain or played after much rain had fallen; in 1921 the fielding side was granted a new ball every 200 runs, in 1948 every 55 overs. So cleverly did Bradman plan his tactics that a new ball after 55 overs meant that Australia could take it, on average, every 130 runs. One effect was the instant demise of the wrist spinner:

AUSTRALIAN WRIST SPINNERS IN TESTS

| | Percentage of | |
	Overs	Wickets
New ball every 200 runs		
1921	36	28
1926	46	69
1930	33	38
1934	75	74
1938	63	74
New ball every 55 overs		
1948	3	1

Bradman's was the last great touring party to play in England before the revolution brought about by the change of the lbw law in 1935 changed cricket for good. In 1930, the year of Bradman's first visit, five English googly bowlers and four slow left-handers took 100 wickets, in 1948 4 and 6 respectively. By 1953, the year of Hassett's Australians, the three 'English' googly bowlers to take 100 wickets were all imports from Adelaide, Melbourne or Sydney; when Benaud's team arrived in 1961 prolific wrist spinners had disappeared, though exponents of the seam were twice as numerous as they had been in 1930. Then cricket encouraged Bradman's genius: of his 254 at Lord's, 73 were scored from cuts. As Sir Leonard Hutton would say in retirement: 'It was in 1950 I realized bowlers were no longer trying to get me out but contain me.'

The six weeks' prelude to the first Test at Trent Bridge in 1948 found the Australians at their warming-up exercises, especially at Bradford where snow threatened. Twelve games were played and two drawn, play being limited to two days at Old Trafford; of ten victories, eight were by an innings and such margins as 171, 296, 451, 158 and 325 runs. At Worcester Bradman was content with 107 (in three pre-war innings on this ground he had totalled 700), and a BBC commentator watched Lindwall ambling into action and assured the nation the pace was brisk but certainly playable. The nation pursed its lips when an Australian voice broke in, 'But he's only bowling at slow-medium!' Gradually Lindwall loosened up so that against Nottinghamshire he sent down 91 balls and took 6 for 14; in this, and in the ensuing match with Sussex, his tally was 17 wickets for 73. Batsmen agreed he was fast.

A Cambridge undergraduate at this time trying to bowl fast was Trevor Bailey. Invited to play for Essex, he had the privilege of being a member of the only side to dismiss the 1948 Australians in a day.

Southend, Saturday, 15 May: the Australians are not playing their fast scoring team – Lindwall suffers from a strain, Morris, who will make 290 in 5 hours at Bristol, is resting. Now at Southend Barnes and Brown open with 145 in 96 minutes, a probing exercise to detect the enemy's weakness. Barnes out for 79, spectators stand and strain their necks, hundreds of cameras are pointed – Is it HE? It is! The pre-lunch artillery bombardment lasts 22 minutes, HE scoring 42 including five boundaries from the morning's last over. Six would have meant taking a risk.

After lunch both Brown and Bradman see the ball well. At ten minutes to three, the Australians 364 for 1, Brown decides he's had enough – that is 153. A fighter takes off from the visitors' dressing room, its mission to strafe eleven men of Essex peering out of their trenches. K. R. Miller is not interested, he allows himself to be bowled first ball. Bradman considers court-martial proceedings, then shakes his head: 'Keith will learn.' (He never does.) The bombardment is resumed until, at eight minutes to four with the score 452, Bradman is out for 187. His run rate of 90 an hour exceeds by 2 Macartney's at Trent Bridge in 1921; Macartney, of course, made 345. After tea the Generalissimo orders his cavalry to mop up any Essex survivors; Loxton and Saggers score hundreds, their partnership 166 in 65 minutes. Unfortunately the Australian dish-washers fail to apply themselves (no Lindwall) so that the innings stutters to a halt 10 minutes before 6.30. 10 minutes wasted. 721 all out. The Australians have hit eighty-seven boundaries; Essex, for want of something better to do, have averaged 22·1 overs an hour.

No Essex player was picked for England in the first Test at Trent Bridge, though the county's 83 did not seem all that poor a score when England's 8th wicket fell at 74. It was a good toss to lose – the pitch hard and true but with a touch of green, the light dull and sometimes murky, and occasional showers. Two Surrey bowlers, Laker and Bedser, acknowledged the absence of Lindwall after tea by adding 89, Laker's 63 containing a half-century made in an hour. Here tribute must be paid to the man mainly responsible for England's meagre 165, the ever cheerful Bill Johnston with figures of 25–11–36–5. Whether at fast-medium left-arm over the wicket, or at slow-medium in a remarkable impersonation of Hedley Verity, he was magnificent. If Lindwall and Miller were great fast bowlers, Johnston was no less great as the Australian work-horse; without him Bradman must have turned to one or other of his leg-spinners, McCool and Ring, both unsuited to the pitches of 1948. Johnston not only finished the series with as many wickets as Lindwall (27), he conceded fewer runs an over than any other bowler.

The rest of the Trent Bridge Test was, inevitably, a tactical struggle: with four days left, the powerful batting at Bradman's command (Hassett at six and Lindwall at nine) could let runs accrue while England must prevent even that. Both teams succeeded – Australia totalled 509, England restricted them to 2·3 runs an over. The latter's method – much bowling directed wide of the leg stump – was not pretty to watch but was undeniably effective. Bradman responded with a three and a half hours' century; 130 at the close on the second day, he seemed set for a big score. Not so. Overnight O'Reilly emerged from the press box to congratulate Bedser, adding, 'You've got your field set wrong for inswingers to the Don. Bring leg slip round to backward short-leg.' Next day Bedser did as he was told and promptly had Bradman caught in the prescribed position by Hutton. Between 12 and 24 June, and including this occasion, Bradman in three Test innings faced 115 deliveries, made 38 runs, and was out three times – caught Hutton at backward short-leg off Bedser. A chink in the armour or the result of dulled reflexes in the batsman's fortieth year? More probably the latter; if the former, discovered too late!

Two days and two hours left for play, and 344 in arrears, England had to score that number of runs without getting out; put another way, strokes must be played but no risks taken. The odds were against England to start with, more so when Washbrook and Edrich were out with only 39 on the board. But Lindwall was off the field and would remain so. Compton joined Hutton, the pair supremely great batsmen, the difference between them one decided by temperament: Hutton the legitimate successor to Hobbs, Compton the English equivalent of Macartney, though lacking (it seemed) that player's ruthlessness. Obliged one Sunday to play against Lesser Sodbury, Hutton would bat in a vacuum, his 100 retired quite perfect and suggesting wry humour; Compton would at once join in the fun, every stroke an act of daring improvisation and capable of being brought off by the village champion once – and just once – in a lifetime.

By six o'clock at Trent Bridge Miller was bowling off-breaks round the wicket. Hutton glanced him for 4, then drove effortlessly past cover; a faster ball was delicately late-cut. Hutton the artist roused Miller to a fury. He tossed back his mane. A ball not far short of a length leapt at Compton, then the bouncers. Bouncers at Trent Bridge where every man present thought Larwood had been hard done by! In the day's last over a

KEITH ROSS MILLER, 1946–56
Sir Robert Menzies's favourite cricket photograph

bouncer hit Hutton painfully on the shoulder; the batsman was doubtless relieved it had not struck his left forearm sadly mutilated by a war injury. Surely Miller would not bounce yet another? He did not – and Hutton leaned into his stroke to glance another 4. England 121 for 2: Hutton 63 and Compton 36. Miller contrived to be behind the other Australians as the players left the field. The Notts members concentrated their boos with zest.

Peace broke out over the weekend. Before play resumed on Monday an appeal was made to spectators: Be good, and Mr Miller won't bowl bouncers. 'These Australians are great sportsmen. They stood by the Empire in the war* and we should always be pleased to greet them.' The announcement was applauded; so, too, were the Australians. When Mr Miller took the new ball, he bowled a length.

Murk dissolved in thunder, a heavy shower drove the players off. Then at 150 Hutton went half-forward to Miller, the ball skidding through his stroke. One definition of a stylist is that he captivates when not scoring; Hutton had scored – 74 – and looked a great stylist. The crowd roared gratitude but mourned its loss. Hardstaff entered and was promptly dropped at slip; the other side of Bill Johnston's unexpected success was McCool's absence from the Tests. When Lindwall bowled in county matches, McCool and Miller ensured the slips were graded at least A + +; in Tests, with Miller bowling and McCool in the pavilion, the rating sometimes fell to B−. So Hardstaff continued to bat as usual, all wrists and golden aplomb. Compton permitted himself an occasional square drive, once or twice his own patented sweep. Things were looking up for England when, at 243, Hardstaff aimed a blow to the on from the bowling of Toshack, still nagging and appealing to be heard in all adjacent counties. Hassett was exactly placed. Barnett touched Johnston to slip where the catch was marvellously taken by Miller. 264 for 5.

---

* Should this ploy be tried in the mid-eighties, the response will be, 'What Empire? And which war?' The ploy amended may be, 'If you're not good, Mr Rupert Murdoch will close *The Sun*.'

Compton's vigil continued. Thirteen minutes less than 4 hours at the completion of his hundred. Self-discipline for the National cause, a smiling enjoyment of duty. Now he must start his innings again and make a second hundred. But only after giving a chance to slip, missed because Miller was the bowler. At the close on Monday, England had advanced to 345 for 6, Compton 154 and Evans 10; 1 run in the lead and one day to go. Less than a day, for at noon on Tuesday rain once more intervened. Back came the players, Evans excelling with many a drive. 400 for 6: England *must* draw! Keith Miller looked at his close friend Denis Compton, breathed deeply – and bowled the fastest ball he was to deliver in 1948. It was a bouncer which Compton made to hook, then lost against the dark pavilion background. At the last minute he decided not to play it; he overbalanced, tried to straddle the stumps but broke them. Hit wicket bowled Miller 184: this superb innings lasted six and a half hours spread over three days, and included ten starts. Compton was England's pride in 1948 as he must have been if born to play at the turn of the century. Although he achieved mastery and heroism in five-day Tests, his temperament was more attuned to a briefer span and to the company of Trumper, Ranji, John Tyldesley, and others of the heavenly host.

Set 98 to win in 3 hours, Australia were driven home by Barnes's 64 not out, rampant with square cut and hook. The lesson of Trent Bridge was salutary to Englishmen who thought that Australia had won without Lindwall. Of the 222 overs they bowled, 147 were by Miller* 63 and Johnston 84, whose 16 wickets averaged only 21·62 runs each; of 222 overs Lindwall was fit to bowl only 13. How effective might he be when free from strain?

A great side is able to shrug off moments – even hours – of adversity and still reach for the stars. At 22 minutes past two on the fifth day Australia had won the Lord's Test by 409 runs; at

---

* In the England-West Indies Test at Lord's in 1963, Wesley Hall bowled 58 overs and was not the same man again for the remainder of the season. Miller, of course, was also one of Australia's leading batsmen.

the close on the first day they had been 258 for 7. Arthur Morris's 105 was the batting gem of the match; hitherto prone to shuffle across instead of playing back, this time he confronted his tormentor of the years to come, Bedser, with assurance. When in the mood, Morris was by far the most charming of all post-war left-handers, every stroke a gracious acknowledgement of the sweetness of the game he adorned. But 258 for 7 heartened England, particularly the unease displayed by Bradman at the commencement of his innings. Bradman, a few weeks from his fortieth birthday, appeared, and was, very human.

So, too, the next day were William Johnston and Ernest Toshack, two happy clowns with the bat. Inspired by Tallon's immaculate half-century, they indulged in rich stroke-play. Off-drives shot over, through, and (was it possible?) under the slips, pulls bemused extra-cover, square cuts disturbed long-leg. In a few minutes over the hour, Australia had added 92. Then came Lindwall with pace so devastating that 4 England wickets fell for 46. A partial recovery by Compton and Yardley – but 207 for 9 at the close meant the ruin of England's hopes. By five o'clock on Saturday Australia were 222 for 1 in their second innings: Morris again had charmed for 62, Barnes was verging on his century, Bradman had reached 52. His target attained, Barnes mounted an assault on Laker; after Bradman had taken a single from the first ball of an over, 2.2.4.6.6. (Readers may take solace in what the future held for Laker; after 1948 Jack Fingleton could write that the bowler's 'even-spinning off-break lends itself to big hitting'.) By the time stumps were drawn for the weekend, Miller had casually hit a ball on his leg stump high into the grandstand behind square, and Australia were 343 for 4 – 478 ahead. The second Test awaited its funeral rites.

As in Australia eighteen months previously, England were two-down with three to play. There was only one thing to do, and the selectors did it: they took steps when announcing the England side for Old Trafford. Pollard, the Lancashire fast-medium bowler, was brought in for Coxon of Yorkshire – a change that produced snorts at least in Coxon's neighbourhood.

The second step taken by the selectors (A. J. Holmes, R. W. V. Robins and J. C. Clay) was to omit Hutton – a decision that reduced neighbourhood, county and country to gaping disbelief. In retrospect the move was a wise one: Hutton *had* waved his bat once or twice in the second innings at Lord's, though after receiving a crippling blow on the hip, and he did return for the fourth and fifth Tests when he played four innings of distinction. He never again missed a Test for which he was available.

Ironically, this was a match England came close to winning – or persuaded themselves and their supporters they would have won but for rain. And yet. A bad England start, 28 for 2; Compton retired 4 runs later after mis-hooking a Lindwall bouncer (a no-ball) on to his forehead, returning at 119 for 5 with stitches holding the wound and his head swathed to face a new ball taken at 87! Two Englishmen made 37, Compton 145 not out; England's 363 more than commendable with Barnes – badly injured when fielding close in at forward short-leg – out of the game. Australia struggled to 221, Bradman lbw to honest Dick Pollard for 7. By the close on Saturday the England lead was 316 with 7 second-innings wickets standing. Without the weekend's rain, England *must* have won. And yet.

Had an earthquake terminated the fourth Test at 12.30 p.m. on the last day, England would have claimed another moral victory. The ball was turning sharply, the spinners were in control, the close fielders swooping like vultures and the peerless Godfrey Evans behind the stumps – Australia did not have a hope in Headingley. There was no earthquake. The close fielders did not swoop like vultures, and Evans had a bad day. The spinners were not in control because the selectors had misread the pitch and omitted any leg-break bowler or left-hander. In 1934 Grimmett and O'Reilly had been the dangers at Headingley, in 1938 O'Reilly, Fleetwood-Smith and Wright; 1948 saw England relying on Laker's off-spin – this in an age when Test batsmen still preferred the ball coming in to the bat to that going away.

Headingley 1948 was not a great Test match, England's

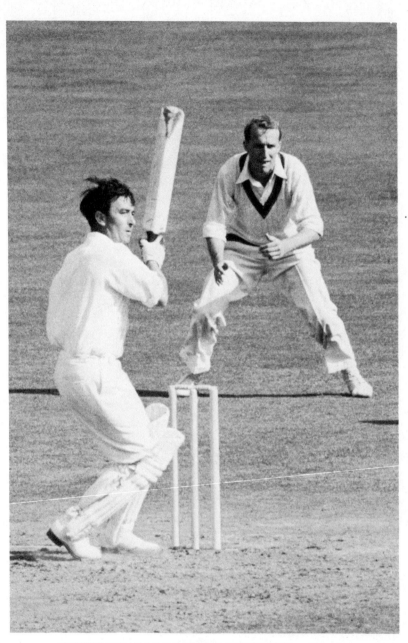

DENIS CHARLES SCOTT COMPTON, 1938–56
Romantic

bowling on the final day precluded that. But it did contain six hours of bliss on the Saturday, the delirious start of one career, and the sunset glory of the greatest of all. The pitch was perfect, the outfield as glass; it was in accordance with the desires of the multitude that Hutton and Washbrook should bat like elder statesmen and make 168 for the first wicket, and England finish the first day on 268 for 2 – Hutton 81, Washbrook 143, and Edrich 41 not out. Next morning the nightwatchman Bedser refused to get out; soon he began to score even to the extent of hitting Ian Johnson and Morris for 6. It was mid-afternoon before Bedser was out for 79 with England 423 for 3. Seven Australians had turned their arms (Lindwall, of course, had done rather more than this) but England were on top and wondering when a declaration might be possible. None came. England subsided to 496 all out, and Australia lost Morris overnight. Bradman's reception matched the one Nelson would have received in 1805 had he returned to London from Trafalgar on two legs and not in a cask.

Australia 63 for 1. 2 runs are added, then Hassett (Barnes's deputy) is caught at slip off Pollard. 65 for 2. Miller joins Bradman, listens attentively to words of advice, and scores 3 from his first ball. Bradman faces Pollard and loses his off stump. 68 for 3. Headingley roars, dances and indulges in song. Yorkshiremen like Bradman to make 300 provided England can win the match. This will do. A diminutive child strolls out to the middle, smiles up at Uncle Keith who would probably like to offer him a toffee. But Neil Harvey does not want a toffee, only the best bowling England can offer. As Miller drives, pulls and cuts, Harvey follows him; a mighty Miller pull off Laker for 6 threatens heads massed behind square-leg. 50 are added in 43 minutes, then Laker spins one past the left-handed Harvey. Miller decides to shatter Laker's length and drives him twice to the boundary. 'I see what you mean,' says Harvey to himself, and also drives Laker twice for 4. 100 in 85 minutes. A Miller 6 into the stratosphere off Laker (the same stroke played at Old Trafford would have interfered with the cloud belt and produced rain) persuades Yardley to put himself on. Two 4s to Miller and – leg-theory! – Miller swings, the ball just touches the bat, and passes via Evans's head to fine-leg. Edrich dives full length and gets the catch in his finger tips. Miller 54, Australia 189 for 4. 15 more runs and the players go off for lunch, Harvey 70.

The other Victorian now at the crease, Sam Loxton, is not happy. It transpires he is waiting for England to take the new ball. The umpire shows it to the scorers, Bedser and Pollard bowl it at Loxton who strikes it in divers directions. Harvey, too, relishes the new ball, it will help him to 100 in his first Test against England. He reaches it in under three hours, with fourteen 4s, but at 294 swings unwisely at Laker. Bradman seems shocked that a nineteen-year-old should be content with 112; the mature Bradman of twenty-one would not have been. Loxton now takes over with four 6s off Laker, then is bowled trying to cross-bat Yardley when 93. Australia slump hereabouts to 355 for 8; England sigh with relief as they visualize Lindwall left on 10 not out. Bill Johnston smiles his way to the wicket, he will be there two hours later; first he shares in a partnership of 58 with Lindwall, batting brilliantly – then he runs for Toshack whose injured knee has collapsed on him. Johnston running for himself resembles a giraffe playing cricket, running for Toshack a giraffe playing baseball – that is to say neither fielders nor umpires know whether he is at first, second or third base when completing (or in the middle of) a run.

England's Monday morning predicament, after Australia's innings closed for 458, was clear: not only this match, but the final Test at the Oval, must be won to square the series. A target for Australia, also time to get the enemy out. Hutton and Washbrook set out on this occasion like elder statesmen rejuvenated before, at 129, the latter hooked Johnston to long-leg where Harvey ran yards at full speed, caught the ball with both hands ankle-high, then drop-kicked it to the wicketkeeper. On the final morning Yardley batted on for a couple of overs so that he might use the heavy roller to break the pitch. Australia were set 404 to win in 344 minutes; almost at once Yardley turned to spin, the ball turning and lifting. The odds were on England.

At 33 Hassett should have been stumped; at 55 Morris, on 32, moved out to Compton and missed the ball which Evans fumbled. 2 runs later Compton caught and bowled Hassett: 57 for 1 in 75 minutes. This time Bradman entered to a reception that suggested Nelson returning to London after Trafalgar having risen from the dead. Bradman at once drove Laker. Yardley brought on Hutton whose leg-breaks were so vaguely directed that any self-respecting Yorkshire colt would have ordered two dozen for breakfast. (Hutton, a non-county bowler, pitted against Morris and Bradman in a Test!) Bradman misread a Compton googly and was missed at slip, Australia lunching at 121 for 1 – Morris 63 and Bradman 35. Between lunch and tea the batsmen added 171, Morris being missed at 136 and Bradman at 50 and 108. The end came 15 minutes before stumps were due to be drawn – a tremendous Australian victory, the runs scored at 74 an hour. Bradman clearly refrained from hitting the winning boundary in the game's penultimate over so that Harvey might have the honour.

Instead of mass suicide, the England selectors said, 'Back to the drawing board!'

The final Test at the Oval bore some resemblance to the corresponding game of 1938. England again won the toss and batted; Hutton made top score, and Bradman's contribution was the same as when he had been 'absent hurt'. Now he was 'bowled Hollies o'. In 1938 England won by an innings and 579 runs after making 903 for 7; in 1948 Australia won by an innings and 149 runs after dismissing England for 52, Hutton first in and last out for 30. Morris made 196 (run out) for Australia, and Hollies replied with 5 for 131 – grand leg-break and googly bowling which must have won the fourth Test at Headingley. But the Oval game of 1948 belonged to one man, Raymond Russell Lindwall.

Tom Richardson would have watched Lindwall and blinked.

RAYMOND RUSSELL LINDWALL, 1946–59
Perfection

ENGLAND *v* AUSTRALIA
Played at Headingley
22, 23, 24, 26, 27 July 1948

ENGLAND

L. Hutton	b Lindwall	81	c Bradman b Johnson	57
C. Washbrook	c Lindwall b Johnston	143	c Harvey b Johnston	65
W. J. Edrich	c Morris b Johnston	111	lbw b Lindwall	54
A. V. Bedser	c & b Johnson	79	(9) c Hassett b Miller	17
D. C. S. Compton	c Saggers b Lindwall	23	(4) c Miller b Johnston	66
J. F. Crapp	b Toshack	5	(5) b Lindwall	18
N. W. D. Yardley	b Miller	25	(6) c Harvey b Johnston	7
K. Cranston	b Loxton	10	(7) c Saggers b Johnston	0
T. G. Evans	c Hassett b Loxton	3	(8) not out	47
J. C. Laker	c Saggers b Loxton	4	not out	15
R. Pollard	not out	0		
Extras	(B2, LB8, W1, NB1)	12	(B4, LB12, NB3)	19
Total		496	(8 wkts declared)	365

Fall of wickets: 1–168, 2–268, 3–423, 4–426, 5–447, 6–473, 7–486, 8–490, 9–496, 10–496.

2nd innings 1–129, 2–129, 3–232, 4–260, 5–277, 6–278, 7–293, 8–330.

AUSTRALIA BOWLING (6-ball overs)

	O.	M.	R.	W.	O.	M.	R.	W.
Lindwall	38	10	79	2	26	6	84	2
Miller	17·1	2	43	1	21	5	53	1
Johnston	38	13	86	1	29	5	95	4
Toshack	35	6	112	1	–	–	–	–
Loxton	26	4	55	3	10	2	29	0
Johnson	33	9	89	2	21	2	85	1
Morris	5	0	20	0	–	–	–	–

AUSTRALIA

A. R. Morris	c Cranston b Bedser	6	c Pollard b Yardley	182
A. L. Hassett	c Crapp b Pollard	13	c & b Compton	17
D. G. Bradman	b Pollard	33	not out	173
K. R. Miller	c Edrich b Yardley	58	lbw b Cranston	12
R. N. Harvey	b Laker	112	not out	4
S. J. E. Loxton	b Yardley	93		
I. W. Johnson	c Cranston b Laker	10		
R. R. Lindwall	c Crapp b Bedser	77		
R. A. Saggers	st Evans b Laker	5		
W. A. Johnston	c Edrich b Bedser	13		
E. R. H. Toshack	not out	12		
Extras	(B9, LB14, NB3)	26	(B6, LB9, NB1)	16
Total		458	(3 wkts)	404

Fall of wickets: 1–13, 2–65, 3–68, 4–189, 5–294, 6–329, 7–344, 8–355, 9–403, 10–458.

2nd innings   1–57, 2–358, 3–396.

ENGLAND BOWLING (6-ball overs)

	O.	M.	R.	W.	O.	M.	R.	W.
Bedser	31·2	4	92	3	21	2	56	0
Pollard	38	6	104	2	22	6	55	0
Cranston	14	1	51	0	7·1	0	28	1
Edrich	3	0	19	0	–	–	–	–
Laker	30	8	113	3	32	11	93	0
Yardley	17	6	38	2	13	1	44	1
Compton	3	0	15	0	15	3	82	1
Hutton	–	–	–	–	4	1	30	0

AUSTRALIA WON BY 7 WICKETS

'*Him* a fast bowler? Why, he's . . .' And Tom, noting the Lindwall variations – two or three balls bowled at fast-medium pace veering this way and that, the yorker, the bouncer, and the despatching ball of fearsome velocity – Tom would not have understood. He was a cataclysmic force of nature; Lindwall thought batsmen out long before their exit. His thirteen strides began easily, then accelerated almost imperceptibly. At the long delivery stride he was moving at top speed, batsmen were aware of his left shoulder pointing and the arched back; the right arm was not high enough for purists but the ball tended to skid through. If Miller was a histrionic bowler, Lindwall represented austere professionalism. In method he reached back to Spofforth, or rather the two Spofforths of 1878 and 1882, of speed and of applied cunning. Ray Lindwall was the most compelling bowler of his age to watch, even when he did not take wickets – from England's point of view too infrequent an occurrence. Lindwall was, not to exaggerate, simply wonderful.

The rest of 1948 was the Generalissimo. His gesture at Headingley, when Harvey was permitted to make the winning hit, meant a frustrating career Test average of 99·94 when just one more boundary would have given him 100·00. Either figure seems inviolable. Bradman's last three innings on English soil were 150, 143 and 153; four tours had seen him play one hundred and twenty innings with an average of 96·44 helped by forty-one scores of over 100 (twelve over 200). His thirty Test innings in England averaged 102·84. He took good care his 1948 side should go through the season undefeated, this record complemented when *Wisden* (for the first and only time) chose as its Five Cricketers of the Year members of one team – Hassett, Johnston, Lindwall, Morris and Tallon.

If an umpiring decision at Brisbane in 1946 did influence Bradman, then cricket is for ever in debt to George Borwick.

Armstrong or Bradman: whose team was the greater? The question produced much heated argument:

'Armstrong's side would have eaten Bradman's!'

'They'd have suffered a duodenal if they had!'

At the end of 1948 Jack Fingleton ventured to put matters into perspective by picking a composite Australia XI for the years 1920–48, a gesture meriting a belated response.

AUSTRALIA	ENGLAND
Ponsford	Hobbs
Morris	Hutton
Bradman (captain)	Hammond
Macartney	Duleepsinhji
McCabe	Compton
Jackson	Jardine (captain)
Miller	Ames
Gregory	Tate
Tallon	Larwood
Grimmett	Verity
O'Reilly	Wright

Of the above sides, little remains to be said. Bradman, who regarded both Gregory and Miller as glorious cricketers prone to lapses in concentration, would almost certainly insist on the inclusion of Lindwall. On the other hand, he would see the point of having two slip fielders who could do the work of three.

'Jack! When you hear Keith whistling Beethoven, that means he is about to take a blinder – or miss a sitter because he's thinking of Egmont's chances in the 2.30. Make sure you cover him.'

The England side prefers Ames to Evans – a great batsman – wicketkeeper to a great wicketkeeper who could bat – because every run will be precious. Tate is chosen advisedly, Bedser not reaching his peak until after 1948. Wright, of course, is essential; should the awful Australian batting machine show signs of realizing its full potential, Wright may be England's only hope.

As both W. G. and Peter May believed four days were long enough for any cricket match, that will be the game's duration.

It will take place at Lord's – England winning the toss and making a satisfactory total before rain falls on an uncovered pitch and a sun of Brisbane intensity takes over.

The Test achievements of the 1921 and 1948 Australian teams cannot be compared, so different were the prevailing conditions. What Armstrong's and Bradman's teams did have in common were three-day games against the counties.

1921		1948
21	Matches played	20
14	Matches won	15
445	Average Australian first innings	448
85	Runs an hour	72
160	Average county first innings	160
62	Overs dismissed in	70

Clearly, the only way to decide the issue is to hold a Tug of War.

Poor Bradman!

CHAPTER EIGHT

A Revolution

Before the next Australian tour of England in 1953 an astonishing change took place in cricket. One moment there was joy for batsmen, the next misery – or at least much cause for cogitation. The change had nothing to do with Bradman's retirement, though a great deal to do with what Bradman had stood for. We may assume that on 1 January 1951 wise men at Lord's cast sinister spells on English pitches.

First the background: in 1947 South Africa's batsmen did well (though Compton and Edrich did even better), in 1948 Bradman's Australians averaged 48 runs a wicket in the Tests. Two great New Zealand left-handers, Bert Sutcliffe and Donnelly, did more or less as they liked in 1949, and the following year the West Indies trio of Worrell, Weekes and Walcott waxed fat on runs. At which someone cried, 'Enough!'

During the early post-war years England lacked fast bowling. But the revolution of 1951 was not brought about by fast bowlers, nor by anyone relying on the seam. England's success was based on finger spin. Between the wars a slow left-hander was an integral part of any English attack, but off-spin was a rarity. In ten Oval Tests during the thirties, off-spinners (J. C. Clay and Tom Goddard) took 3 wickets for 197 runs.

Excluding 1952 when Trueman frightened most of the Indian batsmen, the seasons 1951–7 revealed the nature and extent of cricket's revolution. The visitors were South Africa, Australia, Pakistan, South Africa, Australia and West Indies.

AVERAGE TEST INNINGS BY TOURISTS

	Grounds other than Oval	Oval
1947–50 (4 years)	397	405
1951, 1953–7 (6 years)	238	185

Australia's average score in Oval Tests when Bradman batted, including 1948 when he failed, was 528.

And the agents of cricket's revolution?

ENGLAND SPINNERS

	Grounds other than Oval	Oval
1947–50	108 wkts at 35·90	32 wkts at 41·68
1951, 1953–7	176 wkts at 24·27	69 wkts at 11·94

When the South Africans of 1955 arrived in England the captain Jack Cheetham expressed hopes for the tour, adding that to share the series South Africa must go to the Oval one-up. They went two-all, and lost the series.

Surrey won the County Championship seven times between 1952 and 1958, though possessing only one great batsman: May. Their bowlers were Bedser, Loader, Laker and Lock. Laker's Test career had begun before the revolution:

LAKER

	Grounds other than Oval	Oval
1948–50 (3 Tests)	10 wkts at 55·80	4 wkts at 22·25
1951, 1953–7 (16 Tests)	62 wkts at 15·41	34 wkts at 14·02

Surrey's other spin bowler of the fifties was often more lethal than Laker, helped perhaps by a suspect action. Lock's Test career began after the revolution:

LOCK

	Grounds other than Oval	Oval
1953, 1955–7 (12 Tests)	23 wkts at 32·13	28 wkts at 9·96

Test matches at the Oval illustrate the nature of cricket's revolution. During the thirties the most formidable opponents came from Australia and South Africa, in the late forties from Australia, South Africa and West Indies.

	England spinners at the Oval
Thirties (4 Tests)	14 wkts at 50·57
1947–8, 1950 (3 Tests)	23 wkts at 43·39
1953, 1955–7 (4 Tests)	52 wkts at 12·25

The England spinners of 1953, and 1955–7 were, of course, Laker and Lock. To put their figures in perspective, we must recall that the greatest pair of pre-war spinners seen in tandem at the oval were Grimmett and O'Reilly. In the 1934 Test they took 12 wickets at 26·50.

Laker, a supreme master of flight, line and length, was a great bowler on any pitch. Whether cricket's revolution was wise to encourage him as it did, is a matter of opinion.

The Australian reader has been warned.

CHAPTER NINE

A Different World

How much longer would Australia remain on the summit? Had England begun to rise from the depths? These questions accompanied the *Stratheden* across the world in September 1950. By standards less exacting than those set by Bradman's teams, English cricket was not in the depths. All comparisons are relative. A captain of the eighties would smile and sleep soundly if told he could have Hutton, Washbrook, W. J. Edrich and Compton to lead his batting. 'And you can have Evans to keep wicket, Bedser to open the bowling . . .' Here our captain of the eighties might interrupt his benefactor: 'Are you quite sure Bedser won't break down?' A phone call to the Oval – 'A word, please, with Alec Bedser' – and a detailed explanation of the meaning of 'break down' must inevitably produce a snort from the bowler. It seems he does not suffer from ailments, real or imaginary; he will be in perfect condition for the first Test in mid-June, by when he will have bowled about 600 overs for his county. A little testily perhaps, Bedser says he *may* consider putting his feet up in late August – but only *after* capsizing Australia ten times.

Alec Bedser, the greatest of England bowlers since the Second World War, is the key to a puzzle as yet (and most likely for ever) unsolved – the change in Australian batting effectiveness after 1948. Granted Bedser developed his skills between then and 1950–1; granted, too, that the Australian pitches of the latter year differed vastly from those of 1946–7, that the seasons of 1950–1 and 1953 were both helpful to masters of swerve and cut. Yet bearing all this in mind, some may conclude the change in the response of Australian batsmen was, at least in part, psychological. Put simply – in the ten Tests of 1946–7 and 1948 Bedser's 34 wickets each cost 46 runs, while Bradman was loud in the bowler's praise. Then in the ten Tests of 1950–1 and 1953 Bedser increased the number of his wickets to 69, and reduced their cost from 46 to 16. A more finished technique and sometimes helpful conditions, or batsmen who no longer believed in their own invulnerability?

The unbeaten post-war Australian run was impressive – fifteen wins in twenty Tests against England, India and South Africa. England, on the other hand, had just lost a four-match series to West Indies. Normally those on board the *Stratheden* would have talked in terms of Lindwall, Miller and Johnston; now was added the query, 'Have Australia got any good spinners?' Englishmen shuddered at the memory of 1950 when West Indian fast bowlers had taken 4 wickets, and the spinners Ramadhin and Valentine 59. When played from the crease, their web was a compound of penetration and thrift. In 1934 Grimmett and O'Reilly had conceded 31 runs per 100 balls, in 1950 Ramadhin and Valentine fewer than 23. Thank goodness O'Reilly was safe in the press box, and Grimmett harmlessly attending to his garden.

With both Yardley and F. G. Mann unavailable, the captaincy of MCC in 1950–1 fell to F. R. Brown. Since visiting Australia as a redundant leg-spinner with Jardine's side, Freddie Brown had spent some years as a prisoner of war, a hiatus in his life he was obliterating from the mind by hitting cricket balls with blows of much violence. Some felt he might be too old for the job in hand – a fortieth birthday between the first and second Tests. In the event, preferring seam to spin, he took more wickets and at a better average than Lindwall, and finished third in the England batting after Hutton and R. T. Simpson! The Brown countenance grew even ruddier as the series progressed; his leadership inspired and the crowds loved him.

His side was oddly constituted. Edrich, a fearless hooker of fast bowling, had been omitted; so, too, had the leading wicket-takers of the recent English season, Laker and Wardle. Two spinners who were chosen, Hollies and Berry, seemed unlikely to turn on Australian pitches – and didn't. However the selectors achieved a record of sorts; they gave Brown eight opening batsmen – that is eight men who either had gone in first for England, or would do so in the course of their careers: Bailey, Close, Dewes, Hutton, Parkhouse, Sheppard, Simpson and Washbrook. What the selectors could not foresee was the total eclipse of Compton; recovering from a cartilage operation, he scored 53 in eight innings, the most heartbreaking reverses of any great batsman since those of Fry and Ranji in 1902.

Robertson-Glasgow thought yet another Brisbane farce after rain should have been called 'The Marx Brothers at the Test'. Australia won the toss and batted more or less as they had in 1948 – more in the sense that they included nine men who had appeared under Bradman, and less in their ability to score runs. They tottered to 228, only Harvey's 74 (terminated by a miraculous leg-side catch by Evans off Bedser) suggesting permanence and domination. Bailey, Wright, Brown, and especially Bedser, bowled superbly; one man who might have taken root, Barnes, sat writing his bumper fun column full of unpleasing comment. After their pathetic display, the Australians prayed for rain. It came, and prevented further play until 1 p.m. on Monday when Washbrook and Simpson batted nicely until lunch. Afterwards wickets fell, and Hutton came in at 52 for 4 – the idea being he would stiffen the middle. He did but only at one end. It was Hutton at his most intellectual, reason assuring him that no ball could leave the pitch at an angle of more than 90°. However, with England 68 for 7, Brown declared – Hutton 8 not out and wondering what all the fuss was about.

Australia opened their second-innings account after 20 minutes' batting; somehow 1 for 3 wickets looked better than 0 for 3 wickets. Bedser and Bailey bowled, Australians came and went. At 32 for 7, captain Hassett said 'Fie!' – and also declared. Brown responded by asking for the heavy roller. The ground-staff located the heavy roller, then went in search of the horse whose duty it was to pull the heavy roller. This Australian animal was first cousin to the British TUC horse created by the cartoonist David Low: it moved slowly and thought hardly at all. After each journey down the wicket the Gabba horse was unhitched, re-adjusted, and then urged back into the shafts. No oats until you stop working to rule. Freddie Brown did not get his – or rather the pitch's – 7 minutes' rolling.

At 4.50 p.m. England set out in pursuit of 193 runs. An hour later – 23 for 3 – nightwatchman Bedser (this England side consisted of Hutton and ten nightwatchmen) drove extravagantly and was caught; inspired, Bailey smote a harmless delivery to long-leg. Play ended with England 30 for 6, McIntyre having run himself out going for a fourth run. England's reserve wicketkeeper was in the team for his batting, which said much for the current form of the specialists, actual or potential. From the day's final moments there was lacking only Harpo Marx and a blonde. Next morning the pitch had rolled out; Hutton, No. 8, began to enjoy a net in the middle. But when at 46 Evans and Compton departed to successive balls, Hutton was roused to his Golden Age grand manner – jumping out to spin, driving and pulling Miller for 20 off 3 overs. The 9th wicket fell at 77 and Wright waited upon Hutton. Now Lindwall found himself hit high over extra-cover and toyed with – Lindwall, the age's fast bowler with deep and three-quarters deep fielders everywhere. To the last ball before lunch Wright succumbed, hitting at a long-hop. The morning's 23 overs had brought 92 runs, 62 of them to Hutton. Once again he was cheered into memory. Australia had won a match after which they deserved to be at least one and a half games down.

At Brisbane Jack Iverson made his highest Test score – 1 not out – a feat twice equalled during the series. He was a thirty-four-year-old shambling oddity whose off-breaks, top spinners and occasional leg-breaks were the result of a two-finger exercise. The ball was held by the thumb and a doubled-over second finger (the other digits not engaged) and bowled – as Iverson put it – 'like a man flicking a cigarette stub'. Not surprisingly, the most frequent victim was F. R. Brown, an inveterate pipe smoker. Just before lunch on the second day of the first Melbourne Test Iverson appealed against Hutton for a lobbed catch to leg taken by Tallon. A photograph suggests the ball came from the batsman's pad, and one or two Australian close fielders saw fit to agree – in private. This infamy is emphasized because Englishmen insist it cost them the game, meaning this was another encounter Australia deserved to lose. A humid atmosphere – fine bowling by Bedser and Bailey – a mightily struck 62 from Brown – England required only 179 in the last innings: and who got out playing his only ungrammatical stroke of the tour? Hutton, promoted on this occasion to No. 4.

Australia retained the Ashes by winning at Sydney when injuries to Bailey and Wright when batting (the latter 'run out and pulled muscle, o') reduced England to three bowlers – Bedser, Brown and Warr. A Miller hundred lasted 6 hours, Iverson took 6 for 27 in England's second innings, and John Warr proved less effective as a Test bowler than he would a couple of decades later as an after-dinner speaker. At Adelaide Arthur Morris stopped shuffling across the crease to Bedser and made 206, Hutton then carrying his bat for 156 out of 272; the margin this time in Australia's favour 274 runs. And so to the return match at Melbourne when, to the delight of everyone on the continent save presumably eleven home cricketers, England won by 8 wickets. Brown 5 wickets for 49 in Australia's first innings (Bedser 10 for 105 in the match): England, in the persons of Hutton and Simpson, were perched happily at 171 for 1 before subsiding to 246 for 9. Whereupon an odd thing happened: Reg Simpson remembered he had packed a glittering array of strokes before leaving Trent Bridge. At last he played them. The 10th wicket put on 74, Tattersall – flown out with Statham as reinforcements – pushing down the line as Simpson advanced to 156 not out, compelling spectators to say 'And Hutton's quite good, too!'

In 1950–1 the ball so dominated the bat that the two sides

found runs harder to come by than any of their predecessors on Australian pitches during the present century. If England's bowlers did at least well – and often magnificently – none doubted what decided the series. In thirty-eight innings Parkhouse, Washbrook, Sheppard, Bailey, Compton, Dewes and Close between them averaged 11·94. In the light of these failures it was quite irrelevant that the world's greatest batsman should average 88·83.

Hutton was now quite simply 'the Master'.

1953

The year was a day – 2 June. The Australians said they did not wish to play cricket on this day – wisely, because if they had, no one would have watched them. Not even Trumper with the promise of a century before lunch, followed by every ball of an over passing through the Doctor's beard, could have vied with the Coronation. News had also reached London that a New Zealander, Edmund Hillary, and Sherpa Tensing were sitting on top of Everest – well, standing briefly, the temperature at 29,002 feet being even lower than at sea level in England during 1953.

In the story of the Ashes, the year was a quarter of an hour round three o'clock on 18 August. In the course of sixteen balls, Australia lost 4 wickets; exactly a day later, they had lost custody of the Urn.

A different world: cricketers should seek to be born at the right time. An Australian coming into the game during the middle or late twenties suddenly found himself facing Larwood with half a dozen short-legs in position, Englishmen of like vintage who did not relish playing leg-breaks and googlies soon learned to fear Grimmett and O'Reilly. In 1953 four Australians – Hassett, Harvey, Miller and Graeme Hole – filled the No. 3 position in Tests, scoring two hundreds, a 59 and a 71. Today a first wicket down batsman who averaged 43 in a series would be considered, if not sent from heaven, most welcome. Over six series in England, 1921–48, Australia had two regular

No. 3s – Macartney and Bradman. They managed 96 an innings. In the first two post-war series when Barnes opened for Australia, the openers obliged with 59; in the next two, after Barnes had disappeared, nineteen 1st-wicket partnerships each averaged 15.*

1953 was a summer of sweet irony. Wet weather generally prevailed as it had five years earlier, so that Lindwall and Miller must have wondered what it was like to attack on hard fast English wickets. When they made their third and farewell tour in 1956, conditions were much the same. Bill Johnston, who in his slower guise might have proved best suited, badly injured a knee in a one-day knock-about before serious games began. Out of hospital, he was obliged to re-model his delivery stride, so putting less strain on the leading foot. A cricketer the Australians would have welcomed (even if he had not been permitted to bat) was the slow left-hander Macartney. 1953 was indeed a summer of sweet irony, the principal wicket-taker being an Australian googly bowler playing for Notts, Bruce Dooland. Omitted from the 1948 party, he had entered English league cricket before being lured to Trent Bridge. Those who batted against him in the fifties had no doubts as to his quality – the best of his type since 1939.

The captains, Hutton and Hassett, regarded one another with suspicion during the first four Tests, neither willing to take a risk. This was to England's advantage because the final match was scheduled for the Oval where the home side *should* win unless confronted by an Act of God – five days' rain, or a remarkable geese-into-swans transformation among the Australian spinners. Hutton's holding operation from Trent Bridge to Headingley was therefore logical; Australia held the Ashes but England (in a negative sense maybe) the initiative. She could change players from one Test to another and did – the

---

* England-Australia Tests have known several successful 'firms'. In twenty-one excursions Hutton and Washbrook averaged 49, also in twenty-one Lawry and Simpson 58; in thirteen Woodfull and Ponsford 40. Hobbs and Sutcliffe opened for England twenty-nine times and averaged 83.

eighteen chosen being only three fewer than in 1948. England also had Bailey. We have noted how, on 29 August 1882, Dr W. G. Grace was bloody; on divers occasions during 1953 Trevor Bailey was, from an Australian point of view, even bloodier.

The Trent Bridge Test began, and continued, in perfect Bedser conditions: in the first innings the great bowler turned in 38·3–16–55–7, in the second 17·2–7–44–7, figures less amazing than those of the Australian scoresheet. Morris 67, Hassett 115 and Miller 55 promised much to start with, then eight other Australians made 7 between them. Lindwall (5 for 57) bowled out England for 144 before Bedser returned to business – this time Morris made 60 and eight other Australians 31. Set 229 to win, England reached 120 for the loss of Kenyon. Rain, perhaps a moral victory for England. Moral victories don't count in a fight for the Ashes, neither do self-inflicted humiliations. In the rain-ruined third match at Old Trafford Australia had 55 minutes' batting in her second innings and made 35 for 8, the method used to play Wardle and Laker being a charge down the wicket finishing in a wild hoick. In the press box Sir Donald Bradman watched impassively.

Meanwhile Bailey had contributed the first of his party pieces at Lord's. Fine weather for a change – excellent batting by Hassett, Harvey and Davidson – eight other Australians make 99 – in the circumstances 346 adequate. Three catches missed by Hutton (cares of captaincy?) – vast crowd not amused; superb Hutton 145 – vast crowd stands in acclamation; lovely 78 by Graveney – happy assurance from Compton; eight other Englishmen make 72 – in the circumstances 372, all that could be expected. Australia batting again reach 227 for 2. Morris 89 and Miller 109 – will it happen yet again? It does – seven Australians make 60. England need 343 to win in 7 hours. Lindwall strikes, not once but twice – Hutton and Kenyon are out for 10. Johnston gets Graveney, Compton and Willie Watson hang on till the close of the fourth day. At 12.40 on the morrow, Compton is out – 73 for 4; England must survive for nearly 5 hours. The crowd is heavy with woe.

Trevor Edward Bailey feels histrionic. (Feels? felt? – the tense does not matter with Bailey. Spectators watched him in the present yet were conscious they had aged since his arrival. Australian bowlers referred to him as past, present and future indefinite – and *most* bloody.) T. E. Bailey's histrionic act is something of a contradiction; he thinks, 'Once more unto the breach' but the line comes out as 'No!' It may be spoken in different ways: firmly but with respect to Lindwall, with a sense of playfulness, 'You won't get me, Keith' to Miller, petulantly as a schoolmaster reproaching Benaud for errant length. While all 'No's' echo round Lord's, some reach St John's Wood Underground where men emerging from the darkness pause, then say 'Ah! Bailey.' A defensive forward stroke is multiplied by X, a backward defensive stroke divided by Y; the Bailey equation – very far from being simultaneous – goes: 50 minutes = 10 runs, 100 minutes = 25, 185 minutes = 39, 220 minutes = 50. Hell and damnation! Bailey is caught off a leg-break after a vigil lasting 4 hours 17 minutes. Runs? Those incidental things? 71. A great silence falls over St John's Wood. But surely Bailey had a partner? Willie Watson's 109, the finest innings of a distinguished career – but Willie is not histrionic. He merely bats.

England reached the Oval all-square after drawing the fourth Test at Headingley, but it was a close-run thing with Bailey firing an air gun at the Australian steed only a furlong from home and forcing it into the rails. 99 behind on the first innings, England next time crawled to 275 at precisely 2 an over – Bailey 38 in 260 minutes. With just under 2 hours left, Australia needed 177 for victory; they could hardly get out in time, so they played strokes inventive, wild and hopeful. Bedser, Lock and Laker each took a wicket but in 27 overs gave away 130 runs; Bailey, too, took a wicket – for 9 runs off 6 overs. Had he pursued his wide of the leg stump attack ('attack' – there is no alternative word) at Sydney, he would rightly have been lynched; his final words, 'That was a far better thing that I did than I have ever done before. But remember, I shall resurrect myself for Melbourne.'

In the story of the Ashes, 1953 was a quarter of an hour round three o'clock on 18 August. England's side at the Oval included Aircraftman Frederick Sewards Trueman of the RAF, of whom the Australians had heard much – and more than much if meeting the aircraftman. For the first time since the Oval in 1938, when Kenneth Farnes played his last Test at home, England had a fast bowler against Australia. The crowd anticipated fire from Fred, and were not disappointed – his first-innings victims Harvey, Hole, de Courcy and (fittingly!) Lindwall, although only after the last named had driven and pulled for 62, the highest score in Australia's 275. England topped this by 31 – Lindwall, Miller and Johnston bowling 111 overs, the tour's spinners having been found wanting and left out. Hutton's 82 was not the Master at his best; Bailey's 64 in 228 minutes was that lesser master doing his best to raise Australian blood pressures. AND in mid-afternoon on the *second* day, Johnston caused a spurt of dust to rise from the Oval wicket.

Bedser and Trueman bowled only 5 overs to Morris and Hassett before Hutton brought on Laker. At once the off-spinner got Hassett lbw, bat caught up in pads. Australia 23 for 1, their most 'professional' batsman gone. Morris and Hole raised the 50 in 55 minutes – exhilarating but feverish. Woodfull, Ponsford and Kippax, all competent on this kind of wicket, would have dug in with three days and four hours left, seeking to set England 250 on a crumbled surface against Johnston, holding an end, and Dooland. In reality Laker showed what he thought of the conditions by bowling round the wicket. Hole lbw to Laker: 59 for 2. A single to Harvey who, trying to on-drive Lock, hit across the line and missed: 60 for 3. Miller lunged forward to Laker and edged a catch to Trueman at short-leg: 61 for 4. Lock did everything but kiss Trueman; resorting to propriety, he persuaded Morris to put his legs in front of a straight ball: 61 for 5. 16 balls, 2 runs, 4 wickets – some thrilling strokes from Ron Archer and Davidson, but Australia were out for 162 scored (if we exclude the time taken for batsmen to come and go) at a run a minute. Laker 16·5–2–75–4, Lock 21–9–45–5. Just before three

ALEC VICTOR BEDSER, 1946–54
Greatly indomitable

o'clock on the fourth afternoon, Compton – in partnership with Edrich – hit the winning boundary. Victory for England by 8 wickets.

The Ashes had come home after a bowler's series in which two accepted giants, Bedser (39 wickets at 17·48) and Lindwall (26 at 18·84), again proved their supremacy. When England had regained the Ashes at the Oval in 1926, it was with their second win to Australia's twelve since the First World War; now with a second win to Australia's eleven since the Second World War. 1953 was a happy series when the two captains, Hutton and Hassett, had respect and affection for each other, when Sir Donald Bradman and Douglas Jardine sat side by side in the press box. It was a year when the Coronation concentrated the pride of a family, when the Tests made one branch of the family feel life really was worth living. Only one thing was missing – a picture of the Abominable No-Man Bailey playing steadfastly forward on the top of Everest and shouting defiance to the elements.

Leonard Hutton's problem was how to retain the Ashes.

1954–5

Pace – the greater the better. Hutton was a believer in fast bowling, providing those responsible for its violence were on his side. As a young man he had faced – and been dismissed by – Larwood; had been disturbed by the Australian McCormick, and assaulted by the West Indian Martindale. In the Lord's Gentlemen and Players match in 1938, he had made 52 while Farnes shattered the Players with 8 for 43, and the Long Room asked, '*Was* Larwood faster?' (This was the occasion when the Players' captain, Woolley, used only four bowlers in a total of 411, as Hugh Bartlett made 175 not out with two 6s on to the roof of the grandstand. Perhaps at Brisbane in 1954, Hutton forgot about Woolley and his four bowlers.) Since the war Hutton had opened for England twenty-three times to the barrage of Lindwall and Miller. He knew the meaning of stress, of continual ducking and weaving; he admired Lindwall and Miller, and wished they had been playing for England.

If MCC's bowling of 1954–5 was not collectively the strongest to visit Australia, it is hard to think of any better balanced: Tyson, Statham and Loader for speed; Bedser and Bailey also to use the ball when, or almost, new; Appleyard and McConnon (the latter sustained injury and returned home early) for off-spin; Wardle equally adept at orthodox or back of the hand left-arm. Laker, Lock, Tattersall and Trueman had been omitted, in itself a rare tribute to those chosen. Hutton had the bowlers he wanted, had long prayed for. Could he command his formidable artillery with sound judgement?

England's captain made three grave tactical errors during the series – all at, or rather before, Brisbane. First, he opted to play only four bowlers, something Chapman had done successfully in 1928–9 but always with Hammond in reserve; secondly, with Bedser the slowest of the bowlers, there was precious little variety; and thirdly, having won the toss, Hutton put Australia in on a pitch which proved to be perfect. The reward for these eccentricities was Compton's broken finger on the first day – he trapped his hand in the pickets – sore feet for everyone by the second, and the unbecoming sight of Tyson off a run of such inordinate length that he resembled not a bull charging a gate but one in search of a gate. After twelve hours Australia untied its napkin, belched thanks for the dozen dropped catches, and declared at 601 for 8. The match was completed with more than a day to spare, England's two innings 154 short of Australia's one. The sole link with more spacious days was provided by a citizen of Brisbane who suddenly offered £100 to the batsman hitting the fourth day's first 6. In 1884 Scotton had come by mining shares for top scoring at Gympie; in 1954 the £100 (comparable purchasing power today £650) went to Trevor Bailey, gloating most horribly.

Hutton's attitude was one of, 'That didn't count, let's begin again.' England did so, controversially. Heavy overnight rain at Sydney, and a cloudy morning, suggested ideal conditions for Bedser. Hutton thereupon dropped Bedser (still recovering from a severe attack of shingles) and relied on Statham, Tyson, Bailey, Appleyard and Wardle. So ended Bedser's career against Australia: 104 wickets in twenty-one Tests, he had been on the losing side twelve times, the winning but twice. As Hutton believed in pace, Bedser was no longer wanted. As Jardine, too, had believed in pace, Tate was not wanted in 1932–3 – being saved up for Wagga Wagga.

Hutton lost the toss at Sydney and Morris, deputizing for Ian Johnson, put England in. The ball swung and sometimes lifted from a length: 34 for 2 at lunch after 90 minutes, England were 99 for 8 at four o'clock. Johnny Wardle now applied himself with comic song and custard pie, his strokes played from yards down the wicket, the ball bisecting reason. Hutton probably watched the scoreboard and not the antics. A last-wicket stand with Statham added 43 and carried England to 154; little more than a day later Australia had succumbed to Statham, Bailey and Tyson for 228. Tyson's shortened run – less than a pitch's length – produced co-ordination; the bull had found its gate beyond which were Australian batsmen clad in red. The stumps behind them appeared match-stick thin.

The 1954–5 series began for England after lunch on the third day at Sydney with the score 55 for 3 – arrears of 19. At the fall of the 4th wicket Edrich would appear, then four bowlers and the wicketkeeper. But the fourth partnership of the innings lasted 3 hours; more, it saw England's cause prosper by 116 runs; most of all, it announced the coming-of-age as Test batsmen of May and Cowdrey – the former aged twenty-four, the latter twenty-one. Both, like Sir Jack Hobbs, were modest, even self-effacing, men; both were superb technicians, perfectly drilled and batting to the book of logic. Where May and Cowdrey differed was in temperament; at the crease May was steel translated into destructive power, Cowdrey was still modest and apt to play for his own self-delectation. At his best, Cowdrey could make May seem almost vehement; then moments of broodiness intervened. 'Can I' – one could see Cowdrey asking himself – 'Can I really be as good as this?' To see May in command was to be aware of a very great batsman; Cowdrey was content to reveal cricket as a beautiful and civilized pastime.

On 20 December 1954 at Sydney Cowdrey made 54, the next day May completed his century before departing in the most honoured manner (honoured if one had completed a century), bowled Lindwall. The best way of dealing with a Lindwall bouncer was not to duck and place the back of one's head in the path of the ball. Tyson did this and lay unconscious. 'He will take no further part in the game,' announced the pundits. Tyson disagreed – and later completed his innings: bowled Lindwall. England's lead was only 176 when the 9th wicket fell; it was 222 after Appleyard and Statham had expressed themselves. Two 10th-wicket stands accounted for 89 of England's 450 runs. At close of play, Australia were 72 for 2, needing 151 for victory.

Harvey, not out overnight, batted easily. Tyson, a strong wind behind him, heaved mightily in; the dauntless Statham accepted the hard alternative as ever, philosophically. Statham's greatest virtue as a fast bowler was his straightness, a fundamental quality which put him at the very top. Suddenly Tyson yorked Burke; in the same over he yorked Hole. Speed. Australia 77 for 4. Benaud lingered, then hit across Appleyard's line to be caught, somehow, by Tyson at square-leg. The fielder seemed uncertain which was the ball and which the bump on his head. He held the ball while the bump throbbed. After lunch Tyson bowled Archer with a break-back as vast as any Tom Richardson achieves at will on Olympus; Evans accounted for a Davidson snick off Statham in front of second slip. Australia sank to 145 for 9 before Harvey and Bill Johnston caused English palpitations by adding 39. Harvey's undefeated 92 promised twice as many with a little more help. England had won by 38 runs – her two last-wicket partnerships 43 and 46.

Tyson 18·4–1–85–6; Statham 19 – 6–45–3.

Miller had missed the second Test through a knee injury. Told by the doctors he could play in the third at Melbourne on condition he did not bowl, Miller said 'Right!' – and had England 41 for 4 at lunch. He permitted 5 runs to come from 1 over, otherwise his figures were both aggressive and virginal: 9–8–5–3. This was Miller exultant, heroic and sublime. After lunch Colin Cowdrey began to stroke the bowling benignly, or as benignly as fifteen balls reaching the boundary would permit. O'Reilly declared it to be one of the finest centuries he had seen in Test matches. The highest stand was 74 during which Bailey played forward. England 191 – Cowdrey 102, the rest 80. Hutton clucked; a day later Ian Johnson clucked for Australia finished 188 for 8.

Was the pitch watered during the weekend? All agreed it had changed by Monday but was the cause moisture applied from a hose or did it – as two learned professors insisted – work its way up from below? If the latter, Old Trafford may have overflowed. At all events, batting became a more rational business. May drove superbly for 91: hereabouts the prose-poet in Alan Ross saw May as 'a player of the Renaissance, lean, hungry, adventurous', and Cowdrey as 'a Georgian, discreet, handsome, and of some substance'. Wardle whirled his pies, Bailey dropped anchor for nearly 3 hours. With England expiring for 279, Bailey was still contemplating his anchor as the ship left. Australia ended the fourth day 75 for 2 – 165 runs from victory. Victory – a figment! Fifty thousand spectators gathered on the morrow; after 75 minutes they went home. Statham bowled four shooters in a row to Miller, Evans caught Harvey yards wide on the leg side; Tyson required 50 deliveries, from which 16 were scored, to take 6 wickets. England were home by 128 – Australia demoralized.*

England clinched the series at Adelaide where little happened until tea on the fourth day, Australia's 323 having been headed by 18. Then Appleyard, varying his pace beautifully, had Australia 54 for 3 at the close. Would the off-spinner confound the remaining batsmen? We shall never know, for Hutton next

---

* On the first day of this Melbourne Test, Australia bowled 67·5 overs, the equivalent of about 108 six-ball overs in an English six-hour day. (In 1936, Australia had averaged about 72 overs daily.) England followed with 54 overs on the second day, about 86 overs in an English day. Was Hutton the first captain to achieve intentionally what is now taken for granted?

day reverted to pace – Tyson and Statham with an old ball. 7 wickets fell for the addition of 57, leaving England with only 94 to get. A formality, on paper – not to Keith Miller who swept Edrich, Hutton and Cowdrey aside for 18, almost caught and bowled May 5 runs later, then at 46 swooped to catch him at cover. But it was too late for an Australian miracle; Compton stood firm with assistance from Bailey. A mentally exhausted Hutton wiped his brow; in Yorkshire Mrs Dorothy Hutton said, 'Thank God!'

The final Test at Sydney did not matter. Rain prevented any play until after lunch on the fourth day when Ian Johnson put England in. Tom Graveney obliged with one of his most cultured Festival hundreds, an innings fit for the Sydney where MacLaren and Hammond had once ruled. Hutton declared at 371 for 7; the Ashes safe, he then permitted Wardle to indulge in wrist-spin. Australia wrinkled the brow, forgot where Fleetwood-Smith, Jack Walsh and Tribe had been born, and followed on. The last gesture of the series was made by Hutton himself. At 116 for 5 he put himself on to bowl – for the first time against Australia since Headingley 1948. His sixth ball evaded the bat and hit the stumps. Hutton's face showed no emotion, though mind-readers felt sure his unspoken words were, 'And you can't play leg-breaks either.'

The recipient's name was Richie Benaud.

1956

A quarter of a century later, it is tempting to remember 1956 as a dream or – if one is an Australian – a nightmare. James Charles Laker took 46 wickets at 9·60, an average superior to that of S. F. Barnes in 1913–14 on the South African mat. At the time, and certainly now, Laker's achievement encouraged one to seek excuses for the batsmen rather than reasons for their humiliation. No bowler could be that good, no batting side could be that feeble. Even if we concede the truth – that Laker was supremely good, and the batting for the most part unbearably awful – we must still account for both. Laker, of course, was in his eleventh season of first-class cricket; his length, line, spin and flight were those of a master craftsman. In several of the Tests he bowled on helpful, though not unplayable, pitches. But on no occasion was he favoured with anything like the Edgbaston horror of 1953 (the year when batsmen collected pebbles and miscellaneous objects); against Warwickshire's Hollies, turning and popping, Hassett batted nearly 3 hours for an undefeated 21. Lindsay Hassett was a pre-war batsman capable of countering and annoying O'Reilly.

If, as was certainly the case, Australia's woes of 1956 were partly psychological, how did this come about? In the past Australian sides had generally trampled over the counties, coming to the first Test with an air of, 'We are the greatest!' Not so in 1956 when Ian Johnson treated the early games as occasions for batting practice; six county games were drawn (rain interfered more than once), that with Surrey lost. This latter fiasco – the first time the Australians had been beaten by an English county since 1912, the year when the 'Big Six' refused to tour – set the pattern for the whole summer. At 12.20 on the first day, Laked bowled from the pavilion end at the Oval, resting himself at a quarter to six with figures of 46–18–88–10, the Australians' score 259. Johnson's decision to outdo Laker was then welcomed by Surrey. Lindwall was given only 2 overs while Constable (shaky against pace) made a century, and Laker and Surridge 80 between them. Johnson's 60·3–12–168–6 helped the County Champions to a lead of 88, whereupon Lock bowled from the pavilion end and took 7 for 49. Surrey needed 20 to win.

If Johnson's tactical approach appeared odd, the reasons he was appointed captain appeared odder. One was called Miller. When Australia's side to tour South Africa in 1949–50 was announced, the world's greatest all-rounder had been omitted. (He later joined the party when Bill Johnston was injured.) Thereafter, or so it seemed to Englishmen, the Australian selectors were determined to avoid having to make Miller captain of his country. They may have been wise – one great

England contemporary thought Miller a poor captain – they may have been stupid; many Australians saw Miller as an inspiring captain of New South Wales. Certainly, even in his cricketing dotage, Miller was an integral part of his country's team. Johnson, on the other hand, had toured England in 1948 when he took 7 Test wickets at 61, but been passed over in 1953. Whether at the end of 1956, when his Test record in England showed 13 wickets at 57 – and a batting average of 8, Australia's selectors felt their faith in Johnson had been justified, is a secret for ever locked in their comprehensive bosom. Ironically, Johnson's off-spinning record in Tests played on Australian, South African and West Indian wickets was superior to that of Laker.

With the recent example of Tyson and Statham in mind, the Australian selectors opted to rely on the pace of Lindwall, Miller, Davidson, Archer and Crawford in 1956. Had the English summer resembled that of 1921 or 1947, the outcome could well have been interesting. But 1956 was wet, a sure sign that finger-spinners would come into their own. Lock was not chosen for the Lord's game; the four in which he did play saw the Lock-Laker duo capture 58 wickets, 484·4 overs each yielding a mere 1·42 runs. The Grand Inquisitor was Laker with a basic movement into the right-handed batsman; Lock, with the same movement to a left-hander, generally accounted for Harvey. Here, indeed, was a classic contradiction of cricket's long established lore – that the going-away ball is the danger one. Neville Cardus took Laker's success very much to heart; not on personal grounds but on those of Holy Writ. For years he would enter his club, pick up a poker, nominate a few dozing members as Laker's short-legs, and utter the magic word, 'Macartney!'

'I don't know what Macartney would have done to Laker. But, by God, I know what he would have tried to do!'

After the Trent Bridge Test had been washed out by rain, Australia won at Lord's. The pitch was firm, Johnson won the toss, and McDonald and Burke dug in until four o'clock. If Australia's 285 did not threaten England, Miller's bowling did. Fresh from a day at Ascot (with too few legs to run and rather too heavy to steer, he paraded in top hat and tails), Miller took 5 wickets in each innings – 10 for 152 in the match. Benaud devoured all bowlers in a heroic 97, and Mackay lingered eternally (265 minutes) for 31. Spinners on both sides gave best to the seam, Miller and company cantering home by 185 runs. Three Tests later, Australia felt like unveiling a plaque to the Lord's groundsman; conversely, their thoughts on other tenders of turf lay too deep for words.

Shortly before tea on the *second* day at Headingley, Laker bowled. His first ball turned sharply, and three short-legs materialized like vultures. Acknowledging England's fine recovery from 17 for 3 to 204 for 4 – and 325 all out, and the wisdom of bringing back the forty-one-year-old Washbrook whose 98 was as impressive as May's hundred, we are left with a question: 'When, in a match scheduled for five days, should the ball begin to turn?' One answer is that Australia should have included a Hugh Trumble in their side. But this prompts another question: 'Then why not play three-day Tests?' England in 1956 would probably have played Trumble better than Australia played Laker, if not as well as John Tyldesley or Hutton would have played either. Even so, a wise impresario does not engage a Wagner-size orchestra and then ask one quarter of the musicians to play Bach. That the Headingley Test lasted until just after lunch on the fifth day was due to intermittent rain. England's win by an innings and 42 runs was gratifying – in a way. Little could the Australians have guessed when Laker bowled his first ball on the second day that thereafter, until the end of the series, Lock and Laker would together take 48 wickets, and Statham, Bailey, Tyson and Trueman 6.

The day before the fourth Test was due to begin at Old Trafford, the groundsman predicted a fast grassy pitch. Lindwall, Miller and Archer rubbed their hands. On the morrow, when the sides assembled, it was apparent the pitch was shaven bare and marled. England won the toss and batted; Lindwall, Miller and Archer just managed to get the ball stump high. Peter Richardson made 104, Cowdrey 80, and the Reverend D. S. Sheppard (like Washbrook restored to the fold) 113. By 2.20 on the second day England had made 459. As the wicket was brushed, a dust storm materialized. W. J. O'Reilly in the Australian press seats said 'Ho!', adding 'Aha!' Between 2.30 and 3.45, however, nothing happened; Laker, from the railway end, and Lock looked no more than professionally efficient. Seventeen overs of spin produced apathy. Then May switched his bowlers; McDonald pushed forward to Laker and was caught, Harvey played back and was bowled. The tea score of 62 for 2 was good.

Good in view of what was to come. Lock had Burke caught off his glove, the bowler's last Test wicket for a month. Laker bowled, Craig played back and missed; Mackay prodded a catch to second slip; Miller, driving, got an inside-edge to short-leg; Benaud whacked a catch to long-on; Archer charged down the wicket and missed; Maddocks and Johnson played back to balls of full length. Since tea Laker had bowled twenty-two balls, and taken 7 wickets for 8 runs. Without bothering to inspect the pitch, sniff the breeze, or enquire after Laker's fitness, May thought it would be nice if Australia followed on. This they did at 5.25. After 20 minutes, and a similar number of runs off Statham and Bailey, Laker re-appeared. McDonald having left the field with an injured knee, Harvey came in; his first ball from Laker he drove to short and wide mid-on. At the close Australia were 53 for 1; three days remained.

The third and fourth days, and 2 hours before lunch on the fifth, saw Australia score 57 runs for the loss of Burke. Hour after hour was lost to rain: could Australia survive? When the sun stayed in, yes; when it came out, no. Laker at the Stretford end enjoyed one spell of 4 wickets for 3 runs in 9 overs. Lock's idea of the appropriate length grew more and more eccentric, McDonald relishing many juicy pulls. Laker turned yet very rarely popped; this was most surely not a sticky wicket. Length, flight, spin and direction: Laker just went on and on. At 5.27 Maddocks played back and missed. The deed was done. Off 51·3

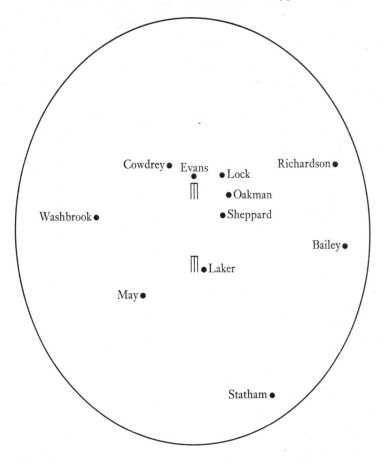

Laker overs Australia had managed only 53 runs; the bowler had managed all 10 wickets.

Off-spinners as a breed are modest men. One of the greatest, Tom Goddard, was told after some remarkable performance that he had bowled well. 'I always bowl well,' growled the hero, 'but sometimes the batsmen don't agree.' Which was at least part of the explanation of Laker's triumph at Old Trafford in 1956.

ENGLAND v AUSTRALIA
Played at Old Trafford 26, 27, 28, 30, 31 July 1956

ENGLAND

P. E. Richardson	c Maddocks b Benaud	104
M. C. Cowdrey	c Maddocks b Lindwall	80
Rev D. S. Sheppard	b Archer	113
P. B. H. May	c Archer b Benaud	43
T. E. Bailey	b Johnson	20
C. Washbrook	lbw b Johnson	6
A. S. M. Oakman	c Archer b Johnson	10
T. G. Evans	st Maddocks b Johnson	47
J. C. Laker	run out	3
G. A. R. Lock	not out	25
J. B. Statham	c Maddocks b Lindwall	0
Extras	(B2, LB5, W1)	8
Total		459

Fall of wickets: 1–174, 2–195, 3–288, 4–321, 5–327, 6–339, 7–401, 8–417, 9–458, 10–459.

AUSTRALIA BOWLING (6-ball overs)

	O.	M.	R.	W.
Lindwall	21·3	6	63	2
Miller	21	6	41	0
Archer	22	6	73	1
Johnson	47	10	151	4
Benaud	47	17	123	2

AUSTRALIA

	First innings		Second innings	
C. C. McDonald	c Lock b Laker	32	c Oakman b Laker	89
J. W. Burke	c Cowdrey b Lock	22	c Lock b Laker	33
R. N. Harvey	b Laker	0	c Cowdrey b Laker	0
I. D. Craig	lbw b Laker	8	lbw b Laker	38
K. R. Miller	c Oakman b Laker	6	b Laker	0
K. Mackay	c Oakman b Laker	0	c Oakman b Laker	0
R. G. Archer	st Evans b Laker	6	c Oakman b Laker	0
R. Benaud	c Statham b Laker	0	b Laker	18
	b Laker	0		
R. R. Lindwall	not out	6	c Lock b Laker	8
L. Maddocks	b Laker	4	lbw b Laker	2
I. W. Johnson	b Laker	0	not out	1
Extras		0	(B14, LB4)	16
Total		84		205

Fall of wickets: 1–48, 2–48, 3–62, 4–62, 5–62, 6–73, 7–73, 8–78, 9–84, 10–84.

2nd innings 1–28,* 2–55, 3–114, 4–124, 5–130, 6–130, 7–181, 8–198, 9–203, 10–205.

ENGLAND BOWLING (6-ball overs)

	O.	M.	R.	W.	O.	M.	R.	W.
Statham	6	3	6	0	16	9	15	0
Bailey	4	3	4	0	20	8	31	0
Laker	16·4	4	37	9	51·2	23	53	10
Lock	14	3	37	1	55	30	69	0
Oakman	–	–	–	–	8	3	21	0

ENGLAND WON BY AN INNINGS AND 170 RUNS

* At 28 McDonald left the field with an injured knee, being replaced by Harvey who was out to Laker's first ball. Craig joined Burke, the latter falling at 55, when McDonald continued his innings.

CHAPTER TEN

Under New Management

The New Age had dawned as Peter May's MCC party left for Australia in 1958. For the first time England would not include a player whose first-class debut was pre-1939. Never again would the selectors be able to put the clock back and wheel out in bathchairs such worthies as Washbrook and Compton who had managed respectively 98 and 94 at Headingley and the Oval in 1956. The New Age had dawned. For the first time in the twentieth century England had no wrist-spinner in the ranks, although this omission had been more or less forced on Lord's *after* Wardle had been chosen. A certain disharmony (rare understatement) in the Yorkshire dressing room led to the termination of Wardle's contract with the county, at which the bowler sprang into print with criticism of his former captain, colleagues and committee. MCC settled down to a perusal of Wardle's articles. Concluding perhaps that its President, Marshal of the RAF Viscount Portal – or indeed one of its immediate Past-Presidents, who included two non-Royal Dukes, two Viscounts, one Earl, one Knight *and* Her Majesty's Consort – might next be in line for unpleasing comment, MCC breathed a collective 'Tut!' and purged Wardle.

While this course of action did not necessarily weaken the bowling under May's command (most would agree it did), it certainly led to an unbalanced attack of four fast bowlers – Statham, Tyson, Trueman and Loader – plus Bailey, with Laker and Lock as the only spinners. Injury to either of the last named did not bear thinking about. On the other hand, Hutton had succeeded with much the same balance of forces – McConnon having been injured – so everything seemed to revolve around the strength, not of England, but of Australia. Had the enemy recovered from humiliations imposed first by Tyson and Statham, and secondly by Laker? In so far as an answer was possible before the 1958–9 series began, it was to be found in South Africa.

Immediately after 'Laker's summer' at home, England had played a drawn series in the then Union, being grievously confined by Tayfield with off-spin and two forward short-legs. Ironically, in view of the future, by far the most successful England bowler was Wardle, generally as wrist-spinner. May used Bailey as opening batsman, though it must be admitted the composition of the party left him with few alternatives. A year later, 1957–8, a 'new' Australia (without Lindwall and Miller) toured South Africa. Alan Davidson at once proved himself a superb fast left-hander, while Tayfield's brand of Chinese torture was welcomed by Mackay who didn't play strokes anyway, and who continued to hold his bat like some teetotal water-diviner wary lest he discover a distillery. Most significant was the emergence of Benaud as a player of the front rank – 329 runs average 54, and 30 wickets at 21. Although Ian Craig was captain, Benaud appeared to be tactical adviser-in-chief.

All true Englishmen believe to this day that Australia's 4–0 win in 1958–9 was the outcome of including a 'bowler' who threw, at least his faster ball. Now unless Ian Meckiff's action changed *after* 1958–9, there seems little doubt that he did throw: five years later he was no-balled out of Test cricket by umpire Colin Egar. However, the fact that Meckiff 'chucked' does not make moral judgement any the easier. In 1951 Frank Chester had referred the matter of the South African McCarthy's very fast delivery to Lord's, only to be told he must not provoke an incident. The following year Tony Lock was called for throwing; in the Oval Test of 1953 Keith Miller gesticulated angrily after receiving a Lock thunderbolt whose pace suggested Statham warming up. But the acknowledged king of all modern 'chuckers' was the Australian Burke, who professed to purvey off-spin but whose action reminded Ian Peebles of a policeman applying his truncheon 'to a particularly short offender's head'. In 1958–9 or thereabouts a 'chucker' was bitterly resented but only when taking wickets for the other side.

To the reader who insists on cherishing records, the first Test at Brisbane was the most memorable of the series – 518 runs being scored on the first four days. On the first, when the wicket was green, England strove hard to reach 134; on the second, when conditions were more favourable for batting, Australia advanced to 156 for 6. As the hourly run rate was thus far 29 – and this was, after all, a Test match – onlookers expressed themselves by yawning. Certainly England's bowlers had fought back splendidly; when, just before lunch on the third day, Australia were out with a lead of only 52, England looked forward to batting for a couple of days and then to spinning out the opposition. At least, these appeared to be May's tactics. His first wicket fell at 28; coming in at No. 3 (a place formerly filled by J. T. Tyldesley, George Gunn, Woolley and Hammond) was T. E. Bailey. Finding his forward defensive prod to be in good working order, Bailey went to work. The hourly run rate on the third day accountably fell to 25; onlookers, suspecting mental as well as physical lethargy, expressed themselves by more than yawning.

In 90 minutes before lunch on the fourth day – during which time Graveney was run out – Bailey scored 8. At 2.50 p.m. Burke threw a ball that turned (waiting for Laker!), 5 minutes later a member of the press woke up and asked how long it was since Bailey had last achieved a run.

'Twenty past two,' replied George Duckworth, the England scorer.

'Today or yesterday?' continued the inquisitive one, dropping off again before Duckworth could answer.

Since lunch, when he had been fortified by Brisbane's best carbohydrates, Bailey had increased his hourly run rate from 8·4 to 9·5. Undismayed by Cowdrey's controversial dismissal (caught at short-leg off Meckiff, the film seemed inconclusive),

Bailey pressed on. A hard-earned half-century in three minutes under 6 hours persuaded him that this – with yesterday and tomorrow – was his day. Alas, he reckoned without Australia's new captain, Benaud, who called up Mackay. The Queenslander's bowling, like his batting, was unusual. Approaching the crease furtively, as though suspecting ambush, he delivered at friendly medium-pace with the wicketkeeper standing back. This enabled Mackay to pretend he was Lindwall. Bailey was not deceived. He would attack Mackay; he swung mightily and was bowled. He had scored 68 runs off 40 balls. That his innings lasted 7 hours 38 minutes was due to his not scoring off 388 balls. On the fifth day, requiring 147 for victory, Australia's batsmen agreed the pitch was not one for stroke-making. Then Norman O'Neill, playing in his first Test, made an undefeated 71 in under 2 hours. A glorious talent marred by ignorance of the occasion.

England began the 3rd over of the second Test at Melbourne with 7 on the board. She ended it 7 for 3, Davidson dismissing Richardson, Watson and Graveney with his first, fifth and sixth balls. Using a cross-breeze, the left-hander swung late and viciously. Clearly he was unplayable. Not by Bailey who, sent in first, surveyed the multitude as if to ask, 'Who says I have no strokes? Just you watch.' Bailey* scored only 48 but made the Australian bowlers conscious of a minor miracle in the middle. At the close England were 173 for 4, with May 89 and Cowdrey 28. The match was certainly not lost. On the morrow May became the first England captain to make a Test century in Australia since MacLaren in 1901–2. A total of 259 was poor, yet acceptable after that dreadful start. Australia soon lost Burke before cruising to 96: McDonald's bat was monumentally straight, Harvey's 60 in 2 hours ominously prophetic of what might come.

The third day – Friday – saw May set defensive fields and two

---

* In the England-New Zealand Test at Lord's in 1949, Bailey came in at an awkward time to reach 50 in 67 minutes. His partner, whom he outscored, was Compton – then at the peak of his powers.

great cricketers in opposition: Harvey fluent though restrained, Statham's every ball compelling respect. By five o'clock Australia were 255 with only two men out; a few minutes later Statham had O'Neill caught by Evans, and Loader yorked Harvey. 257 for 4. Simpson at once fell lbw to Loader, and Benaud to Statham – both without scoring. The third day ended with Australia a mere 23 ahead with 6 wickets down; England were still very much in the game despite that start. The deficit was limited to 49 on Saturday when Statham was cheered from the field with figures of 28–6–57–7 and thoughts of putting his feet up till late on Monday. His rest lasted 3 hours. For now came Meckiff.

The roar which accompanied him as he tore in was equalled only by that committed to paper by the *Daily Telegraph*'s correspondent, E. W. Swanton, who roused not only every retired colonel in England, but a few million others who were neither retired nor colonels. The chairman of the Australian Board of Control, W. J. Dowling, on the other hand, did not think the problem of throwing even existed. Clearly, there was room for compromise, perhaps on the lines of 'You gave us some queer pitches in 1956, now we're giving you some "chuckers".' Jack Fingleton, who had passed judgement on English pitches, wrote in the *Sunday Times* that he thought Meckiff's faster ball should have been 'called'. So England slumped to 27 for 4 in an hour, and to 57 for 6 at tea. By 5.30 they were out for 87, leaving a somewhat disgruntled Statham the task of skittling Australia for 37 to ensure an England win.

Meckiff with his jerking elbow was undeniably fast, his trajectory hard to pick up; the Australian close catching brilliant in the extreme. But England's batsmen also made heavy weather of Davidson (whose action was above suspicion) as they had in the first innings and, indeed, at Brisbane – as they would of Sobers, and as no less a batsman than Boycott would of the gentle medium-pace of the Indian Solkar. Left-arm over the wicket bowlers present problems whether their actions are legitimate or not. What no one could fathom at Melbourne were May's reasons for batting himself and Cowdrey at five and six; not until the fourth Test did they move up to what seemed their rightful positions of 1st and 2nd wicket down respectively. Meanwhile Australia had won two Tests both by 8 wickets. England must somehow square the series to retain the Ashes.

About now Edward Ralph Dexter had been plucked from his table at the Folies Bergères, his absinthe and nodding acquaintance with Jean-Paul Sartre (which was how Alan Ross might have indicated that Dexter was working in Paris), given a few shirts and a bat, and told to report to Sydney. His omission from the original party had caused Robertson-Glasgow to call the selectors 'gibbering dolts'. Had he been chosen, and then failed, he might have won the Australian Amateur Golf Championship and carried back a trophy to Lord's. At twenty-three he was – as we now see – the last of the cricketing romantics* and capable of almost anything. Another newcomer to the MCC party was John Mortimore, the Gloucestershire off-spinner, who was supposed to cover Wardle's absence.

The third Test at Sydney was drawn, partly because Benaud employed defensive tactics on the fifth day when England were 3 wickets down in their second innings and still 74 behind Australia. Odd! However, coming to Adelaide, May was in a predicament – he had to win the last two Tests to retain the Ashes. With Laker unfit, his attack *had* to consist of Statham, Trueman, Tyson, Bailey and Lock; if the pitch did offer life, it would be on the first day. Accordingly, on winning the toss, May put Australia in. The score at the close on the first day was 200 for 1, on the second 403 for 6; McDonald batted 8 hours for 170, and England knew that with only three and a half days left, Benaud could close up the game. Cowdrey, May and Graveney all played good innings, Cowdrey's 46 in 50 minutes (adjudged run out, and the picture told a story) the aesthetic joy of the season. Benaud followed his 9 for 177 in the third Test with 9 for 173, Lindwall aged thirty-seven replaced an injured Meckiff,

---

* Ian Botham is a first Elizabethan pirate who, from time to time, will sing 'Yo-ho-ho! and a bottle of rum', and then singe a few Australian beards.

and Rorke dragged – the ball still in his hand when the back foot passed the popping crease. Australia won by 10 wickets, then by 9 wickets in the final game after Benaud had put England in. The last captain to gamble successfully in matches between the two countries had been Douglas at Melbourne in 1912.

The New Age did more than dawn in 1958–9, it proclaimed itself. The fastest scoring batsman was not Harvey, O'Neill, May or Cowdrey but the dogged master of placements, McDonald. 1958–9 was the first series when statisticians ceased announcing a batsman had made his runs in so many hours and minutes, preferring from balls received. Although both sides used slow bowlers for 4 overs in 10, Australia averaged 4 minutes 40 seconds per over, England 5 minutes 5 seconds. When a stopwatch was used on Lindwall in the final Test, he was found to complete an over in 3 minutes 46 seconds – so making sense of the 46 six-ball overs bowled pre-lunch at Headingley (Bradman 105) in 1930.

Trevor Bailey played the last of his twenty-three Tests against Australia in 1958–9. His 42 wickets and many brilliant catches close to the bat underlined his usefulness; his batting was a sign of the times, of the nature – and strength – of English cricket in the Welfare State. The majority of his twelve 'major' innings came in the middle of the order, the twelve totalling 345 runs and occupying 31 hours 20 minutes – 11 runs an hour. In short, Bailey at No. 6 restored a balance which Herbert Sutcliffe had once tilted towards his side at No. 2. Australians will never forget Bailey if only for an over he bowled at Headingley in 1953. It took – or so Australians insist – 7 minutes to complete. England drew the match. Opponents gradually took to Bailey; Australians were particularly appreciative in 1958–9 of his Brisbane marathon which effectively gave Australia the game.

England were outplayed. Injuries were many, certain tactics odd: Lock, a slow left-hander, generally bowled over the wicket at the stumps, so requiring a split field. May, Cowdrey, Statham and Trueman alone maintained their reputations. England's opening partnerships averaged only 19 an innings, Australia's

50. For the first time in twenty-eight five-match series with Australia dating back to 1884-5, not a single England innings realized 300 runs. Australia had batting in depth, fine ground fielding and brilliant catching. Davidson was a major force, Benaud with 31 wickets at 18·83 put wrist-spin bowling not too far short of the pinnacle where O'Reilly had left it. A blend of charm and ruthlessness, Benaud crowded the England batsmen, studied their weaknesses, and – apart from one day at Sydney – attacked. On his return home, Peter May was asked about 'throwing'. He replied that Norman O'Neill had the best throw from the boundary he had seen.

1961

The Hill at Sydney is a protuberance where rude fellows foregather to entertain the players. There are no rude fellows at Lord's – at least not in June 1961; if there had been, and had they sought a protuberance to occupy, the second Test must have been summarily halted. Because instead of a Hill, Lord's had produced a Ridge which ran across the pitch at the Nursery End more or less on a fast bowler's length. Those whose duty it was to deliver the ball were happy, batsmen were not. When at the finish of the match the Secretary of MCC solemnly declared the Ridge did not exist, both bowlers and batsmen were taken aback. However, the Ridge or non-Ridge did cause to be played one of Test cricket's greatest innings.

Richie Benaud's twenty-second Australians were not strong in bowling. There was, of course, Davidson, a tremendous performer once Benaud had convinced him his pre-breakfast migraine, pulled ham-strings, lumbago, slipped discs and incipient plague were better than expected. Benaud himself had a creaking right shoulder by mid-June. In support were the fast-medium Gaunt and Misson whose career haul of wickets against England would total 10, McKenzie nineteen and therefore raw, Kline and Quick who sounded like a firm of stockbrokers and bowled slow left-arm, Simpson with leg-breaks – and Mackay. The batting with Davidson at eight and Benaud nine suggested no problems, and so it proved at Edgbaston where Australia followed England's 195 (Mackay 4 for 57 imitating Lindwall) with 516 for 9 declared. Whereupon England played out time with 401 for 4 – Subba Row 112 in his first Test against Australia, Dexter all magnificence 180.

How to get England out? The answer was very soon apparent – play all Tests at Lord's (England's problem was likewise solved). Although May appeared again after missing Edgbaston through injury, Cowdrey retained the captaincy, Harvey deputizing for Benaud, by now paying daily visits to hospital. Harvey called wrong, Cowdrey beamed Pullar and Subba Row into their pads, and Davidson opened from the pavilion end. His first ball was of a good length and passed the batsman chest high. Davidson suddenly felt very fit. The other Australians were fascinated by the pitch and not the ball so that Pullar was missed when 5, Dexter 11, and Subba Row 33. When England's 9th wicket fell at 167, MCC members of riper years recalled the Gentlemen and Players match at Lord's in 1868 when W. G. made an undefeated 134 out of 200, and an honest chronicler wrote that *he* would have risked batting on such a wicket only if wearing 'a single-stick mask, a Life Guardsman's cuirass and a tin stomach-warmer'. By 5.30 Trueman and Statham had whacked England to 206. Davidson had bowled superbly: 24·3–6–42–5. 10 minutes later one of Test cricket's greatest innings began.

Bill Lawry was tall and angular. His backlift was minimal, his strokes compounded of straight lines and no imagination. Elegance and charm had bypassed him at birth, the good fairy in charge of his making temporarily out of curves. But Bill Lawry did have a nose, a long nose – which was the foundation of his batting. As a ball left the bowler's hand, the Lawry nose would sniff and register precise length and direction; feet and bat as accessories, a hunched Lawry was now in position to absorb the ball – perhaps to drive or deflect, better still to hook. If the prospect of an innings by Lawry never emptied a cricket ground, it never filled one; generally a crowd was resigned, the fielding side apprehensive, and ten fellow Australians grateful. Around six o'clock on the first day at Lord's in 1961, Statham and Trueman shot out McDonald and Simpson with the score at 6. Harvey joined Lawry – the latter showing distinct signs of bravado: Australia 42 for 2 at the close, Lawry 32. The match was evenly poised.

23 June belonged to Lawry. Statham soon produced a ball which pitched on middle and leg, and was taken by the wicketkeeper in front of first slip standing wide. Trueman twice hit Harvey between wind and water, a reflex action stroke outside the off stump then accounting for that batsman. O'Neill was bowled by Dexter: 88 for 4. Trueman hit Lawry in the stomach; Statham achieved a bouncer threatening at least decapitation, Lawry's response being to fall flat on his back. Once more vertical, the Victorian continued his vigil, a mis-hit landing fifty yards in front of long-leg – therefore no chance. This ball kept low, that one struck Lawry on the shoulder; runs came if slowly. Burge, a great hooker, made 46 before snicking a short-pitched delivery, Davidson did not long survive. 194 for 6. At 3.55 the battered and beleaguered Lawry reached his century; unaffected by the multitude's acclaim, the nose resumed command.

All bad things come to an end (the England point of view is being presented); 40 minutes before the close, Lawry flashed at Dexter. Lord's rose as it had to Hammond in 1938 after his Rolls-Royce innings; this time it saluted an armoured car caught up for more than a day in cross-fire. The main BBC Television News began with Lawry walking off: the caption '130. HE'S OUT!' Lawry had passed into history. Mackay had not. He was loping up and down the wicket on bent knees. His very presence inspired first McKenzie, and then Misson to display strokes of some nobility; the last two Australian partnerships added 102, the bowlers performing like batsmen and Mackay . . . like Mackay. A jab off Lock (no backlift and no follow-through) reached the cover boundary as though jet-propelled. A lead of 134 made Australia virtually safe. McKenzie bowled from the pavilion in the second innings, Pullar and Barrington alone offering much resistance, and finished with 29–13–37–5. A last day target of 69 did not indicate tension, but Statham and Trueman soon had Australia 19 for 4. Burge was almost caught 14 runs later, then took control in his side's 5 wickets victory. Immediately, an array of little men armed with theodolites and spirit-levels invaded the middle; aligning Father Time with the Tavern, they passed on their findings to the Secretary of MCC. '*Not* a ridge but a number of slight depressions.' Batsmen noted the subtle difference as they attended their bruises.

There was nothing subtle about the Headingley pitch a fortnight later. It reminded John Woodcock of *The Times* of 'an unkempt garden path a few days after being sprayed by weedkiller'. He added that it appeared no better than the Old Trafford wicket of 1956 on which Laker had taken his 19 for 90. To the artistic eye, it was a piebald green and white. At 3.30 on the first day dust rose; even so, Australia were 183 for 2 at tea with Harvey and O'Neill well established. Then at 187 Trueman struck: in 6 overs he swept aside Harvey, O'Neill, Simpson, Benaud and Grout for 16 runs. Australia 208 for 9. Davidson and McKenzie took the score to 237, a total England had passed by a single for the loss of four men by the close on the second day. Bowling round the wicket at reduced pace, Davidson cut the ball disconcertingly but Cowdrey, 93, was his master. By 3.50 on the third afternoon – little more than halfway through the five days allotted to the match – Australia were 99 for 2 in their second innings, the lead 37. Harvey again made the pitch seem possible for cricket. However, in the space of twenty-four balls before tea, Trueman bowling off-cutters, dismissed O'Neill, Harvey, Simpson, Benaud and Mackay without conceding a run. In two spells at crucial moments Trueman had bowled 10 overs and taken 10 for 16. With still two days left, England squared the series with an 8-wicket win.

The fourth Test at Old Trafford was a classic encounter. At five o'clock on Saturday England were in a commanding position; at noon on Tuesday England seemed likely to amble home, 4 hours later a new MacLaren was decimating the

Australian attack to the point of ridicule so that only 106 were required for victory – at a run a minute perhaps but with 9 wickets standing. England should win, at worst draw; the best Australia could hope for . . . Australia could *hope* for nothing. But being an Australian, Benaud shrugged his shoulders and said 'Why not? Let's gamble.'

27 July 1961 at Old Trafford saw Lawry and Simpson open for the first time in a Test. The pair put on 8 before Simpson was caught at the wicket off Statham. Harvey, O'Neill and Burge made 45 between them, and a sadly truncated day ended with Australia 124 for 4, Lawry not out 64. The wicket was greasy – a good toss for May to lose. Next morning Statham soon trapped Lawry lbw for 74, and although Booth batted stylishly for 46, Australia's tail was snipped off by Dexter. 190 – a total poor, weak-kneed and surely inadequate. At the close England had reached 187 for 3, May 90. England's captain was denied a Saturday century by 5 runs, but Barrington embarked on one of his sternest endeavours. A 7th-wicket partnership with David Allen added 86 and must have had Benaud worried. Leg-spin! Not his own but Simpson's. England went from 358 for 6 to 367 all out, the lead comfortable. Lawry and Simpson reduced it by 63 before the weekend.

On Monday England sought an early break-through. It was denied them, Lawry and Simpson pushing on to 113, the only century opening of the series. Hours passed: Lawry, missed several times, made 102, Harvey 35 and O'Neill 67; Allen's off-breaks turned, furrowing many an Australian brow. With one day left, 331 for 6 was a non-committal score, although the Australian lead of 154 meant that England were *almost* in a winning position. After fifteen balls from Allen at the start of the final day, they were – Mackay, Benaud and Grout had succumbed to flight. 334 for 9: Australia were only 157 ahead. McKenzie's lunges at Allen betokened distress, both technical and mental. The mantle of Laker had fallen on Allen, whose figures were 37–25–38–4. Then a single found Davidson at the vital end.

Counter-attack! One 6 sailed over cover, another over long-off, two boundaries filled out the over to 20. May whisked Allen off; this was no time to indulge a brutally hard hitter of the ball. Davidson might score another 50 before being ensnared, whereas the introduction of faster bowlers – even if they did not secure the remaining wicket at once – must surely give away fewer runs than Allen. The logic behind the reason was impeccable. But Davidson and McKenzie made their last-wicket stand worth 98 before the latter was bowled by Flavell for 32. In the context of the game, any game, Davidson's not out 77 was tremendous. He had given Australia time to breathe and think. England could no longer jog to victory, England must play strokes to win. The target was 256 at 67 an hour.

Pullar and Subba Row knew what their task consisted of – to blunt the attack and not to get bogged down. So well did they succeed that 40 came in 42 minutes before Pullar was caught off Davidson. Dexter strode in to find McKenzie replaced by Benaud at the Stretford End. The Australian captain was having a bad patch. His last four innings against England had brought him 3 runs, the last three innings in which he had bowled 2 wickets for 188. It was time he earned his keep. Dexter's intention was to deny any addition to Benaud's wickets and to increase as rapidly as possible the number of runs. Without taking a risk, Dexter and Subba Row advanced England's score by 50 in 48 minutes. 90 for 1. Dexter's mood was imperial; Old Trafford beheld 'Lord Edward' at his most disdainful.

Simpson tried his leg-breaks and googlies: 21 runs from 4 overs, most of them to Dexter whose 50 in 63 minutes contained ten boundaries. With a proud man's contumely he drove Mackay far into the crowd, a stroke unfamiliar to the 'Slasher' in all his guises. Hereabouts, between overs, Benaud made a remark of some significance to his vice-captain, Harvey:

'Neill, we're not going to draw this match.'

What did the foolish man expect? With Dexter in his present mood, there wasn't much hope of applying a brake. In any case, the Australian over rate was verging on 20 an hour. 'We're not

RICHIE BENAUD, 1953–63
Last of the great Australian leg-spinners

going to draw this match.' That left two alternatives, one of which did not appeal to Benaud. He must gamble.

It was 3.55 p.m. England were 150 for 1, with Dexter rampaging like a lion; the target 106 at exactly a run a minute. Benaud decided to bowl round the wicket, aiming at the rough outside the leg stump. Of course, a few loose deliveries would hasten Australia's . . . Benaud did not like the word 'defeat'. The scoreboard showed Dexter on 76, the batsman himself an expression of icy contempt. Leg-breaks round the wicket.

The ball pitched precisely, gripped and lifted; Dexter's square cut got a top edge to Grout. 150 for 2.

May played one ball, then swept at the next; he was bowled round his legs. 150 for 3. The silence asked, 'But when did May last try the sweep?'

Close's answer to Benaud was a straight drive for 6, surrounded by numerous bucolic heaves. Behind square-leg O'Neill waited for the inevitable mis-hit. 158 for 4.

Benaud began the last over before tea and at once yorked Subba Row. 163 for 5. Benaud had taken 4 wickets for 9 runs off 19 deliveries. 6 overs ago England had needed 106 for victory, now Australia needed 5 wickets.

Immediately after tea, they got three more: Barrington, who knew something about leg-breaks, falling to Mackay. 171 for 7. Simpson at slip caught both Murray and Allen off Benaud, the latter by one of those prehensile engulfments which made men forget Hammond – except that men who had seen Hammond never forgot him. For the final blow, Benaud tossed the ball to Davidson; with 20 minutes left, the left-hander knocked back Statham's off stump. Australia's victory by 54 runs: England's last 9 wickets had fallen in 115 minutes for 51 runs.

The Ashes were still Australia's (the fifth Test was drawn to give them the series) partly because a gambler had said, 'We're not going to draw this match.' Benaud's 6 for 70 off 32 overs was the ripest haul by an Australian wrist-spinner in England since O'Reilly's 5 for 56 at Headingley in 1938. Doubtless the mentor was satisfied with his pupil.

The Duke and After

Bernard Marmaduke Fitzalan Howard, sixteenth Duke of Norfolk, Earl Marshal of England *and* President of Sussex, was appointed manager of the thirteenth MCC side to tour Australia. Should the natives of Sydney get above themselves, His Grace had only to appear in Garter robes – floppy hat replaced by a Harlequin's cap – to promote a mood of national abstinence.

To the Duke was added 'the Rev', David Sheppard having taken a Sabbatical leave from his East End Mission. The batting looked strong with Barrington, Cowdrey, Dexter, Graveney, Parfitt, Pullar and Sheppard providing both glamour and solidity. The bowling reflected the bias of the English county game – six fast or above medium-pace men being balanced by three off-spinners. Clearly no slow left-hander was thought capable of containing batsmen in the early stages of a match, or of worrying them as pitches wore. In the event neither side was able to dominate the other, and so it went on throughout the sixties. In Benaud's two victorious series recently concluded, seven of ten Tests had produced a decisive result. Of twenty Tests played between 1962–3 and 1968, again seven were finished – a lower ratio not altogether due to weather. Individual performances tended to eclipse collective achievements. A new breed of great Test batsmen had arisen.

We cherish what we know; today, let alone tomorrow, can never rival yesterday. Nostalgia is most precious. The names of Compton, Cowdrey, Dexter, Graveney and May echo down the years; Victor Trumper, we may be sure, would have watched them all with approval. But when restrictive practices – in-slant bowling and defensive field placings – mark an age, a different temperament asserts itself. 'Accumulators' emerge, make runs, ensure victory – and are acclaimed. The story of the Ashes is concerned with the winning and *saving* of matches. Does elegance count when Australia has to be frustrated? No, men look for the broad bottom and guts of Maurice Leyland. Does an ability to make some Cardus babble of lyric poets and Mozart impress ruthless Australians when they are on the kill? It does not. A house in danger in the sixties and later looked to its insurance policy, especially the small print. Were Barrington, Boycott and John Edrich mentioned?

Pundits and commentators who show displeasure when England are not (a) winning, and (b) playing strokes as frozen in the photographs of G. W. Beldham, and analysed by C. B. Fry, are urged to ponder these figures relating to Tests in Australia:

Trumper	38 innings against England	average 35
Compton ⎫		
Cowdrey ⎪		
Dexter ⎬	124 innings against Australia	average 35
Graveney ⎪		
May ⎭		
Barrington ⎫		
Boycott ⎬	63 innings against Australia	average 53
J. H. Edrich ⎭		

That, in brief, is the lesson of England-Australia Tests in the sixties and later. The pundit or commentator willing to see England lose each game in a series by one run, *providing the stroke-makers delight him first*, is yet to be found. Generously we point out that three artist-batsmen – Hobbs, Hammond and Hutton – played one hundred and eight Test innings in Australia and averaged 57. But that was in the days before restrictive practices took over.

In 1962 MCC flew to Aden where they boarded the *Canberra*, the Duke joining them at Colombo. The first Test was drawn after the captains, Benaud and Dexter, had each displayed personal prowess. Dexter's second innings of 99 in 165 minutes inflicted feelings of inferiority on Australia; here was a batsman who would dictate. He did again at Melbourne where Australia meandered to 316 and then endured a Dexter-Cowdrey 3rd-wicket partnership of 175 made at 54 runs an hour. Cowdrey's 113 was both snug and opulent. Davidson restricted England's lead to 15 before Trueman set about Australia. Booth made his second hundred of the series, but 234 did not seem a large target for England. Sheppard, a couple of missed catches his sole contribution to the game so far ('It's a pity Reverend don't put his hands together more often in t'field,' opined F. S. Trueman, master of out-swing and repartee), had reached 113 when, with the scores level, he made a stroke to waft himself down the wicket on the wings of angels, and England to victory. Sheppard run out 113.

England's lead lasted one match. Discovering the best way to get themselves out on a slow Sydney pitch of uneven bounce was to miscue long hops, they obliged for 279. At 174 for 1, Australia exuded confidence only to find the professorial off-spin and drift-away of Titmus suddenly sinister. Harvey, Simpson, O'Neill and Booth left as the score crept to 212; an Australian total of 319 (Titmus so happy with 37–14–79–7) meant that at 2.40 on the third day England could begin again on more or less level terms. Begin – not continue: Davidson was at his best. 37 for 4 at tea, and 86 for 6 at the close, England lost by 8 wickets. The last two Tests were drawn, leaving Australia with the Ashes and three gaping wounds caused by the retirement of Harvey, Benaud and Davidson. No left-hand batsman has given more pleasure than Harvey. If he flirted outside the off stump, six hundreds against England told of his pedigree; at his best 'brilliant' was too meagre a word to describe him. Davidson was massive, both in build and in achievement: 750 runs and 84 wickets. Harvey and Benaud were superb fieldsmen, Davidson appeared the most wonderful of the three. Benaud's 83 wickets against England marked the end of an Australian tradition which had started with Hordern – that of the googly deceivers. Benaud also ranks as a very great captain.

1962–3 made to shed a fourth Australian tear, then hesitated with the drop 'twixt eye and cheek. Had he really existed? How many hours had he spent at the nets practising his letting-the-ball-go-by-outside-the-off-stump stroke? How many times had he squirted the ball past fieldsmen when they were sure his backlift promised an anaesthetic dab? Was he in his own imagination, when the wicketkeeper stood back, a worthy substitute for Lindwall? Certainly in England he swung the ball prodigiously. He had helped discreetly to win Tests and, most vexingly, to save them. He was unique. As 'Slasher' Mackay loped off the field for the last time, shares in Australian chewing gum fell sharply.

Another Queenslander, Peter Burge, made sure that Australia would retain the Ashes in 1964, a miserable summer when balls bowled seemed likely to be overtaken by millimetres of rain fallen. The first two Tests produced 1,207 runs for 53 wickets with never a result in sight, the fourth at Old Trafford 1,271 for 18 wickets, and the fifth 942 for 24 wickets. The fourth, if inevitable, was not a good advertisement for the existence of Ashes; finding himself one-up with two to play, Bobby Simpson did what any other captain would have done in the circumstances – played safe. Australia batted until 12.30 on the third day for 656 for 8 (Lawry run out 106, Simpson 311 in 12 hours 40 minutes, Booth 98), to which England replied with 611 (Dexter 174, Barrington 256). For England Tom Cartwright bowled 77 overs, for Australia McKenzie 60, Hawke 63 and Veivers 95. All the while Dexter cursed himself for the outcome of the third Test which *might* have been different.

At Headingley England had grafted their way to 268 – an odd statement in view of exciting stroke-play by Dexter and Parks, yet true – Australia being 95 for 1 some 10 minutes before lunch on the second day. Enter Titmus: bowling unchanged until half an hour after tea, he reduced Australia to 187 for 7, his own figures 29–17–27–3. At the other end the slow left-hand Gifford slid to the wicket with restrictive aim and effect. Burge on 38 looked safe if musclebound, a heavyweight contender anxious for his opponent to trade blows but uneasy against a middleweight all head and elbows, Titmus. Whereupon Dexter took the new ball, the obvious way to brush aside the Australian tail-enders Hawke, Grout and Corling.

However, Dexter's shock troops, Trueman and Flavell, seemed under the rhythmic spell cast by Titmus and Gifford, obliging with many a long-hop of genial pace. Burge soon believed his eyes, unlocked his square-cut and hook, indulging in assault and battery. Hawke took the hint, 7 overs with the new ball costing 42 runs; 283 for 8 at the close, Australia continued next day to 389. A hearty deficit instead of a handy lead shook England. Only Barrington made runs in the England second innings, Australia winning by 7 wickets. Burge's 160 was the masterpiece of his career; he, alone, had saved his side from possible defeat, then carried it to a likely victory. His companions could not – and did not – let him down. Since regaining the Ashes on 5 February 1959, Australia had held them through three series and fourteen Tests. Englishmen felt tetchy: 'How long, O Lord, how long?'

Not for a while. MCC in 1965–6 had a Colonel (S. C. Griffith) in place of a Duke as manager, 'Lord Edward' Dexter giving way to a Smith (M. J. K.). In two innings Boycott was England's first change bowler, in the fifth Test the side's over rate was 12 an hour. It was not a series for bowlers – England's most prolific wicket-taker I. J. Jones with 15 at 35, Australia's Hawke with 16 at 26. Meanwhile batsmen gorged themselves: Barrington, Titmus, Cowdrey, Parks, Edrich, Boycott and Barber all averaging over 40, Simpson, Lawry, Cowper and Walters from 88 to 68. England won the third Test by an innings thanks mainly to a glorious 185 in under 5 hours by Barber, Australia the fourth also by an innings after McKenzie had 6 for 48 and Simpson and Lawry opened with 244 *at almost a run a minute*. In the last match Cowper made 307, Lawry increased his aggregate to 592 compiled – so men say, for men work these things out – at 21 runs an hour, and Barrington dashed to 102 from 122 balls. 1965–6 saw England led by Lawry's nose: 'How long, O lord, how long?'

Bill Lawry's twenty-fourth Australians deserved to retain the Ashes because of two strokes played by the captain on the first day of the first Test. Both were off Pocock, both went for 6. England did not recover from this gesture, batted badly and lost the match. However, the series was squared at the Oval where hundreds by Edrich and d'Oliveira were followed by a seven and a half hours' 135 by Lawry. Needing 352 to win, Australia was almost saved by rain; the mopping up was done most effectively – by numerous citizens of south London armed with brooms and blankets, and by Underwood with the ball. Between-whiles the other Tests had their moments: Milburn (tragically to lose the sight of an eye a year later) set Lord's alight with the power of his hooks and drives in 83, after which David Brown and Knight bowled Australia out for 78; at Edgbaston Cowdrey made 104 in his one hundredth Test, at Headingley Ian Chappell suggested a young man with a future. The Australian fielding, with Sheahan oustanding, never failed to impress, though Simpson's retirement did finally convince some Englishmen that he was greater than Hammond.

The 'swinging sixties' had small influence on England-Australia Tests; a dynamic force was sought by Lord's. Why not a poet? The beard owned by Alfred, Lord Tennyson was superior to that of W. G., Byron (a poor cricketer indeed but a master of language) had a profile more thrilling than Dexter's. Yes, Lord's would send a poet to Australia in 1970–1. Was the one they had in mind willing to go? After communion with his Muse, John Augustine Snow was quite willing.

CHAPTER ELEVEN

A Captain's Notebook 1970–1

Who will lead MCC in Australia? That's the talking point in mid-summer 1970. 'Reason points to Cowdrey,' writes John Woodcock. 'But I expect Illingworth to be given the job.'

22 July. What is the opposite of a shop steward? Member of the board? Company director? After I've been appointed for Australia, Woodcock feels I am a 'shop steward rather than a cavalier'. Who is, or was, a Test cavalier captain? Presumably Percy Chapman who ground Australia into the dust at Brisbane in 1928. Perhaps Gary Sobers at Trinidad in 1967–8 when he declared and set England 215 in 165 minutes. West Indies were without Hall in that match, Griffith was unable to bowl – England won with 3 minutes to spare. Gary wasn't lynched by home supporters but he might well have been.

Give me a team chosen from the best English batsmen of the present day *and* from the Rest of the World side we're playing (Barry Richards, Kanhai, Sobers, Clive Lloyd and Graeme Pollock), then put us against Wagga Wagga on an off day – and I promise to be the best cavalier captain in history. Which of the great Australian captains – Noble, Armstrong, Bradman, Benaud – was a cavalier? I am also 'a sergeant-major rather than a brigadier'; Colin Cowdrey is apt to be 'defensive'.

How many captains have England had in the past five years? 1966 Cowdrey for three Tests, Mike Smith and Brian Close one each; 1967 Close for six; then he lost the captaincy after 'time-wasting' in a county match (he refused to apologize) and Cowdrey took MCC to West Indies in 1967–8. He had the job again in 1968 except for one Test when Tom Graveney took

217

over. Colin would surely have been in charge in 1969 had he not snapped an Achilles tendon early in the season when playing in a Sunday slog game. I was then given the job.

Mention of Brian Close and 'time-wasting' brings to mind the case of the Notts ('amateur') captain, George Heane, in 1936. With 5 minutes of extra-time left, Sussex went in needing 9 to win. 1 over produced 7 runs. Slight rain began to fall. Heane appealed to the umpires, and led his team off the field. Sussex threatened to cancel fixtures with Notts, whose Committee said they did not uphold the action taken but expressed their confidence in Heane as captain. Was George Heane a shop steward for insisting on keeping his men dry?

1970–1 will be Colin Cowdrey's fifth tour of Australia – his fourth as vice-captain. He is thinking the matter over.

Notice the first-class batting averages: six of the top seven places held by Sobers, Lloyd, Kanhai, Basil d'Oliveira, Majid and Glenn Turner. Fair comment on 'English' cricket.

September – end of season. What are England's chances in Australia? Very good. Two reasons: we have done well *v* Rest of the World. Losing by four-one *but* almost winning at Headingley and almost drawing at Edgbaston. In the Oval game Mike Procter came in at No. 8! The other reason why our chances are very good is that a year ago in South Africa Bill Lawry's men were thrashed four-nothing, crumbling before the fast bowling of Procter and Peter Pollock. (The Australians had reached South Africa after a lengthy tour of India, moving from slow to fast pitches – even so.) We hope to win by fast bowling.

It used to be easy to pick bowlers for Australian tours. In 1928–9 Chapman's party had four of the top six bowlers in the averages (Lancashire's Macdonald was, of course, Australian and so ineligible), in 1932–3 Jardine had five of the top six, in 1954–5 Hutton six of the top ten.

JOKE! The man who will regain the Ashes finished the English season about fiftieth in the averages. Larwood, Voce, Trueman and Statham never did that. But John Snow is an odd bird. Like all of us since 1963, he is not a 'professional' or 'amateur', just a 'cricketer' who is paid for playing the game. Had he been at his peak in the thirties, I fancy John would have worked as a schoolmaster or in the City, then told some county secretary he was available for matches in August. Cricket seven days a week will never motivate John Snow. The sight of green caps at the other end will. A man has his pride.

The better and faster John bowls, the more the Aussies will find excuses. Fast bowling always produces alibis from the other side. Slow bowling on a good pitch can't!

What is a bouncer? Everyone knows. Do they? In the sense of causing a false stroke, yes. Not in the sense of intimidating a batsman. Imagine a batting order like Herbert Sutcliffe, Milburn, McCabe, Pat Hendren, Peter Burge and Sobers – all at their peak. A succession of short-pitched balls might get them out but I fancy one or two of them would get a lot of runs first. They were all great hookers. So a bouncer is intimidatory when bowled at a specialist batsman who can't hook. Or won't. I don't recall that Fred Trueman bowled many bouncers at Sobers!

For the first time since 'Plum' Warner's tour of 1911–12, MCC's tour will start at Adelaide and not at Perth. In 1911–12 Barnes and Frank Foster did the trick. Good omen?

I'm thirty-eight – if I don't know the game of cricket now I never shall. I know what I can do, and what I can't do, with bat and ball. No excuses if we fail.

ASSETS:

(i) Pity cricket wasn't devised so that two wicketkeepers are required – one at either end – because we have the best pair of keepers ever to tour with the same side. Alan Knott and Bob Taylor – both great.

(ii) Geoff Boycott and John Edrich! Expect Brian Luckhurst to do well, also Basil d'Oliveira.

(iii) Snow and Alan Ward to open bowling, Peter Lever and Ken Shuttleworth in support.

(iv) Derek Underwood on Australian pitches?

2 November. Match *v* South Australia ends with 1,335 runs scored for 22 wickets. Slow pitch, MCC 451 for 9 declared – Boycott 173 (he'll want more practice after that), Edrich, Keith Fletcher and John Hampshire bat nicely. Then South Australia get 649 for 9! Both Chappells make runs, though Ian is apt to slash at fast rising balls outside the off stump; Barry Richards, on an Australian dollar a run, 224 and reminds Clarrie Grimmett of McCabe. Pleasant thought – Richards-McCabe at one end, the Don at t'other. Have it confirmed Barry R. is not qualified to play for Australia. Tell press, especially English, that's a joke.

9 November. Lose to Victoria by 6 wickets, no more than we deserve. 'Froggy' Thomson – Mike Procter-ish sort of action – shot us out for 142 after Bill Lawry put us in. Three of 'Froggy's' first four balls to me were short-pitched, second hit my shoulder. Umpire Figgis said 'Oy!' in Australian, Lawry asked why. A second innings by Colin C. took over 5 hours – way below his old form.

16 November. DEPRESSION. Drawn game with NSW, Colin in charge while I look on. Doug Walters double hundred, usual mixture of brilliance and faulty technique; wonderful to watch if you're not fielding side. Then O'Keefe tied us in knots with leg-spin – 6 for 69. We follow on and make 325 for 1, Boycott and Luckhurst centuries.

Depression caused by foot injury to Alan Ward who will return home. Snow-Ward opening attack now a dream. Replacement will be Bob Willis, twenty-one and not yet capped by Surrey. A fine goalkeeper from what I hear. What I want is some Stanley Matthews who can bowl like Tyson. The last England captain to regain the Ashes in Australia was Jardine – and look at his bowlers!

2 December. Five days ago I should have said, 'Damn Brisbane!' On the first morning of the first Test we had Keith Stackpole run out for 18, but Umpire Rowan said not. Stackpole 207. Next day Australia were 418 for 3; then Redpath, Sheahan and Walters went to Underwood in seven balls, Snow got fierce, and Australia were out for 433. John's 6 for 114 a fine piece of bowling. We got our heads down after this and made 464. The Australian second innings was Lawry – 84 in five and a half hours. To put them out for 214 (leaving us 184 to win if there'd been time) was something to cheer. Puzzle: Underwood 1 for 23 off 20 overs, Illingworth 1 for 19 off 18. We can't both have been bowling at Lawry. Or have we found a way to contain Aussie batsmen?

Try to picture John Snow in his school days at Christ's Hospital, wearing long blue garment and *yellow* socks. Can't. What did he have underneath?

16 December. For the first Test ever at Perth, the WACA produced an easy-paced pitch, the Australian Selectors settled on three regular bowlers (McKenzie, 'Froggy' T. and Gleeson), and Bill Lawry put us in! 257 for 2 at the close was satisfactory – Luckhurst 131 outscoring Geoff B. 70. Opening stand of 171. Next day John Edrich ran himself out and we closed for 397. Garth McKenzie bowled well but we should have got many more. Anyway on the third day Australia were 107 for 5 when Greg Chappell joined Redpath. We kept Greg down to 1 run in 40 minutes, let him know what Test cricket is all about. 42 at tea, he went to his hundred in about an hour. Lovely method – if he's not already a great batsman, it won't be long before he is. Fancy Yorkshire would prefer brother Ian!

John Edrich's not out 115 saved us when we were in a sticky position in the second innings – great Test match batsman. Make token declaration setting Australia 245 in 145 minutes. Snow and Lever got three out for 40; Lawry and Redpath then played out time. Should we have dropped Underwood for this game? Must think about it.

17 December. Still thinking about it, and other things, on the flight to Adelaide when we read in the evening papers that David Clark, our manager, has been talking to the Australian press. Apparently both teams have been thinking too defensively. Asked if he'd prefer to see the next four Tests drawn, or for

Australia to win them 3–1, he replied 'I'd rather see four results.'

Immediate response of team – outrage. As the manager is part of England, not wise to be drawn by the press in this way. I suppose you could say that two easy-paced pitches have guaranteed two draws; put another way, neither side is *collectively* strong enough in bowling to make a result likely. Hutton's bowlers of 1954–5 might have done, so Bradman's of 1946–7 but even they had to be content with a draw at Adelaide.

Anyway, is a cricket match left unfinished necessarily dull? Because if so, the only way to make sure you get a result is to have play-to-a-finish matches. Pity David Clark spoke.

2 January 1971. More trouble. This is the third day of the Melbourne Test – the third blank day, and the ground fit for water polo. The Australian Board, led by the Don, then consulted Sir Cyril Hawker, president of MCC and therefore chairman of the Cricket Council (here for business and pleasure), Gubby Allen, the vice-chairman, and David Clark, and suggested another Test in place of the return game with Victoria at Melbourne in between the scheduled fourth and fifth Tests. I didn't like the idea and said so – some of the players very much against it. And as the Aussies will be paid extra, how about the cash?

I've worked out that if the revised tour goes according to plan – if all matches go the distance – we shall now have twenty-eight days of cricket, and sixteen off, in the space of six weeks and two days. Including *four* Tests! Point is not so much the cricket as the travel: counting 5 January when we have a 40 overs' slog at Melbourne, we shall be playing at Melbourne, Wagga Wagga, Sydney, Newcastle, Melbourne, Adelaide, Canberra, Sydney, Parkes and Sydney. Ten grounds in forty-four days. Not the way to run a tour. What happens if there's an airlines' strike? Walk, I suppose.

9 January. Perfect Sydney morning, England 100 for none at lunch in fourth Test. Geoffrey B. 64, never seen him bat better. Beautiful strokes. Can't say I've often seen him get out caught on boundary hooking a long-hop which he did when 77. Still we were 200 for 2 and happy. Then in 8 overs after tea Ashley Mallett took 3 for 6 – very fine off-spinning. We end the day 267 for 7, big disappointment considering that start. Mallett runs through on a line close to the stumps – useful for Underwood in fourth innings?

12 January. Now we are happy, more or less, at the close of the third day – 274 ahead with 7 second-innings wickets in hand. Team effort. On Sunday morning we pushed on to 332 – the fast bowlers Snow, Lever and paleface Willis making 88 between them. To my surprise, Lawry took Ian Chappell in with him; remembering Ian's fondness for open-blade slash to off-side bouncers, I posted a fly-slip some twenty-five to thirty yards in from the fence. It worked! Trouble is I don't suppose Chappell, I. M. will ever fall for that one again. But after we'd got rid of the openers, our slip catching grew constipated; Redpath and Walters settled in for a while so that Aussies closed 189 for 4. Derek Underwood was only turning the odd one but that was enough, he put fear and desperation into the batsmen. Today we put Australia out for 236 (Underwood 4 for 66), and are now 178 for 3. Apart from running out Edrich, Geoffrey had been perfection itself – a brick wall sprouting strokes. Basil d'Oliveira equally admirable; just to think I had a bit of a fight to get him included in the party.

13 January. Very happy! No more or less about it (unless rain comes which seems unlikely). This morning I told Geoffrey to stay put and increase our lead. With 12 hours left, I suppose he'd have liked to bat until halfway through the last day, giving us 3 hours to bowl out Australia with fast shooters or hope they'd all run themselves out. Dolly went soon after play began – 181 for 4 – then I settled in and scored faster than my partner. Interesting to study the Boycott technique at close quarters; decide the best way to get him out would be some Arthur Mailey-ish oddments – double bouncer followed by a full-toss. Geoffrey would regard this as an affront to his dignity and probably miscue. In 2 hours before lunch we increased England's lead to 350 with 10 hours left. When to declare? A good declaration is one which gives *you* every chance to get the other side out while *appearing* to give the opposition a chance. So we went on for 40 minutes, adding 65.

Australia 416 to win in 9 hours or so, with some dusty spots at one end. Bill Lawry had already told the press there was no way Australia could win (that was at start of play), 47 an hour for a day and a half. Well, if five batsmen each played the innings of a life-time there was – assuming we missed all our catches and if all our bowlers sent down rubbish. Enter John Snow. His first ball to Ian Chappell lifted viciously from a length: 1 for 1. Don't see how any batsman could have avoided playing such a brute of a ball with the edge. Then he had everyone apprehensive. He bowled as straight as Brian Statham, on a good length, and cutting the ball away. He was *very* fast – the only way of telling if Tyson was faster in 1954–5 would have been to measure the distance the respective slips stood back. Bad light stopped play an hour early with Australia 64 for 4, Lawry still there with 24.

14 January. Task completed in first over after lunch, England by 299 runs. Lawry took out his bat for 60. Most memorable of course the bowling of Snow, 5 for 20 off 8 overs, giving him an innings of 7 for 40. One word to describe him – SUPERB! Two remarkable catches close in: by Peter Lever left-handed at full stretch (and Bobby Simpson would have taken this one with both hands), the other by Bob Willis with two hands – and Simpson wouldn't have taken this because he's not 6 ft 5 ins tall! Wonder how Corinthian-Casuals are progressing without Bob in goal? McKenzie hit in face by good length ball. Bad.

One-up with three to play. Hope to win the toss three times, score 600 and then sit back – waiting for manager to react with interview.

21 January. Awful day to start fifth Test at Melbourne. Colin Cowdrey, back in the side after being omitted at Sydney, dropped Ian Chappell before he had scored – this was off Snow, then at 14 off Dolly. Ian went on to make 111 – at 100 an invading mob stole his cap and Colin's sun-hat as well as a stump. At least they didn't leave a bomb on the pitch.

26 January. Inevitably, the game was drawn. I stopped counting when our missed catches reached eight in Australia's first innings of 493 for 9, at which point Lawry declared with Rod Marsh on 92! (Bill won't be welcome next time he visits Perth.) Geoffrey failed for once, so did John Edrich; but a fine hundred by Brian Luckhurst – most of it made with a broken finger caused by 'Froggy' T. – and another by Dolly put things right. Dolly they wished to omit from party; never forget that. 'Froggy' enjoyed himself bowling bouncers at Luckhurst and Cowdrey but Umpire Rowan seemed not to object. He even bowled a couple at John Snow, not a very sensible thing to do. Anyway, when Australia went in a second time – and crawled though one match down – John pitched short at Doug Walters. Doug's method of playing the short stuff is to go to earth with his bat stuck up like a periscope. What fast bowler could resist the invitation? Still, Umpire O'Connell spoke warning words. I ran over and pointed out that John was bowling fewer bouncers than 'Froggy' had in one over at us. Well, an umpire can object to a certain number of short-pitched balls per over – we're agreed on that. But he must apply his objections impartially to both teams. I met with a frosty response. Proving a Snow bouncer is better than a Thomson one?

Lawry declared setting us 271 to win in 4 hours. Boycott and Edrich spent the last 40 minutes batting to a background of boos, hand-clapping and the banging of empty beer cans. The umpires conferred. If the mob had again invaded the field, I'm sure Geoffrey would have defended *his* cap to the death. Whose death? Ah!

29 January. Ridiculous! 72 hours ago we finished the fifth Test at Melbourne, now we've completed the first day of the sixth Test at Adelaide. Happily (a) we're not caught up in an Adelaide heat-wave and (b) we're batting first – 276 for 2 at close. And there was the 'Boycott Incident'. At 107, with Geoffrey on 58

(John Edrich had opened with him in Luckhurst's absence), a fine throw from Ian Chappell at mid-wicket hit the stumps towards which G was running. Facts: G did not appear to be hurrying, and he did not have his bat down. Australian appeal, brief pause from Umpire O'Connell – out! It was a close thing either way. However, G cast his bat aside and glowered; Greg Chappell returned bat to its owner and pointed the way to the pavilion. Muggins – me – now concocting an apology.

1 February. An hour from the close this evening we put Australia out for 235, exactly that number of runs behind us on the first innings. I decided NOT to enforce the follow-on. Ammunition for the pundits and the press! Reasons: I consulted the England players, particularly the fast bowlers Snow, Lever and Willis. They agreed with me. This Adelaide strip is getting easier as the game progresses, therefore the possibility of a strong Australian recovery were I to make them follow-on. We're one-up in the series because we're the better side (doesn't always show in the slip fielding). But should Australia set us an awkward target here – and should the wicket be wearing – things might turn out unpleasant. I have a higher opinion of John Gleeson than most people; what if he stopped bowling the odd bad ball and had a purple patch? It's happened before. In a nut-shell: we've bowled well enough to make Australia bat badly more than once. The law of averages suggests they may continue to bat badly – but make a lot of runs.

3 February. Since I didn't enforce the follow-on, we've made 233 for 4, and Australia 328 for 3. Total 561 for 7! The Adelaide wicket was dead; so should I be in the eyes of the English press if we'd come a cropper! All to play for in the seventh Test at Sydney where (I trust) eleven fit Englishmen will beat the best the Aussies can put against us. Western Australian fast bowler Dennis Lillee sprayed the new ball in our first innings at Adelaide, later picked up 5 wickets. Good action. Fast.

8 February. Something had to happen. It has. Today at Sydney we played a limited-over farce on a damp pitch. A ball from McKenzie lifted from a length and struck Geoffrey Boycott's left forearm. Broken. In ten Test innings on this tour G's averaged 93. Irreplaceable.

We were playing Western Australia, the champions out here in limited-over stuff. Who cares?

Funny world. Australia have not only taken the captaincy from Bill Lawry and given it to Ian Chappell, they've dropped him from the side. I ask how many Australians have played a comparable number of innings with a superior average. The answer is three – Arthur Morris, Bob Simpson and, of course, Bradman. If I were a spectator I wouldn't pay to watch Bill Lawry, but if I were picking an Australian Test team . . . For the past ten years he's been the foundation of their batting. Chosen in his place Ken Eastwood, another Victorian – didn't play against us earlier in tour. We enjoy the prospect of *not* bowling at Lawry.

11 February. Tomorrow's pitch is bound to help bowlers. Glad McKenzie is back home in Perth.

12 February. Seventh and final Test. A good toss to win. Ian Chappell won it – and put us in. (We're playing six bowlers, including Dolly and self.) Lillee and the left-arm Dell made the ball lift. John Edrich, the man the Aussies most wanted to get rid of, was caught at third slip off Dell for 30. Ian C. pressured us with close fields until I broke them up a bit. O'Keefe's wrist-spin was given a three-man leg-trap and a slip; wrist-spin at the other end from Jenner, the pair took 6 for 90. I top-scored with 42, our total 184. Ian C. certainly an aggressive captain. But was he lucky – is he lucky? If Colin had caught him for nil in the fifth Test (when he went on to make 111), his run would have been 17, 12, 0 and 0. Possibly would have been dropped – not on merit for he's a good bat, but because selectors do funny things. In which case the Australian captaincy for Redpath?

I read somewhere once that at Trent Bridge in 1948 Bradman was not keen to have too long batting on the first day after England had collapsed early, so used more friendly bowlers. Sounds the sort of thing Bradman would have thought of. From the Australian point of view, Ian C. might have tried to keep us in this evening. As it was, we had time to take 2 Aussie wickets – Eastwood caught low down on the leg side off Peter Lever (any other keeper, a wonderful catch; for Knott routine. I doubt if anyone could be more brilliant than Knottie has been in this series), and Stackpole bowled by Snow. A couple of balls seaming away from the off stump, then an incutter that hit the off stump. Lovely bowling! Australia 13 for 2 at the close.

13 February. Oh dear! Oh dear! Not a day I want to live through again. Why can't Dougie Walters *hook* John Snow? But first things first. Early in the day Rod Marsh played a nice leg glance for 4 off Lever, except it wasn't 4 but out. Our goalkeeper Willis launched himself into space (bet he grew six inches during the night) and caught a blinder. Not content with that, Bob then bowled Ian C. Australia 66 for 4. After lunch I set Snow and Lever at Redpath and Walters. Redders doesn't like the ball whistling past him but he plays the short stuff well, sways out of its path. But Doug either goes to ground or backs away aiming square-cuts. Bradman's 'harpoon' shot to Larwood? Neither Doug nor anyone else is Bradman. Luck was Walters's way, so I took Snow off – whereupon we missed Doug off Underwood, then off Willis. Still he was stumped off Derek for 42, who caught and bowled Redpath for 59. O'Keefe was caught behind off me. Australia 178 for 7, Greg Chappell left with three bowlers to support him.

In the 66th over of the innings I brought Snow back to take the new ball. Jenner faced the first ball of his second over, it rose to the batsman's ribs and he edged it away for a single. Greg C. faced the next four balls, then Jenner again. The sixth ball – *short* – he evaded. If I could, as it were, re-play what now happened, I most certainly would. I brought over Willis from mid-off to the on side, so that Snow's field consisted of Underwood at long-leg, Hampshire at backward short-leg, myself short-leg, and Willis mid-on. Ideally, this was perhaps the time for a Snow yorker; instead he bowled one short of a length which cut in. Jenner ducked into it and was hit on the left side of the head. As Frank Tyson did to Lindwall in 1954–5.

The crowd erupted. We helped Jenner to his feet, eventually the Australian masseur and Peter Lever helped him walk from the field. Dennis Lillee came in. As Snow began to move back to his bowling mark, Umpire Rowan said something to him. John took no notice. Maybe he should have. Rowan said something else. Again no response from John. Rowan turned to Umpire Brooks at square-leg and raised one finger. I rushed to the bowler's end and asked what was going on. 'I'm giving the bowler a first warning,' said Rowan. I emphasized it was unfair to warn a man for one bouncer in an over. And I questioned Rowan's interpretation of the row.

Worse to come. As Snow ran up to complete his over – to Lillee – the Hill started hooting. We then had drinks; as we did, some cans were thrown on to the field at the north-east corner of the ground. The 'little Hill' area. I sat down while an attendant shoved the rubbish in the gutter at the foot of the fence. I told John Snow to go to third man rather than to long-leg but he went to his normal position. There were shouts, John replied and started to fraternize. Not sensible! A drunk grabbed him by the shirt, other people pulled the drunk away, and John walked in fifteen yards from the boundary. More cans were hurled, Bob Willis rushed down as reinforcement; still more cans. I ran down, pulled Snow in field, then a couple of bottles flew past our heads.

I waved to the England players and we left the field. When bottles hit a man, they make a mess. Before long the umpires came into our room. Rowan asked me if my side was going back or if we were forfeiting the match. I replied I had a duty to safeguard my players. First thing was to clear the ground of cans and bottles. A loudspeaker announcement informed the crowd the ground would be cleared and play resumed. 7 minutes after England had left the field,* they returned.

---

* Writing in *Wisden* a few years later, Richie Benaud – a former captain of New South Wales and Australia – said that in similar circumstances he would have done the same.

7 minutes wasted out of 30 hours, no one hurt. Alternative? I can think of one, not likely to be approved by MCC. If I'd had a Colin Bland in the side, I could have ordered him to throw the bottles back where they came from, aiming at the heads of offenders. Too much the reaction of a shop steward.

We now returned to a game of cricket. Greg Chappell batted very well till the close when Australia were 235 for 7, a lead of 51.

14 February. We were applauded when we took the field this morning. Jenner came in at Lillee's dismissal and carried his runs to 30, Greg C. last out for 65. Australia 264, a lead of 80. We had to get a good start, and Brian Luckhurst (very good) and John Edrich obliged with 94. We didn't capitalize on that, due partly to Ian C.'s low cunning. Just before tea he put Eastwood on; the hand suggested George Tribe, the length me bowling left-arm when blindfold. Full-tosses mostly. Somehow Keith Fletcher managed to get himself caught. I hope Ian C. was ashamed of himself! John Hampshire was hitting the ball well when miraculously caught by Ian running back from slip. I joined Basil d'Oliveira at 165 for 4, only 85 ahead. We added 64 before the close, Dolly 37 not out and me 25. Lillee and Dell with the new ball were painful, not to watch but to play. Dell hit me mid-ships two or three times, then on the left knee. Moral: Don't get hit on the knee by a sixteen-stone giant.

16 February. Spent yesterday having my knee repaired, this afternoon wondering whether I should cry. Come to that in a minute. Dolly went for 47, and I for 29, before a spot of batsmanship by Snow and Lever took us to 302 – Australia needing 223 to win. Ian Chappell asked for the light hand-roller. Drama at once. Snow yorked Eastwood: 0 for 1. Then, in Peter Lever's second over, Stackpole hooked high to John at long-leg – a swirling catch. John misjudged the flight, came in, then went back – and jammed his right hand between the pickets. Little finger torn and dislocated. The bowler we relied on off to hospital and out of the game.

But in Lever's next over a perfect outswinger touched Ian Chappell's bat. 22 for 2. Stackpole clearly the danger man because he's always likely to smash any ball just the slightest bit off-line or over/under-pitched. Thought I'd better have a go. It worked. At 71 Redpath was neatly taken at backward short-leg by John Hampshire. For Doug Walters I baited a trap with Dolly deep down the gully. Bob Willis bowled one to slash, Doug obliged – Dolly didn't have to move. 82 for 4. Stackpole joined by Greg Chappell: vital stage of the innings. Men to come can bat, some of them, but these the last two specialists. At 96 Stackpole tried to sweep me and was bowled for 67, the highest score in the match – so far. It had better be, or we shall lose! I'm patted on the back. Felt pleased. Now Greg Chappell and Marsh. MIRACLE! At 103 for 5 Marsh gave a very easy off-side stumping chance. Our genius missed. Knott missed. Knott missed a chance. Go on repeating this.

The bowler me. Australia 123 for 5 at the close, exactly 100 short.

17 February. Just after 12.30 we did it. By 62 runs. Proud to say I made the break-through when Greg came out after me only to miss the out-floater. Dolly and Derek Underwood got two each. At the end John Hampshire and John Edrich hoisted me, strong men both.

As we were made presentations in front of the pavilion, I saw the greatest cause for pride – Geoffrey Boycott with left arm in sling, John Snow with right likewise. We're the first side since Jardine's in 1932–3 to regain the Ashes in Australia, the only one since time-limit 30-hour Tests began in 1946–7 to prevent Australia winning at least one game in a rubber. Someone points out it's twelve years and twelve days since Richie Benaud grabbed the Urn back. Too long. Now the fight begins to keep it.

Long after that tour I am tempted to write down two representative sides chosen from men I played with or against during my years in first-class cricket, 1951–78. Tactfully, I give twelve names for each side – to be selected from. On Australian pitches:

ENGLAND	AUSTRALIA
Peter May (captain)	Richie Benaud (captain)
Len Hutton	Bobby Simpson
Geoff Boycott	Bill Lawry
Denis Compton	Neil Harvey
Ted Dexter	Greg Chappell
Ken Barrington	Keith Miller
Alan Knott	Ian Chappell
John Wardle	Alan Davidson
Fred Trueman	Rod Marsh
Frank Tyson	Ray Lindwall
Brian Statham	Dennis Lillee
Bob Appleyard	John Gleeson

For a game to be played in England I would substitute Alec Bedser and Tony Lock for Tyson and Wardle, Ashley Mallett for Benaud – Ian Chappell becoming captain of Australia.

Could I be more controversial?

CHAPTER TWELVE

Then and Now

In 1895 W. G. Grace performed the then unheard-of feat of scoring 1,000 first-class runs in May. His rewards were a national testimonial promoted by the *Daily Telegraph*, a Grace Fund collected by *The Sportsman*, and a Gloucestershire county fund. In due course the Doctor noted the nation's response – £9,073 6s 5d. Had he been well advised and invested this sum in property, today's value would be somewhere in the region of £1·6 million. To any appalled that an amateur could do so well out of the game, and who point to the many professional cricketers who ended their lives in penury, we would recall the case of Lancashire's R. G. Barlow. When he toured Australia in 1886–7, he received from the promoters – the Melbourne Cricket Club – £320 *plus* first-class expenses. Since the purchasing power of that sum would today be £30,000, England's current Test players may hope future tours of Australia will be in the hands of the Melbourne C. C.

In 1903–4 the Marylebone Cricket Club sent its first side to Australia, the professional Wilfred Rhodes being hired for £300. At this stage of his career, Rhodes was regarded as a bowler who went in last and sometimes made runs. It is therefore unlikely that he took many bats. Indeed, as Jessop used only one bat during the 1897 season (and this one smote 101 in 40 minutes against Yorkshire at Harrogate), we shall allow Rhodes two bats for Australia. Assuming he chose the most expensive equipment available, his kitting out bill then was as follows – and we have converted shillings and pence into our own prosaic p:

Cricket bag, one		£1·50
Pads, two pairs	@ 40p pr.	·80
Gloves, three pairs	@ 40p pr.	1·20
Sweaters, three	@ 42p each	1·26
Shirts, six	@ 24p each	1·44
Boots, three pairs	@ £1·10 pr.	3·30
Trousers, four pairs	@ 75p pr.	3·00
Bats, two	@ 90p each	1·80
		£14·30

Although it is unlikely that many professional cricketers of the Golden Age could afford to drink whisky, we should note that a bottle of the best Scotch then cost 25p. The finest pipe tobacco was 2p an ounce; if Rhodes packed the latest *Wisden* for serious reading, it cost him 5p. All of which suggests that although many cricketers did fall on hard times, those at the top did quite nicely. Everything is relative, so we point out without comment that England's Test players of the 1980s are less well rewarded than those who played against Australia in 1934. In that year the average industrial worker earned £141 – or £2·71 a week – the average school teacher £230, a country bank manager at his maximum earned £580. For twelve weeks' coaching at Harrow School, Rhodes received £300 – his habit being to wander down the wicket after a less than perfect stroke and say, 'Jack Hobbs did it this way.' In 1934 the match fee of an England Test player was £40, its 1982 purchasing power £2,200.

We have emphasized the matter of cash payments because of the increasing influence of money on first-class cricket. If W. G. or Spofforth could return, they would surely scratch their heads at some of the goings-on. For example, when New Zealand met Australia at Christchurch in 1977, the promotions men briefly took over:

'[As] Lillee bowled the last over, to Congdon, he had every fieldsman in a line from wicket-keeper to a point position –

a ploy repeated at Auckland – so that a picture could be provided for the cover of a new book by Chappell.'

Wisden

At least the above incident did not waste time, and we may wish that some brilliant photographer had been present with sophisticated camera when Spofforth bowled at Grace in 1882. Of another occasion, when Lillee strode forth at Perth carrying an aluminium bat, opinions will differ. The Lillee bat gave forth an odd sound when striking ball; England's captain, Brearley, objected – perhaps on musical grounds. A bat wielded by a Hammond, Cowdrey or Greg Chappell should sound like an expertly played 'cello; to have Lillee's bat suggesting a haphazardly struck xylophone was all wrong – funny perhaps, but only if heard once every hundred years.

Certain oddities of contemporary cricket would have bewildered the ancients – as they may do the future. Polishing the ball on some part of the anatomy is now obligatory for all non-spin bowlers, and sometimes even for them. How Maurice Tate obtained movement through the air and off the pitch *without* polishing never seems to be considered. Fast bowlers are probably no faster than they were during the first decade of the century; at least Jack Hobbs, who faced everyone from Cotter to Larwood, expressed relief he did not have to face another Surrey player, N. A. Knox. Twenty years ago Frank Lee refused to believe that anyone had, or could bowl faster than Larwood whom he had met in the thirties, or Tyson whom he had watched as umpire in the fifties. Yet batsmen survived without crash helmets, Woolley going so far as to say he thought Larwood an eminently fair bowler. (Once rudely assaulted by Larwood, Woolley said in an aggrieved voice, 'Are you trying to hit me, Harold?') However it must be conceded that had Woolley, Hobbs or George Gunn been obliged to bat on some of today's so-called Test wickets, even they might have seen the point of helmets.

GREGORY STEPHEN CHAPPELL, 1970–
The Aristocrat

It depends on what we expect from cricket. The most delectable of writers may sometimes find himself eating his own words. In 1956, irked after seeing much of Mackay, Alan Ross defended – if not the wickets of that year – wickets that were less than perfect. 'If one is going to discount completely cricket's more subtle skills and graces, then let wickets be specially prepared by turf consultants to a uniform specification, and transported to all Test match grounds in suitable containers.' Nearly a quarter of a century later Kerry Packer's staff did just that, leaving Mr Ross to regret that he hadn't thought of the accompanying pulchritude of young women in high heels and without skirts – grown more or less to a uniform specification. But Mr Packer in Australia and limited-overs cricket in England have produced a new species of spectator seeking instant excitement. Granted any intelligent person would prefer to watch a Macartney in a 40-overs match to What's-his-name in a five-day Test. But careful conditioning has persuaded many they would prefer to watch Macartney in 40 overs to Macartney in a Test.

The current proliferation of cricket tours inevitably deprives each of the accompanying sense of suspense which was once a joy. There can be a surfeit even of genius. Whether spectators are as well catered for as they were fifty years ago is a matter for disagreement. The reader who is not altogether happy about the entertainment provided is urged to read an article in the 1981 *Wisden* by the former captain of England, G. O. Allen, who played in the Lord's Test of 1930 and who watched the Centenary match in 1980. More in sorrow than in anger, Mr Allen pointed out that the runs per 100 balls in 1930 was 53, and in 1980 48·4. But whereas the former year saw 69 runs scored every hour, in 1980 the figure was 48·4. The inevitable explanation shall be stated simply:

1930		1980
21·50	Overs per hour	15·82
129·00	Overs per day	94·92

Put another way, in 1930 the Test cricketers of England and Australia could achieve 387 overs in three days, in 1980 380 overs in four days.

Of course, the Centenary Test was more thrilling; that was the occasion when certain MCC Members physically man-handled the umpires. Their punishment, alas, remains a closely guarded secret.

CHAPTER THIRTEEN

Blood, Thunder – and Dennis Lillee

D. K. Lillee was bloody-minded.

The time was 2.30 on the afternoon of Saturday, 15 August 1981, the place Old Trafford. Had various cricketers stared at Lillee and asked, 'Cripes! Why are you so bloody-minded?' he would have answered, 'Think not, my friends, that I am bloody-minded. Indeed not; I am a loyal Australian. Yet consider the scoreboard and the clock. Since play began this morning – 140 minutes ago – those Pommie bastards [for such is the way in which Australians refer to the flower of England's batsmen] have made 34 runs from God only knows how many overs. [The Almighty did know – it was 34 overs.] And here am I with only ONE wicket, while Terry Alderman has got four. *One* wicket! because the . . .' – here Lillee choked – 'aren't good enough to get a touch. Am I, or am I not, a Demon?' To which question ten Australians gave the answer, 'Verily, thou art!'

As on another occasion at the Oval, the men of England trembled, swallowed hard and – had they known the courage – looked out of the pavilion at a sky which loured upon the field. Our passion for accuracy compels us to observe that three men of England did not tremble and swallow hard – one was on his way out to bat thinking the while of shooting rabbits, another (Tavaré) was already at the crease practising a kind of cricket yoga which had this day brought him 11 runs, while the captain Brearley exercised his guru's rights by reading *Crime and Punishment*. Oddly, in the circumstances, no spectator named Spendlove took it upon himself to drop dead, though many thousands had dropped off. And certainly, as the Australians had journeyed to England a few months previously, no one observed a tall, sinewy Mephistopheles with eyes that burned casting his spell at a fancy-dress ball. Airliners in 1981 lacked the facilities for fancy-dress balls. Even so, the world recognized in Dennis Keith Lillee an authentic Demon.

The ten years of England-Australia Tests prior to 1981 were dominated by Lillee – either in the flesh or *in absentia*. Not infrequently they were ugly years. Players on both sides used foul language on the field, so echoing declining standards in the world at large. (In the mid-seventies Lindsay Hassett, whose international career spanned the years 1938–53, could say that during his time he had never heard a single player of either side swear at another.) Crowd behaviour deteriorated in England and Australia, mob violence often threatened to disrupt a game. Lillee himself, in *Back to the Mark*, had written: 'I bowl bouncers for one reason and that is to hit the batsman and thus intimidate him.' Perhaps publishers were partly to blame. More than half a century earlier, Cotter had enjoyed 'pinking' a batsman, but he did not commit his delight to print. Without pen or aluminium bat, Lillee dominated his decade in the flesh too often for England's comfort.

In absentia he was mourned by spectators – not in 1974–5, his first serious season after suffering four stress fractures in the lower vertebrae and spending weeks in a plaster cast – but in 1977 and 1978–9. During those latter years he missed eleven Tests against England. Between 1974 and 1980 he played in fifteen, only ten when the Ashes were at stake. At Melbourne in 1975 he left the field with a foot injury after bowling 6 overs for 17 runs and 1 wicket. England went on to win the match. Of the remaining fourteen Tests in which Lillee played, Australia won nine and England none. In 1977 and 1978–9 when he was not playing, Australia won one Test and England eight. By the start of 1981 Englishmen regarded the great athlete of the glorious action, the master of cut and swerve, of the perfect yorker and fearsome bouncer, and wondered if they ever would see him put to the sword. Just once – they were not asking for the dismemberment of Lillee to become a habit, merely one innings played by some Ranji or MacLaren. Something to remember in old age.

The message of the seventies was delivered by bowlers with the support of captains: 'If we don't bowl, you can't score.' The logic behind this was remorseless; no great batsman in history could have gainsaid it. Over rates became so low that stroke-makers languished. A hundred in 4 hours was exceptional, one in 5 hours the norm. New standards prevailed; that Bradman had reached each of his eight double-centuries against England in an average 5 hours 15 minutes was irrelevant. Bowlers had sought to dismiss him and given of their best *without delay*. Bradman in the seventies must have perished from sheer boredom – if, of course, he had been able to remember the spirit and tempo of the thirties. The message of the seventies was implicit: the bowlers' union was working to rule.

Illingworth and Ian Chappell were again the captains when the 1972 Australians arrived without Lawry, Redpath and McKenzie. The sides were evenly balanced: after England had won by 89 runs at Old Trafford on a seam bowler's pitch – Snow and Lillee each took 8 wickets, Greig's 57 and 62 the top scores for England, and Marsh's 91 a defiant last shout for Australia – there followed Massie's triumph at Lord's. Robert Arnold Lockyer Massie was, in effect, a one Test match bowler. Within a couple of years he had lost his place in the Western Australia side, but at Lord's in 1972 his medium-pace swing (from both over and round the wicket) brought him 8 for 84 and 8 for 53. Baseball players may have been able to fathom his art, not England's cricketers. Greg Chappell's aloof poise in an innings of 131 ensured an Australian victory by 8 wickets. Lord's 1972: a cricket quiz question emerged. Which bowler took one-tenth of his first-class wickets in one match, and where?

A dead pitch at Trent Bridge, with hundreds by Stackpole and Ross Edwards, and a 96 by Luckhurst (England's highest score in the series), spelled a draw. Whereupon Illingworth took one glance at the Headingley pitch and gloated; winning the toss, he put Australia in. They made 146 (fungus-affected wicket), England replying with 263, an 8th-wicket partnership between Illingworth and Snow realizing 104 at a time of trial and tribulation. By now Underwood was licking his lips, his 6 for 45 capsizing Australia for 10 runs fewer than in their first innings. England retained the Ashes with a 9-wicket victory, the match neatly summarized by the figures of Underwood and Illingworth: 92·1–38–146–14. Recovering technically, and forgetting their outraged emotions, Australia squared the series at the Oval. The family Chappell supplied two hundreds in the tourists' first innings after Lillee, 5 for 58, had found little opposition save that of Knott, 92. Lillee had to work harder next time against Wood, 90, and Knott 63. But 10 for 181 was a good haul. Sheahan and Marsh guided Australia to a win by 5 wickets. A fine series – England felt sure of doing well in 1974–5.

As news of Lillee's injury ('My dear chap, one doesn't bowl fast after *that*!') and fight to recover sank in, England felt very sure of doing well. True, Boycott had withdrawn from the party at the last minute – Luckhurst taking his place – saying he needed a further rest from Test cricket. But even without Boycott there was confidence. After all, the last Scots-born captain, Douglas Jardine, had been successful; there, surely, was a hopeful precedent for Michael Denness of Kent. Soon after the start of the tour, the Englishmen encountered and overcame Thomson – one problem solved. They remembered they had brought five fast or fastish bowlers, plus Greig. They were happy. Who, they asked, would open the Australian bowling? Lillee – they were glad that Dennis felt better. And who? Thomson. But they'd already played against him. No, not 'Froggy' – Jeff. Who on earth was Jeff Thomson?

A former surf rider and, seen retrospectively, a man who might well have won an Olympic medal for throwing the javelin had he been plucked from the sea and trained, Thomson ambled to the wicket and discharged the ball with something akin to the old-fashioned slinger's action. It was this action which enabled him to make the ball rise abruptly from only just short of a length; going on to the back foot in the prescribed manner, batsmen found themselves in danger of decapitation, actual or imaginary – the latter psychologically more damaging if one hoped to go on batting. On several occasions from Adelaide to Brisbane England's faster bowlers had pitched short. On a Woolloongabba pitch prepared by the Lord Mayor of Brisbane, Alderman Clem Jones, who went about his task clad in shorts, wellies and a crash helmet, England again bowled what they considered a fast bowler's length. Alas! Willis, though fast, was slower than Lillee; Lillee was slower than Thomson. It was blood and thunder with lightning added.

Of 78 England wickets to fall to bowlers in the first four Tests, Thomson and Lillee accounted for 46, and the fast-medium Max Walker 15. Halfway through the fifth Test Thomson wrenched his right shoulder playing tennis, yet he and Lillee still totalled 11 wickets. In Sir Donald Bradman's view, the two killers (the word is used in its complimentary sense) 'were probably, as a pair, the fastest and most lethal opening pair in Australia's history . . . with a willingness to exploit the short-pitched ball to an extent which would have unnerved any side'. England's batsmen were shell-shocked. Greig, provoking Lillee to gladiatorial conflict, made a superb century at Brisbane, Edrich fought as only he knew how to, Amiss batted splendidly once, Knott was impishly productive, and the forty-two-year-old Cowdrey (flown out after the first Test) pitted a consummate technique against odds. All to no avail. Denness dropped himself for the fourth Test at Sydney where Australia regained the Ashes 3 years and 326 days after losing them to Illingworth's side.

Was Mallett now probably the best off-spinner in the world? Was Greg Chappell's disdainful elegance unrivalled in Test cricket? Could Walters play one innings in a series more entertainingly than anyone else? Such questions were irrelevant. When Lillee limped off after bowling 6 overs in the final Test, and England made 529 (Denness 188, Fletcher 146) to win by an innings, the lesson of the tour was merely underlined. Neither Boycott nor Hobbs, Woolley and George Gunn was the answer to Thomson. Only two England cricketers could have persuaded Ian Chappell to call off his dogs of war; ironically, both were living in Australia. But the combined ages of Larwood and Tyson exceeded a hundred years. Their yesterdays were Australia's today.

Finding themselves in the England of 1975 for the Prudential World Cup one-day games, the Australians graciously agreed to play Test cricket. (It was now that the seventies matches between the two countries began to proliferate – thirty-three in all as opposed to the twenty-five one might have expected.) Finding the thought of Lillee and Thomson obliterating his ewe lambs on a fresh Edgbaston pitch distasteful, Denness put Australia in to bat. A score of 359, followed by rain, gave the visitors victory by an innings and 85. At this the England selectors appointed Greig captain for Lord's; more, they reached into the basket of county players and brought up David Steele of Northants. Losing his way in the pavilion as he left the dressing room to bat – no map having been provided – he took guard, adjusted his spectacles, and played resolutely forward to a surprised Thomson. Had the bowler been performing on the Lord's ridge of 1961, the wicketkeeper Marsh would probably have occupied a tennis umpire's chair in front of the sight screen. 1975 was altogether more placid. Fast bowlers do not like being rebuffed by a grey-haired man with sweat-bands worn just below the elbows; after 19 hours of Steele at Lord's, Leeds and the Oval, Lillee and Thomson said 'Bother!' – and waited for the hero to draw his old-age pension. Also put out was Mrs Steele. 1975 was her husband's benefit year, the local butcher promising one chop per run scored. A larger deep freeze was the answer.

1975 was a season unique in Test history. If Steele was first among the heroes, there were others: Edrich with 175 in 9 hours at Lord's, where Greig and Ross Edwards fell in their 90s, at Headingley with the slow left-arm Phillippe Henri Edmonds taking 5 for 28 in the first innings of his first Test, at the Oval where McCosker and Ian Chappell made hundreds only to see England saved by a Woolmer six and a half hours' century. 1975 was a season unique in Test history because it boasted of heroes *and* an anti-hero – one Peter Chappell. His immediate aim in life was to secure the release from prison of a bank robber. With the aid of accomplices, one of whom held a degree in anthropology (for these were the seventies), Mr Chappell broke into Headingley one night. Next day Australia, with McCosker 95 not out, would require 225 to win with 7 second-innings wickets intact. There was no next day – in the cricketing sense of the term. Mr Chappell and accomplices doctored the pitch with holes and a gallon of crude oil on a good length. Yorkshire sticky pitches were once part of the game but not this kind; the Lord Mayor of Leeds, unlike Alderman Jones of Brisbane, omitted to turn up in shorts, wellies and crash helmet – a gesture which would have impressed even if it had failed to appease McCosker, and the match was abandoned. The bank robber was in due course released; a year later he was convicted of another armed robbery, so returning whence he had come.

In 1975 Lillee was acknowledged as a supreme fast bowler.

The Melbourne Centenary Test of 1977 does not enter a story of the Ashes save that during its progress the captain of England, Anthony William Greig, acted as chief liaison officer between Mr Kerry Packer and the players. The magic word, uttered discreetly, was 'Money!' World Series Cricket accordingly gave birth to its first-born, named Super Test, nine months later. On 13 May 1977 the Cricket Council arose in outraged majesty and declared that Greig would not be considered for the England captaincy during the coming season. When the Australians flew in to London, most of them had Packer contracts tucked away with bats and boxes. What they did *not* bring was the impressive trio of Ian Chappell, Edwards and Lillee. Chosen to captain England was John Michael Brearley, aged thirty-five. A Cambridge first in Classics and top place in the Civil Service examination behind him, he was (like Jeeves – save that Jeeves would have batted like Hobbs and bowled like Verity) one who knew all about the psychology of the individual.

Woolmer with 79 and 120 saved England's face in the first

D. K. LILLEE
1971–80

In Tests for the Ashes

Year and Tests		Balls	Runs	Wickets	Average
1970–1	(2)	499	199	8	24·87
1972	(5)	1,499	548	31	17·67
1974–5	(6)	1,462	596	25	23·84
1975	(4)	1,242	460	21	21·90
	(17*)	4,702	1,803	85	21·21

In Tests not for the Ashes

Year and Tests		Balls	Runs	Wickets	Average
1977 (Centenary)		383	165	11	15·00
1979–80	(3)	1,241	388	23	16·86
1980 (Centenary)		204	96	5	19·20
	(5)	1,828	649	39	16·64

In all Tests v England 1971–80

Tests	Balls	Runs	Wickets	Average
22	6,530	2,452	124	19·77

Test at Lord's where Willis took 9 wickets. Greg Chappell, now leading Australia, made his side's only hundred of the series at Old Trafford, England winning easily by 9 wickets. After three years of self-imposed exile, Boycott now made himself available; 107 and 80 not out at Trent Bridge, and 191 at Headingley (his

---

* In reality sixteen Tests: excluding the sixth in 1974–5 where he bowled only 6 overs, 84 wickets at 21·26.

DENNIS KEITH LILLEE, 1971–
The Demon Mk. 2

one hundredth century in first-class cricket made in the right place) persuaded him he was in form. England won the third Test by 7 wickets and the fourth by an innings and 85 runs, so regaining the Ashes. Yet Australians in search of excuses could rightly point to the absence of Lillee. In 1978–9 they could point to the absence of almost everyone, thanks to World Series Cricket. England averaged a mere 256 per completed innings but won five of the six Tests, Australia nine times dismissed for less than 200. A new fast bowler, Rodney Hogg, rocketed to the top for Australia. His 41 wickets suggested superb attacking line and length, his average of 12 inadequate batting techniques, helpful pitches or odd shaped balls. The following season, 1979–80, saw Lillee back in the Australian fold, his skill as remarkable as ever. But these three matches were not played for the Ashes. Would Lillee make the tour of England in 1981?

Excluding the sixth Test of 1974–5, Lillee had appeared twenty-one times against England, his 123 wickets averaging 19·79 – a wicket every 52·69 balls.

1981

On 29 July – about the time a good opening pair would be settling in for the day – England's cricketers were informed they had a Princess of Wales for the first time since 1909 when Noble's Australians had triumphed. So determined were the batsmen of England not to compete with a wedding that they sank into anonymity, hiding whatever strokes they possessed and advancing the doctrine of unplayable pitches. They succeeded so well that in four finished Tests they had been reduced by Australia to these unpromising scores: 185 and 125, 174 and 135 for 7, 189 and 219, 175 for 9 and 104 for 5. But because an all-rounder of parts had not been made aware of the doctrine of unplayable pitches, 135 for 7 blossomed into 356 and 104 for 5 into 404. So England won the series by three matches to one and retained the Ashes. The greatest Australian Demon since

Spofforth asserted his magnificence, though on one occasion suffered the bloodiest nose since Ned Kelly pounded, and was pounded by, Isaiah 'Wild' Wright.

For England joy came out of misery in 1981 – for Australia an unbearable collapse on the verge of victory. On 22 June England lost the first Test; at the close of the second on 7 July, her selectors sacked the captain at a time when he told them he did not wish to continue his command on a match by match basis. The gamble had failed. Little more than a year previously, Ian Botham, aged twenty-four, had been pushed to the summit – perhaps because, more than anyone else, he was an integral member of the team; perhaps because he clearly had years of cricket ahead of him and would learn from experience; probably in the hope he could transmit the magnetism of his achievement into terms of leadership. But England's opposition in successive series was West Indies. Botham failed – as most likely anyone else would have failed – to inspire England above a normal potential. Worse, his own form suffered; he became something like a contemporary cricketer. A genius of instinctive rhyme and rhythm when the mood took him, he struggled vainly in search of reason.

If Trevor Bailey was right in saying the 1981 Australian batting was the worst he had seen from that country, it was at once apparent that Botham's batting would be more vital than his bowling. That any England seam bowler could dismiss Australia was an exaggeration; that the Australian batsmen could get themselves out to any England seam bowler was not. Australia's strength lay in bowling – in Lawson who could be decidedly fast, in Hogg, the medium-pace of Alderman, *and* Lillee. Soon after reaching England, the last named had succumbed to pneumonia. But a Demon, though weakened, is not put out by minor ailments; at fast-medium pace he does what he likes with the ball – and therefore with English batsmen. And so it proved. At Trent Bridge, under heavy skies and on a pitch that might have been ordered by Lillee and Alderman, England's two innings totalled 310 – Australia winning by 4 wickets. Much of Australia's close catching was brilliant, much of England's was not.

At Lord's the pitch was good, so the match was drawn. No individual made a hundred though Gatting, Willey, Boycott and Gower for England, Border and Wood for Australia, all passed 50. Botham fell leg-before-wicket to Lawson for 0, and was bowled by Bright (first ball, sweeping) for 0. As a captain of England is not meant to get a 'pair' at Lord's – especially against Australia – both the selectors and Botham reacted. The former very sensibly said, 'Let's send for Dr Brearley!' Pointing out perhaps that an England captain could no longer rely on some of the most successful batsmen in English county cricket – Zaheer and Javed Miandad having been born in Pakistan, Lamb, Rice and Kirsten in South Africa, and Richards in West Indies – the selectors otherwise gave Brearley a free hand. And so to Headingley.

Sunshine and showers: the weather experts were right. The sun shone on the Australian batsmen who, though not approving of the pitch, discovered they could play on it; England's bowlers rivalled the showers in being intermittently effective. The fielding – brilliant in Brearley's earlier reign – was undistinguished. Around five o'clock on the second day, with only 4 Australian wickets down and over 300 on the board, Brearley brought back Botham: 'You used to be able to move mountains, remove this lot.' Botham pranced in, took 5 wickets for 35 runs, prompting a declaration at 401 for 9. Had the series just started for England? Not yet. On the third day Lillee, Alderman and Lawson bowled them out for 174, with Gooch gone in the second innings. The ball swung and cut, batting an impossibility; Botham made 50, Extras 34, ten other England batsmen 90. Botham's innings was interesting. It was as though George Gunn, a product of the Golden Age, had whispered, 'Never take any notice of the wicket.' That, surely, was one message of the Golden Age. How else can one explain Trumper and J. T. Tyldesley on unlikely surfaces? It is one thing to bat scientifically, another to be overawed by science.

England began the fourth day needing 222 to avoid an innings defeat. At lunch they were 78 for 4 – Brearley, Gower and Gatting out. Still 124 in arrears. Half an hour after lunch Willey left: 103 for 5. The new batsman (and at moments of crisis we should note vital statistics) stood, or rather marched, an inch over six foot, weighed sixteen stone, and carried an implement shaped like a bat but clearly – in the hands of a Botham – about as subtle a weapon as a Stone Age club. To emphasize further his non-contemporary character, Botham did not wear a helmet. He did however have a beard; a tolerable affair as beards go, but not one to tuck inside his shirt. Were a fast bowler to send one through Botham's beard, the ball would strike the batsman on the jaw or cheekbone. Then it would be too late for Botham to walk down the wicket and borrow Boycott's helmet. Too late anyway. Boycott departed at 133, Taylor 2 runs later, England 135 for 7: the 92 runs still required to make Australia bat again were out of the question. Or so the jubilation of the fielders suggested. Dilley, Old and Willis had their pads on. Three straight balls? How the Australians rejoiced!

Their three bowlers were, of course, tiring a little. In a day and a half, Lillee, Alderman and Lawson had sent down 99 overs; a fourth bowler, Bright, had not been used – being a slow left-arm over the wicket bowler, he probably did not expect to be used in the circumstances. True Dilley batted left-handed – and Bright's normal delivery would have pitched in the rough outside his off stump (Benaud round the wicket to Close, Old Trafford 1961). But one of the three faster men would soon account for Dilley. Meanwhile Botham was getting a sight of the ball. Negative his methods were; he did not score from 37 of 57 balls he received. As he hit the 57th to the boundary, the crowd applauded his half-century – eight 4s, two 3s, three 2s, and seven singles. Botham's rate of progress was not rapid, a mere 28 runs an hour. The Australians were bowling only 11 overs to the hour, containing Botham while they snipped off England's tail. However, Dilley was thumping anything pitched up past cover. He looked most un-snip-off-able.

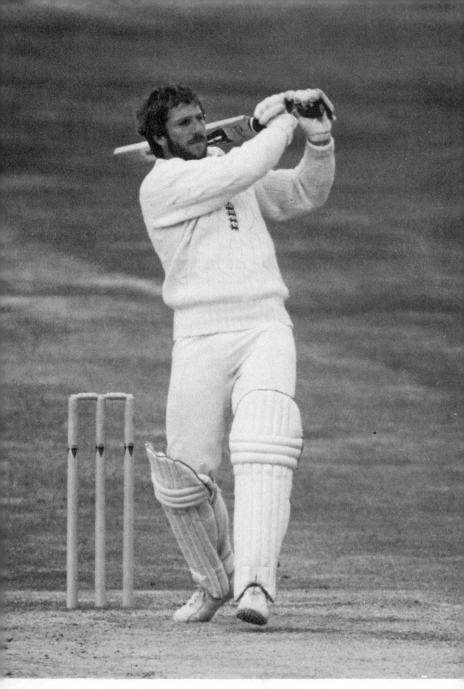

IAN TERENCE BOTHAM, 1977–
The Pirate

Botham's method was simple. If someone had mentioned to him that the pitch precluded stroke-making, he wasn't listening. Besides, what is stroke-making? An expression of self. Balls of a fast bowler's length on the off stump he either slashed or thumped from the back foot, those on the leg stump he despatched to mid-wicket. When captain of England he had too often hit across the line of flight, now he was hitting through the ball. Noting an oddly happy Dilley, Botham became more selective *yet more violent*. From the next thirty balls bowled him, he did not score off sixteen. Those he felt safe to plunder realized one 6, eleven 4s, and two singles. Seven men patrolled the boundaries; twice or three times their number would have been welcomed by Australia's bowlers. Botham's hundred came in just over two and a half hours – in far distant days a commendable though hardly remarkable time. But 103 from 87 balls and 31 scoring strokes: incredible at any time. Had Australia bowled their overs in 1921 fashion, Botham's century would have been made at about a run a minute. At the close on the fourth day England were 351 for 9 – Dilley 56, Old 29, and the Man Without A Helmet 145 not out.

Australia had not won with an innings to spare, but a target of 130 suggested a need for concentration rather than a reason for consternation. Willis and Old had opened the bowling when they began batting five days ago, now Brearley tried his two heroes, Botham and Dilley. Dilley wasn't very straight and Botham, in spite of an early wicket, appeared relatively amiable. So Brearley hastily erased Dilley and substituted Willis. But Willis laboured, and when Willis labours no Test batsman should feel anxious. Willis labouring is a bowler conscious of his knees – or lack of knees; the Willis knees have undergone such surgery that the wonder is he can stagger, let alone run, to the crease. But Willis rampant . . . When Willis is rampant, the batsman sees a 6 foot $5\frac{1}{2}$ inch giant with hair uncut since Bob Dylan was mobbed at Heathrow – a species of stampeding ostrich in huffy mood. Half an hour before lunch, with Australia 48 for 1, Brearley brought on Willis at the Kirkstall Lane End, the breeze behind him.

At once Willis began to make the ball lift. At 56 Trevor Chappell got a brute, the wicketkeeper Taylor running forward to take the catch. Then, with only a few minutes to go before the interval, the bottom fell out of Australia's world: Hughes touched Willis to second slip where Botham dived and came up beaming, Yallop fended off a shortish delivery only to see Gatting hurl himself forward at short-leg. If, with Australia 56 for 1, Brearley thought England would win, he was an optimist; at 58 for 4 it was time to discard pessimistic ideas. After lunch Old bowled Border, Dyson was caught by the wicketkeeper hooking at Willis, Marsh hooked and connected with Dilley waiting at long-leg, Lawson snicked and was swallowed up. Australia 75 for 8. Bright and Lillee added 35 in 4 overs before Willis had Lillee caught, then removed Bright's middle stump. In 61 balls Willis had taken 8 wickets, his innings analysis 15·1–3–43–8. England had beaten Australia by 18 runs *after being made to follow on*. It had happened before, at Sydney in 1894. No one could remember that.

Bowlers win matches? Trumble without Trumper, O'Reilly without Bradman, Willis without Botham . . . Does it matter? Let us say that Botham saved England from an inevitable and humiliating defeat. In the context of 1981 he had only just begun. The fourth Test at Edgbaston – when Australia in perfect conditions required 151 to win, reached 105 for 4, 114 for 5, then collapsed to 121 – that was Botham. In twenty-six balls he took the last five wickets for 1 run. However, by then Australia deserved to lose; a side which totters to 114 from 352 balls should not be surprised if some Botham says, 'Enough of this nonsense!' and sweeps it into the dustbin. After Edgbaston England were two–one up in the series with two matches left. Without Botham they would probably have been three-nil down – and the Ashes in Australian hands. One man had saved England. His next achievement was to be of far greater significance. He would save cricket itself.

Two-thirty on the afternoon of Saturday, 15 August 1981, the place Old Trafford, and D. K. Lillee was bloody-minded. Lillee's reason we already know. We may ignore it. What we may not ignore were the feelings of so many Mancunian thousands who had done what Lillee was not called upon to do – pay to watch England bat. Thursday's cricket had tried the patience and patriotism of the multitude as England pushed to 175 for 9, the pitch an impossible one on which to play strokes. Tavaré had lingered long, four and three-quarter hours for 69; Botham had lingered for one ball bowled by Lillee. If Thursday was uninspiring, Friday was eccentric. Allott, a local fast bowling hero, and Willis, added 56 from 12 overs for England's last wicket. Allott's undefeated 52 surprised everyone, especially fieldsmen who watched off-drives finish up at long-leg. Encouraged by these antics, Australia played strokes and charged to 130 from 30·2 overs, exhilarating even by Trumper standards; also pointless, Australia being dismissed from 30·2 overs for 130. Pundits considered the Australian batting to be dire. After the early loss of Gooch, England in the persons of Boycott and Tavaré played out time properly and Test-ily: 70 for 1 off 36 overs.

Modern jargon likes to refer to the 'launching pad' of an innings. England had such a start on the third day of the fifth Test – 171 ahead with 9 wickets standing. The ball was 36 overs old but the conditions overcast; the England 'take-off' would happen after Boycott and Tavaré had acquainted themselves with wind velocities, depth of cloud cover, visibility over the Mersey and such-like. Half an hour produced 9 runs before Boycott fell lbw to Alderman. Gower lasted 25 minutes while making a single, Gatting a full hour for 11. Brearley entered, saw the morning's runs increased by 1 to 29, then adjourned with everyone else to seek refreshment. In 2 hours Tavaré had made 9. A post-lunch consolidation on the launching pad produced 5 more runs before Brearley was caught off Alderman and retired in the knowledge that improving literature was in his bag. Lillee remembered his 150 Test wickets against England *alone*, asked, 'Am I, or am I not, a Demon?', and heard that verily he was.

ENGLAND v AUSTRALIA
Played at Headingley 16, 17, 18, 20, 21 July 1981

AUSTRALIA

J. Dyson	b Dilley	102	c Taylor b Willis	34
G. M. Wood	lbw b Botham	34	c Taylor b Botham	10
T. M. Chappell	c Taylor b Willey	27	c Taylor b Willis	8
K. J. Hughes	c & b Botham	89	c Botham b Willis	0
R. J. Bright	b Dilley	7	(8) b Willis	19
G. N. Yallop	c Taylor b Botham	58	(5) c Gatting b Willis	0
A. R. Border	lbw b Botham	8	(6) b Old	0
R. W. Marsh	b Botham	28	(7) c Dilley b Willis	4
G. F. Lawson	c Taylor b Botham	13	c Taylor b Willis	1
D. K. Lillee	not out	3	c Gatting b Willis	17
T. M. Alderman	did not bat		not out	0
Extras	(B4, LB13, W3, NB12)	32	(LB3, W1, NB14)	18
Total	(9 wkts declared)	401		111

Fall of wickets: 1–55, 2–149, 3–196, 4–220, 5–332, 6–354, 7–357, 8–396, 9–401.

2nd innings 1–13, 2–56, 3–58, 4–58, 5–65, 6–68, 7–74, 8–75, 9–110, 10–111.

ENGLAND BOWLING (6-ball overs)

	O.	M.	R.	W.	O.	M.	R.	W.
Willis	30	8	72	0	15·1	3	43	8
Old	43	14	91	0	9	1	21	1
Dilley	27	4	78	2	2	0	11	0
Botham	38·2	11	95	6	7	3	14	1
Willey	13	2	31	1	3	1	4	0
Boycott	3	2	2	0	–	–	–	–

ENGLAND

G. A. Gooch	lbw b Alderman	2	c Alderman b Lillee	0
G. Boycott	b Lawson	12	lbw b Alderman	46
J. M. Brearley	c Marsh b Alderman	10	c Alderman b Lillee	14
D. I. Gower	c Marsh b Lawson	24	c Border b Alderman	9
M. W. Gatting	lbw b Lillee	15	lbw b Alderman	1
P. Willey	b Lawson	8	c Dyson b Lillee	33
I. T. Botham	c Marsh b Lillee	50	not out	149
R. W. Taylor	c Marsh b Lillee	5	c Bright b Alderman	1
G. R. Dilley	c & b Lillee	13	b Alderman	56
C. M. Old	c Border b Alderman	0	b Lawson	29
R. G. D. Willis	not out	1	c Border b Alderman	2
Extras	(B6, LB11, W6, NB11)	34	(B5, LB3, W3, NB5)	16
Total		174		356

Fall of wickets: 1–12, 2–40, 3–42, 4–84, 5–87, 6–112, 7–148, 8–166, 9–167, 10–174.

2nd innings 1–0, 2–18, 3–37, 4–41, 5–105, 6–133, 7–135, 8–252, 9–319, 10–356.

AUSTRALIA BOWLING (6-ball overs)

	O.	M.	R.	W.	O.	M.	R.	W.
Lillee	18·5	7	49	4	25	6	94	3
Alderman	19	4	59	3	35·3	6	135	6
Lawson	13	3	32	3	23	4	96	1
Bright	–	–	–	–	4	0	15	0

ENGLAND WON BY 18 RUNS

I. T. BOTHAM 1981

Third Test at Headingley

149 not out
out of 251
3 hours 39 minutes
148 balls
one 6 and twenty-seven 4s
40·82 runs an hour
100·60 runs per 100 balls

Fifth Test at Old Trafford
118 c Marsh b Whitney
out of 149
2 hours 2 minutes
102 balls
six 6s and thirteen 4s (one from overthrow)
†58·03 runs an hour
115·68 runs per 100 balls

267*
out of 400
5 hours 41 minutes
250 balls
seven 6s and forty 4s
47 runs an hour
106·80 runs per 100 balls

---

† Jessop's 104 at the Oval in 1902 remains unsurpassed: 83 runs an hour, and 138 runs per 100 balls.

* Botham's two innings totalling 267 runs may be compared with Bradman's 334 at Headingley in 1930 (see page 121). The changes in cricket over half a century are revealing.

Bradman scored at 12 runs an hour faster than Botham (52.40). Botham scored 32 runs per 100 balls faster than Bradman (106.74). If Bradman had equalled Botham's runs per 100 balls rate, he would have made not 334 but 478.

Had Botham received balls as frequently as did Bradman, he would have batted not for 5 hours 41 minutes but for 3 hours 31 minutes.

BOTHAM'S BOUNDARIES

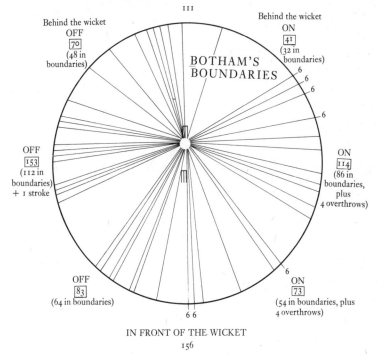

BEHIND THE WICKET

111

Behind the wicket
OFF
70
(48 in
boundaries)

BOTHAM'S
BOUNDARIES

Behind the wicket
ON
41
(32 in
boundaries)

6
6
6

6

OFF
153
(112 in
boundaries)
+ 1 stroke

ON
114
(86 in
boundaries,
plus
4 overthrows)

OFF
83
(64 in boundaries)

6

ON
73
(54 in boundaries, plus
4 overthrows)

6 6

IN FRONT OF THE WICKET

156

Unruly elements in the mob mouthed, 'Why cricket?', then observed Tavaré's yoga exercise and were dumb. England 104 for 5.

The Man Without A Helmet took guard. Where was he? Of course! On a launching pad. When was take-off? That depended. Had it been whispered to The Man Without A Helmet that a new ball was due in 17 overs, he would most likely have looked blank. So what? When Hammond sailed into harbour 210 not out on 24 June 1938 Bradman was asked why he had delayed taking the new ball.

'Because I saw what Wally was doing to McCormick with the old ball, and I knew he would hit the new ball even harder.'

Ian Botham played down the line. So did Tavaré. Lillee and Alderman awaited the new ball. Botham actually scored 5 runs from the first thirty-two balls he received. Tavaré listened to the sound of ball hitting bat; estimated take-off in his view was late summer in 1982 by which time the England space craft would be ready to rise a few feet from the earth, descending at once to appeal against the light.

3.35 p.m. Botham 28 not out in 65 minutes from 53 balls. He was preparing. Alderman, a medium-pace bowler of the highest class, took the new ball. 7 runs to Botham. At the other end Lillee assumed his most terrifying expression and ran in.

'I bowl bouncers for one reason and that is to hit the batsman and thus intimidate him.'

Here we should note that Lillee 1981 had not the pace, or the consistent pace, of Lillee 1974–5, that the Old Trafford pitch was much, much slower than that of, say, Perth. But a Lillee bouncer is a bouncer by Lillee. His first bouncer with the new ball was admirably directed. It made for the batsman's head. Ranji would have swayed outside the line of flight and hooked; had he missed, a split ear might have been the result. Botham did not sway, he permitted the ball to make for the centre of his forehead; had he missed, a split Botham would have been the result. He did not miss. At the precise moment, bat struck ball, ball travelling high into crowd.

Lillee thought he would try another bouncer. In this same over with the new ball he did. Again Botham hooked, again the ball travelled high into the crowd. The crowd danced and waved flags. For want of something better to do, Alderman bowled a bouncer. As it did not rise with the required velocity to compel a hook, Botham pulled it to mid-wicket. For 6. Not being over-ambitious, he was also pleased to hit 4s. After 7 Alderman-Lillee overs with the new ball had brought Botham 66 runs, the Australian captain opted for a bowling change. Bright applied cunning. Botham swept him for 6 to reach a century. Bright applied more cunning. Botham hit him over the sight screen. On 118 Botham was caught at the wicket off Whitney, his last 90 runs made from 49 balls in 57 minutes. For the first time in England-Australia Tests a man had struck six 6s in an innings.

Tavaré's vigil on the launching pad and in orbit lasted seven and one-quarter hours, his runs 78. He read his instruments well. Knott and Emburey cashed in on Botham's act of mayhem with half-centuries, and Australia were set 506 to win. Yallop batted brilliantly for 114. Border 5 minutes under 7 hours for 123 not out. A score of 402 spelled defeat for Australia but recaptured pride. The final drawn Test at the Oval was a match for individuals: Border with 106 not out and 84, Wellham with a second innings of 103 in his first Test against England, Boycott with 137, Botham's 10 wickets in the match and Lillee's 11. The Master Demon was quite at his supreme best.

Pitches were the key to 1981 – to all save one man. Specialist batsmen on both sides had a hard time. For England the least productive twenty-seven innings by Boycott, Brearley, Gatting, Gooch, Gower, Parker and Woolmer averaged 6·85; for Australia the least productive thirty-two by Chappell, Dyson, Hughes, Wood and Yallop 5·00. In twelve innings only one man topped 400 runs, the Australian Border with 533 – the outcome of skill, courage and hard grafting. Australia were sorely handicapped by the absence through injury of Lawson in the fourth Test, and of Lawson and Hogg thereafter. Yet Alderman, the discovery of the season, with 42 wickets and Lillee with 39 –

raising the latter's tally against England alone to 163 – seemed able to shoulder the burden until Botham erupted. Alderman and Lillee with Spofforth and O'Reilly to lend a hand could not have guaranteed victory when, in *four* completed innings (the second of the third Test to the first of the fifth), Australia managed only 538 runs from the bat.

The Ashes are for the moment where they were in 1883 when the Hon Ivo Bligh brought home Miss Morphy's thoughtful gift. To retain them over the next twenty years, England must solve a problem. 'We are both good for each other,' said Brearley of Botham. 'He needs a father figure as I need a younger brother to help me out.' In the event of Botham making his farewell Test appearance against Australia at the same age as Wilfred Rhodes made his, Brearley will be sixty-two – slowing in body if not in mind.

The last word shall be given not to a father figure but to the father of all things, he whose name was first in this book – W. G. Grace.

'Lillee? Yes, Lillee's a good bowler all right. A good bowler. But give me Spoff. Botham? Yes, promising. Reminds me of a young 'un I introduced to cricket – where was it? Old Trafford. Hit Arthur Mold all over the place. Name of Jessop. Mold was fast but Jessop hit him. Always do that to fast bowlers, they don't like it. Botham. Yes. If he lets his beard grow . . . Good prospect. Puts bat to ball, that's what I like about him. Puts bat to ball.'

A proper beard is plucked.

'All the good 'uns do. I DID!'

HOLDERS OF THE ASHES

Season	Held by	Season	Held by
1882	Australia	1926	England
1882–3	England	1928–9	England
1884	England	1930	Australia
1884–5	England	1932–3	England
1886	England	1934	Australia
1886–7	England	1936–7	Australia
1887–8	England	1938	Australia
1888	England	1946–7	Australia
1890	England	1948	Australia
1891–2	Australia	1950–1	Australia
1893	England	1953	England
1894–5	England	1954–5	England
1896	England	1956	England
1897–8	Australia	1958–9	Australia
1899	Australia	1961	Australia
1901–2	Australia	1962–3	Australia
1902	Australia	1964	Australia
1903–4	England	1965–6	Australia
1905	England	1968	Australia
1907–8	Australia	1970–1	England
1909	Australia	1972	England
1911–12	England	1974–5	Australia
1912	England	1975	Australia
1920–1	Australia	1977	England
1921	Australia	1978–9	England
1924–5	Australia	1981	England

INDEX

Numbers in italics refer to
illustrations